SMP interact

Book S1

S1

CAMBRIDGE
UNIVERSITY PRESS

PUBLISHED BY THE PRESS SYNDICATE OF THE UNIVERSITY OF CAMBRIDGE
The Pitt Building, Trumpington Street, Cambridge, United Kingdom

CAMBRIDGE UNIVERSITY PRESS
The Edinburgh Building, Cambridge CB2 2RU, UK
40 West 20th Street, New York, NY 10011–4211, USA
10 Stamford Road, Oakleigh, Melbourne 3166, Australia
Ruiz de Alarcón 13, 28014 Madrid, Spain
Dock House, The Waterfront, Cape Town 8001, South Africa

http://www.cambridge.org

Printed in the United Kingdom at the University Press, Cambridge

Typeface Minion   *System* QuarkXPress®

A catalogue record for this book is available from the British Library

ISBN 0 521 79859 0 paperback

Typesetting and technical illustrations by The School Mathematics Project
Other illustrations by Robert Calow and Steve Lach at Eikon Illustration
Cover image © Tony Stone Images/Darryl Torckler
Cover design by Angela Ashton

The publishers would like to thank the following for supplying photographs:
page 119   Telegraph Group Limited
page 136 (*top*)   David Cassell
All other photographs by Graham Portlock

The authors and publishers would like to thank the staff and pupils of Impington Village College,
Cambridge, for their help with the production of this book.

NOTICE TO TEACHERS
It is illegal to reproduce any part of this work in material form (including photocopying
and electronic storage) except under the following circumstances:
(i) where you are abiding by a licence granted to your school by the Copyright Licensing Agency;
(ii) where no such licence exists, or where you wish to exceed the terms of a licence, and you
have gained the written permission of Cambridge University Press;
(iii) where you are allowed to reproduce without permission under the provisions of Chapter 3
of the Copyright, Designs and Patents Act 1988.

Contents

1 Time

This work will help you

◆ use the 12-hour and 24-hour clocks

◆ calculate with time (including using timetables)

A Happiness graphs

Mary's happiness graph

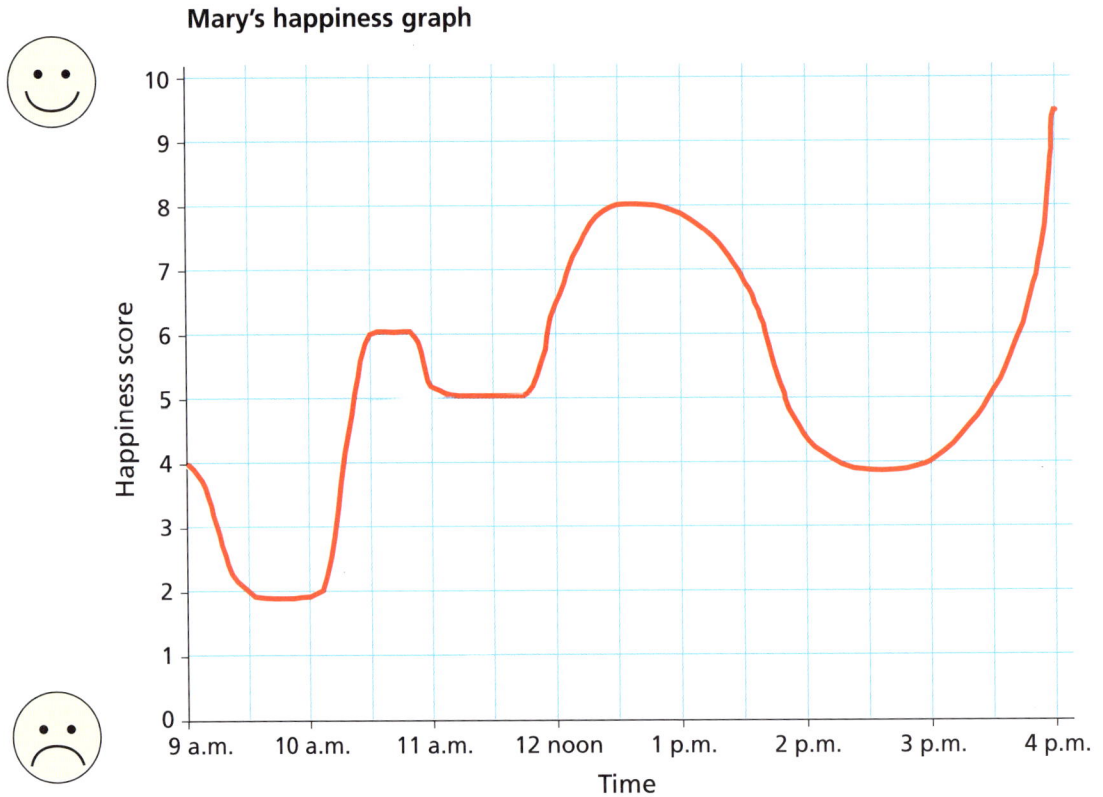

B Time planner

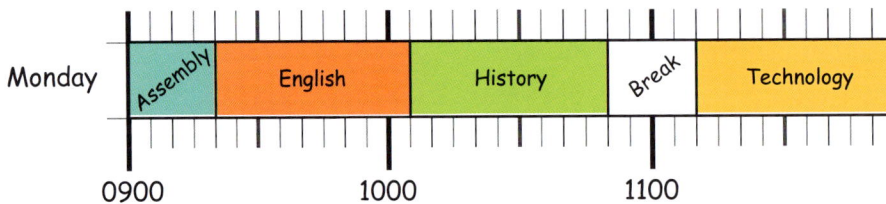

| Monday | Assembly | English | History | Break | Technology |

0900   1000   1100

C The 24-hour clock

A 8:20 a.m.

B

morning

C 25 minutes to 8 in the evening

D

afternoon

E 7:25 p.m.

F 20:05

G 16:35

H 8:50 p.m.

I

evening

J 8:00 p.m.

K 10 minutes past 6 in the evening

L 18:40

M a quarter past 10 in the morning

N a quarter to 5 in the afternoon

O 13:35

P

evening

Q 06:30

R

morning

C1 Write these times using the 24-hour clock.

(a) 2:30 p.m.   (b) 5:15 p.m.   (c) 6:10 a.m.   (d) 12:25 p.m.   (e) 9:50 p.m.

(f) 4:35 a.m.   (g) 6:25 p.m.   (h) 11:15 p.m.   (i) 10:10 a.m.   (j) 7:40 p.m.

C2 Write these times using a.m. or p.m.

(a) 0730   (b) 1600   (c) 1345   (d) 0140   (e) 0050

(f) 1515   (g) 0825   (h) 1240   (i) 1955   (j) 1435

C3 Put these times in order, earliest first.

9:40 p.m.   6:45 a.m.   1:00 p.m.   0205   2209   8:35 p.m.   1600   11:42 a.m.

D How long?

9 a.m.   10 a.m.   11 a.m.   12 noon   1 p.m.

Art   **Lunch break**

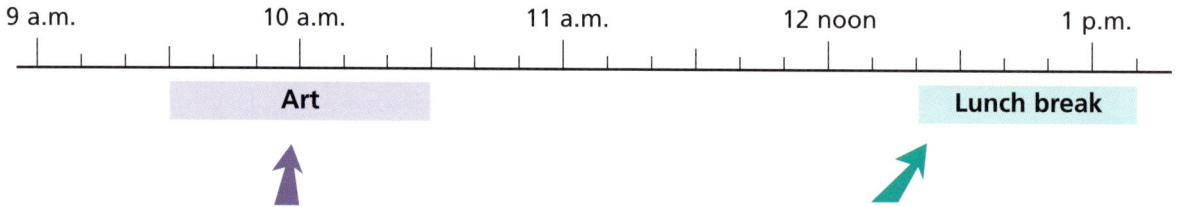

D1 This block shows Jane's art lesson.

   (a) When does it start?

   (b) When does it end?

   (c) How long is it?

D2 This block shows Jane's lunch break.

   (a) When does it start?

   (b) When does it end?

   (c) How long is it?

D3 How long is it

   (a) from 11:30 a.m. to 11:50 a.m.

   (b) from 9:10 a.m. to 10 a.m.

   (c) from 10:20 a.m. to 11:30 a.m.

   (d) from 11:40 a.m. to 12:10 p.m.

You can work out how long it is from 3:50 p.m. to 5:20 p.m. like this.

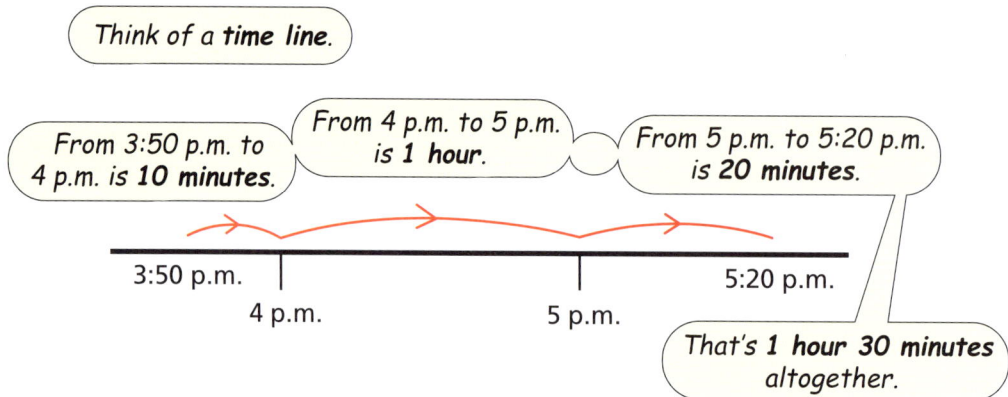

*Think of a **time line**.*

*From 3:50 p.m. to 4 p.m. is **10 minutes**.*

*From 4 p.m. to 5 p.m. is **1 hour**.*

*From 5 p.m. to 5:20 p.m. is **20 minutes**.*

3:50 p.m.   4 p.m.   5 p.m.   5:20 p.m.

*That's **1 hour 30 minutes** altogether.*

D4 How long is it

   (a) from 4:30 p.m. to 6:10 p.m.

   (b) from 2:40 p.m. to 5:10 p.m.

   (c) from 8:20 a.m. to 11:10 a.m.

   (d) from 11:30 a.m. to 1:20 p.m.

D5 How long is it

   (a) from 0645 to 0715

   (b) from 1555 to 1610

   (c) from 0925 to 1040

   (d) from 1935 to 2115

D6 A film starts at 9:30 p.m. and finishes at 11:10 p.m. How long is it?

D7 Sasha wants to go to a film. It starts at 2020. She leaves home at 1945.

How long has she got before the film starts?

Buses leave here at
8:15 a.m.
9:45 a.m.
11:10 a.m.
1:15 p.m.
4:05 p.m.

D8 Gary gets to the bus stop at 10:55 a.m.
How long does he have to wait for a bus?

D9 Sue gets to the bus stop at 12:40 p.m.
How long does she have to wait for a bus?

D10 Misha gets to the bus stop at 3:55 p.m.
How long does he have to wait for a bus?

D11 Paul wants to see *Home Alone* at 2:15 p.m.
It will take him 30 minutes to get to the cinema.

What is the latest time he can leave?

D12 Lana wants to see *Home Alone* at 4:10 p.m.
It will take her 45 minutes to get there.

What is the latest time she can leave?

MASCOT
Cinema

Home Alone

2:15 p.m.	4:10 p.m.
6:20 p.m.	8:45 p.m.

D13 Colin leaves home at 7:45 p.m.
It takes him 25 minutes to get to the cinema.

When he gets there, how long will he have to wait for the film to start?

D14 (a) How long does the first bus take to get from Market Hill to Red Lion?

(b) How long does it take to get from West Gate to Flybridge?

D15 Roddy is at York Road at 10:45.
He wants to go to Flybridge.

How long does he have to wait for a bus?

TURBO TRANSPORT Bus timetable

Market Hill	8:10	10:20
Castle St	8:25	10:35
West Gate	8:40	10:50
York Road	9:00	11:10
Red Lion	9:25	11:35
Tay Cross	9:45	11:55
Oak Hill	10:05	11:15
Flybridge	10:20	11:30

E Round trip

This activity is described in the teacher's guide.

You need sheet 101.

Plan a round trip starting and finishing at Midtown.
Visit each of the other places.
Find different ways of making a round trip.
Which of your ways takes the shortest time?

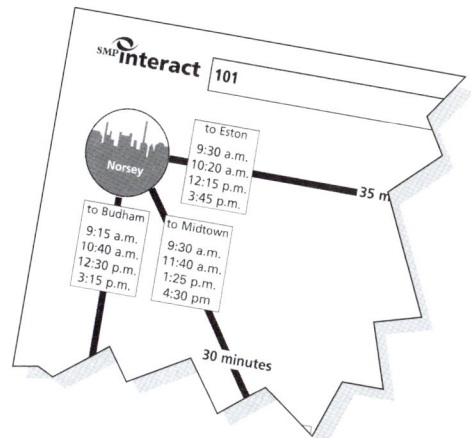

SMP interact 101

Norsey

to Eston
9:30 a.m.
10:20 a.m.
12:15 p.m.
3:45 p.m.

35 m

to Budham
9:15 a.m.
10:40 a.m.
12:30 p.m.
3:15 p.m.

to Midtown
9:30 a.m.
11:40 a.m.
1:25 p.m.
4:30 pm

30 minutes

F Timetables

GREAT EASTERN Train services				Manningtree–Harwich			
Manningtree	1604	1711	1755	1838	1934	2030	2056	2212
Mistley	1608	1715	1759	1842	1938	2034	2101	2216
Wrabness	1613	1720	1804	1847	1943	2039	2106	2221
Harwich International	1620	1728	1812	1854	1951	2047	2113	2228
Dovercourt	1623	1731	1815	1857	1954	2050	2116	2231
Harwich Town	1625	1735	1819	1859	1956	2052	2118	2233

F1 You are at Manningtree at 8 p.m. and you catch the first train to Mistley.

When do you catch the train?

F2 You are at Manningtree at 5:30 p.m.

How long do you have to wait for a train to Harwich Town?

F3 You are at Wrabness at 6 p.m.

How long do you have to wait for a train to Dovercourt?

F4 Find the train which leaves Manningtree at 2056.

How long does it take to get to Harwich Town?

F5 Find the train which leaves Mistley at 1759.

How long does it take to get to Harwich International?

F6 You need to be at Dovercourt by 8 p.m.

What is the latest train you can catch from Manningtree?

F7 You are at Mistley.
You need to be at Harwich International by 9 p.m.

What is the latest train you can catch?

F8 How many trains leave Wrabness for Harwich Town between
5 o'clock and 8 o'clock in the evening?

F9 You are at a friend's house in Wrabness. It is now 6:55 p.m.
It will take you 15 minutes to get to Wrabness station.

What is the earliest time you can get to Harwich Town?

F10 You are shopping in Mistley.
It will take you 10 minutes to walk to the station.
You need to be at Dovercourt by 7:15 p.m.

When do you need to start walking to the station?

What progress have you made?

I can use the 24-hour clock.

1 Write these using the 24-hour clock.

(a) 3:00 p.m.   (b) 6:15 p.m.

(c) 1:35 p.m.   (d) 9:05 a.m.

2 Write these using a.m. or p.m.

(a) 1700   (b) 1420

(c) 0645   (d) 2210

3 Put these times in order, earliest first.

3:30 a.m.   2:05 p.m.   1135   2340

I can work out how long it is between two times.

4 How long is it

(a) from 6:30 p.m. to 7:15 p.m.

(b) from 2:15 p.m. to 3:35 p.m.

(c) from 8:50 a.m. to 10:10 p.m.

(d) from 0540 to 1205

I can use a timetable.

Brock Buses

High Street	1245	1405	1620
Station	1255	1415	1630
Lakeside	1310	1430	1645
Parkgate	1322	1442	1657
Ash Vale	1329	1449	1704
Hill House	1337	1457	1712
Tuxfield	1349	1509	1724

5 Jo is at the High Street bus stop at 1:45 p.m. How long does she have to wait for a bus to Ash Vale?

6 Harry is at the bus stop at Parkgate at 4:35 p.m. How long does he have to wait for a bus to Tuxfield?

7 Shula needs to be at Hill House by 3 o'clock in the afternoon. What is the latest time she can catch a bus from Lakeside?

② Action and result puzzles

These puzzles involve adding, subtracting, multiplying and dividing.
Doing them will help you

- ◆ carry out these sorts of calculations in your head
- ◆ understand more about what happens when you do these calculations
- ◆ explain your methods to other people and listen to their explanations

6 action
add 20

6 result
⁻3

6 result
12

6 action
multiply by 2

6 action
subtract 18

6 result
26

6 result
3

6 action
subtract 9

6 action
divide by 2

6 result
⁻12

- • How do you match the cards?

There are several different puzzles.
Try to solve some of them.

Try making up your own puzzles.

③ Chance

This is about games and other situations where the outcome is uncertain because it is a matter of chance.
The work will help you

♦ use probability as a measure of likelihood

♦ calculate probabilities

A Chance or skill?

Some games are games of skill. Some are games of chance. Many games involve both chance and skill.

There are three games on sheets 111, 112 and 113.

Before you play a game, see if you can tell from the rules if it is a game of chance, a game of skill, or a game which involves both chance and skill.

Then play the game and see if you were right.

Jumping the line

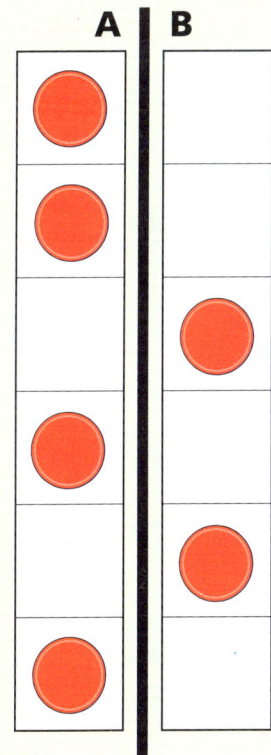

Fours

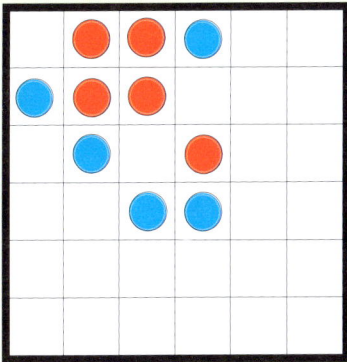

Line of three

1	3	🔵	4	3	3
2	🔴	3	2	2	2
4	2	1	1	🔵	6
1	🔵	6	6	5	3
5	5	5	4	🔴	5
4	4	🔴	1	4	6

B Fair or unfair?

Three way race

For three players (A, B and C)

Each puts a counter at the start of the track.
Two dice are rolled.

If both numbers are even, A moves forward one space.
If both numbers are odd, B moves forward one space.
If one number is even and one odd, C moves forward
one space.

The first to get to the end of the track is the winner.

- Play the game several times.
  Keep a record of who wins (A, B or C).

Winner	Tally	Number of wins
A		
B		
C		

- Is it a fair game?
  Do all three players have an equal chance
  of winning?

- If you could choose to be A, B or C, which
  would you prefer?
  Or doesn't it matter?

- If you think the game is not fair, can you change it to make it fair?

- Can you explain why it is not fair?

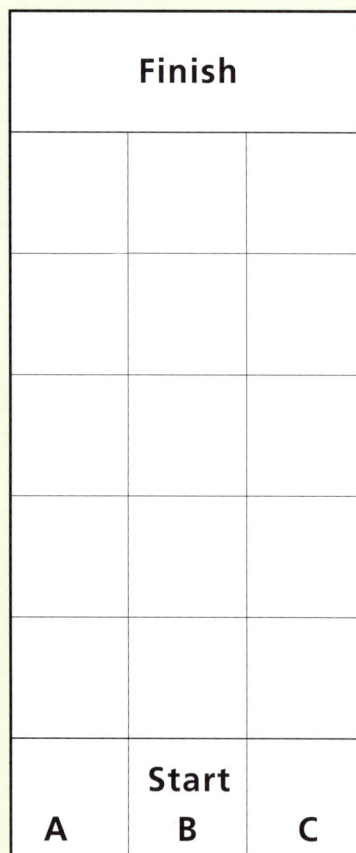

Rat races

For the whole class

You need sheets 114 and 115.

- Are the races fair?
  Does every rat have an equal
  chance of winning?

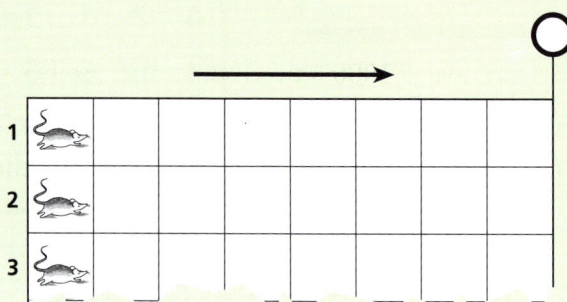

C Probability

Probability is a way of saying how likely something is.

Something which never happens has probability 0.
Something which is certain to happen has probability 1.

Things which have a chance of happening have probabilities between 0 and 1.

Probability scale

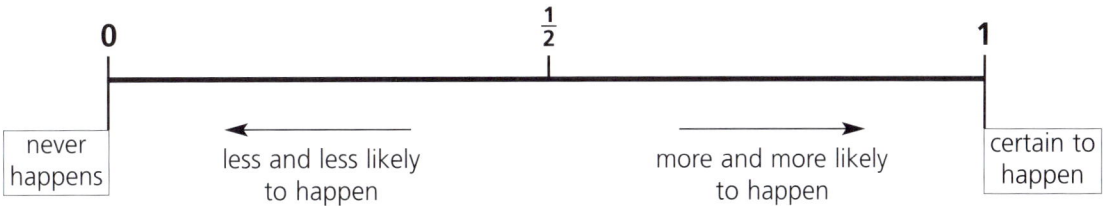

0	$\frac{1}{2}$	1
never happens	less and less likely to happen → → → more and more likely to happen	certain to happen

Where would you mark these on the scale?
- The probability that a coin lands heads
- The probability that rat 1 wins the second rat race
- The probability that the sun will rise tomorrow morning
- The probability that a particular ticket wins the National Lottery

C1 Draw a probability scale like this.

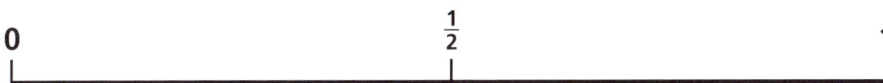

0	$\frac{1}{2}$	1

Mark these roughly on your scale with arrows.
(a) The probability that when you roll a dice you get an even number
(b) The probability that when you roll a dice you get a 6

C2 Out of every 1000 babies born, 515 are boys and 485 are girls.
(a) Is a new-born baby more likely to be a boy or a girl?
(b) On the scale you drew, mark roughly the probability that a new-born baby will be a boy.

D Equally likely outcomes

Sometimes a spinner is used instead of a dice.

This spinner has five equal sections.
You spin the arrow. When it stops it points to a colour.

The five possible colours are called the **outcomes** of a spin.
If the spinner is fair, the five outcomes are **equally likely**.

Suppose you have chosen red.
Red is one of **five** equally likely outcomes.
We say the probability that red will win is $\frac{1}{5}$.

We can also write it as a decimal (0.2) or a percentage (20%).

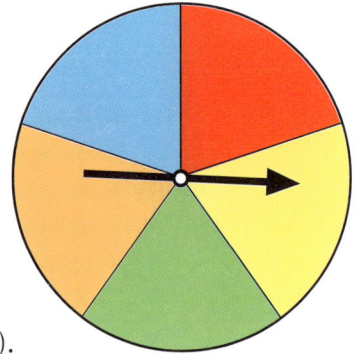

D1 What is the probability that red will win on each of these spinners?

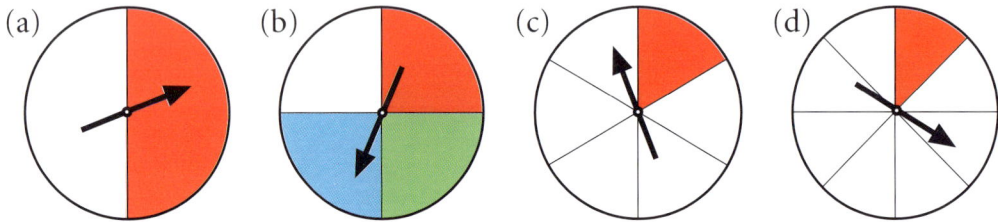

(a)　　　　(b)　　　　(c)　　　　(d)

D2 What is the probability that yellow will win on each of these spinners?

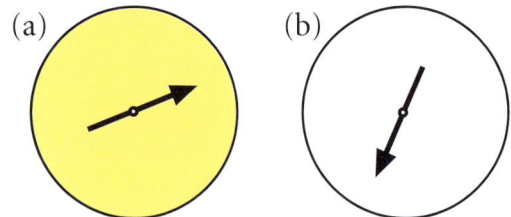

(a)　　　　(b)

D3 On this spinner, the five sections are equally likely.
Two of the sections are green.
What is the probability that green will win?

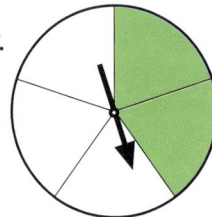

D4 What is the probability that blue will win on each of these spinners?

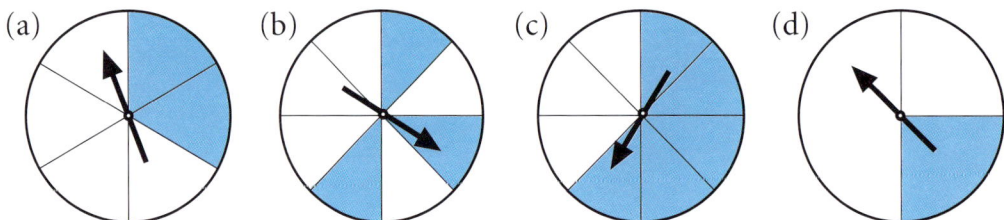

(a)　　　　(b)　　　　(c)　　　　(d)

D5 With this spinner, what is the probability that

    (a) yellow wins

    (b) blue wins

    (c) white wins

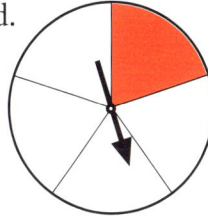

D6 On this spinner, four of the sections are not red.

The probability that red will **not** win is $\frac{4}{5}$.

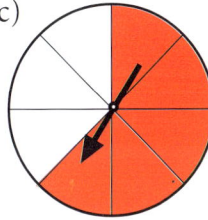

What is the probability that red will **not** win on each of these spinners?

(a) 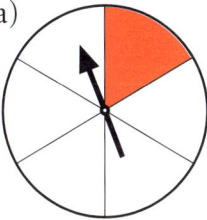   (b) 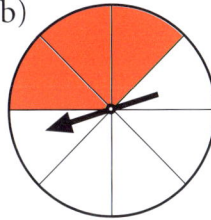   (c) 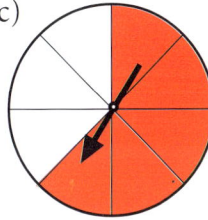   (d)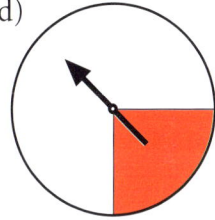

D7 On another spinner, the probability that red will win is $\frac{2}{5}$.
What is the probability that red will not win?

D8 What is the probability that red will not win when the
probability that red wins is

    (a) $\frac{1}{3}$ (b) $\frac{7}{8}$ (c) $\frac{5}{9}$ (d) $\frac{3}{10}$ (e) $\frac{1}{2}$

Odds

The probability of getting red on this spinner is $\frac{1}{4}$.

The probability of getting white is $\frac{3}{4}$.

White is 3 times as likely as red.
Sometimes people say that the 'odds' are 3 to 1 against red.

Odds are used in horse racing and in betting generally.

If you want to tell someone the probability of something,
it is **not** correct to give the odds.
A probability is always a fraction, decimal or percentage.

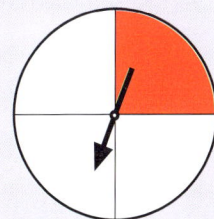

Probability of red = $\frac{1}{4}$

Probability of white = $\frac{3}{4}$

E Equivalent fractions

The probability of getting red on this spinner is $\frac{1}{2}$.

The probability of getting red on this spinner is $\frac{3}{6}$.

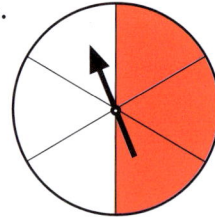

The probabilities of red are equal.

The fractions $\frac{1}{2}$ and $\frac{3}{6}$ are equal, or **equivalent**, fractions.

Here are some other examples of equivalent fractions.

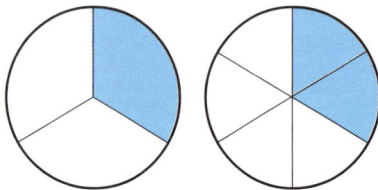

$$\frac{1}{3} = \frac{2}{6}$$

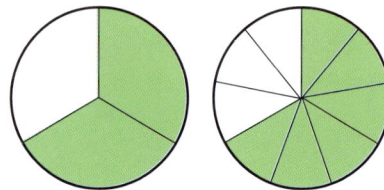

$$\frac{2}{3} = \frac{6}{9}$$

E1 Use these diagrams to help you write down a fraction equivalent to $\frac{1}{4}$.

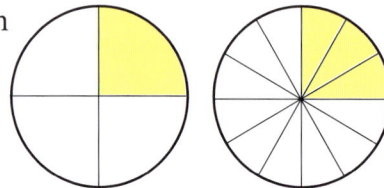

E2 Write down a fraction equivalent to $\frac{1}{5}$. These diagrams may help.

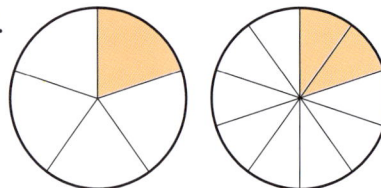

E3 Write down three fractions each equivalent to $\frac{3}{4}$. These diagrams may help.

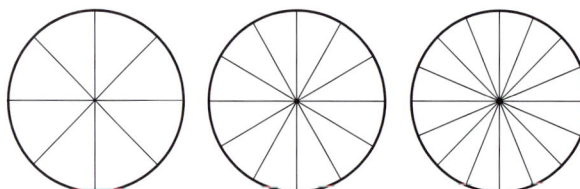

You can make a fraction equivalent to $\frac{2}{3}$ by multiplying the 2 and the 3 by the same number.

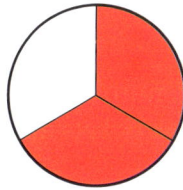

$$\overset{\times 4}{\underset{\times 4}{\frac{2}{3} = \frac{8}{12}}}$$

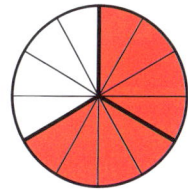

You can reverse the process.
For example, starting with $\frac{8}{12}$ you can divide the 8 and the 12 by 4, to get $\frac{2}{3}$.

$$\overset{\div 4}{\underset{\div 4}{\frac{8}{12} = \frac{2}{3}}}$$

*This is called **simplifying** a fraction.*

E4 Simplify each of these fractions.
Make the result as simple as possible (so that you can't go any further).
(a) $\frac{3}{6}$　　　　(b) $\frac{6}{8}$　　　　(c) $\frac{5}{20}$　　　　(d) $\frac{12}{16}$　　　　(e) $\frac{9}{12}$

E5 Simplify each of these fractions as far as possible.
(a) $\frac{10}{40}$　　　　(b) $\frac{9}{24}$　　　　(c) $\frac{8}{12}$　　　　(d) $\frac{9}{21}$　　　　(e) $\frac{4}{20}$

E6 Simplify each of these fractions as far as possible.
One of them cannot be simplified – which one?
(a) $\frac{20}{30}$　　　　(b) $\frac{15}{24}$　　　　(c) $\frac{12}{30}$　　　　(d) $\frac{9}{25}$　　　　(e) $\frac{14}{35}$

*The 'top number' of a fraction is called the **numerator**.*

To simplify a fraction, divide the numerator and denominator by the same number.

*The 'bottom number' is called the **denominator**.*

E7 Some of these fractions can be simplified and some cannot.
Pick out the ones which can be simplified, and simplify them as far as possible.
(a) $\frac{12}{36}$　　　　(b) $\frac{16}{27}$　　　　(c) $\frac{18}{27}$　　　　(d) $\frac{12}{25}$　　　　(e) $\frac{24}{60}$
(f) $\frac{28}{42}$　　　　(g) $\frac{15}{35}$　　　　(h) $\frac{15}{32}$　　　　(i) $\frac{30}{48}$　　　　(j) $\frac{12}{45}$

E8 Simplify as far as possible the fraction $\frac{48}{72}$.

F Choosing at random

There are 100 raffle tickets in a box, numbered from 1 to 100.
A person shuts their eyes, stirs up the tickets and takes one out
without looking.

This is called choosing a ticket **at random**.
Every ticket is equally likely to be chosen.

Rae has bought the tickets with these numbers: 31, 32, 33, 34, 35.

There is only one prize.
The probability that one of Rae's tickets will be chosen is $\frac{5}{100}$,
which is equivalent to $\frac{1}{20}$.

F1 There are 50 raffle tickets in a box, numbered from 1 to 50.
One ticket will be drawn at random.
Jodie has ticket number 42.

What is the probability that her number will be drawn?

F2 A box contains 200 raffle tickets numbered from 1 to 200.
One ticket is to be drawn at random.
Justin has the tickets with these numbers: 121, 122, 123, 124.

What is the probability that one of his numbers will be drawn?

F3 A box has 250 raffle tickets in it, and one ticket will be drawn at random.
Pam has bought 10 tickets.

What is the probability that one of her numbers will be drawn?
Write it in the simplest possible way.

F4 Imagine these eight cards are
turned over and shuffled.

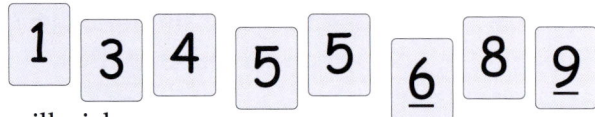

You pick a card at random.
What is the probability that you will pick

(a) the number 4   (b) the number 5   (c) an even number

(d) an odd number   (e) a factor of 12   (f) the number 2

(g) a number which is less than 7

F5 In a fairground game there are 100 sticky labels on a board.

Under one of them is a prize token.

(a) Derek is the first person to have a go. He chooses a label and peels it off.

What is the probability that he will win the prize?

(b) Later the board looks like this. Derek comes back and chooses another label.

What is the probability that he will win this time?

(c) Suppose Derek is unsuccessful. He has another go.

What is the probability that he will win this time?

*F6 Sarah likes red sweets but not green ones.
She can pick a sweet at random from either bag A or bag B.

Which bag should she pick from?

Why?

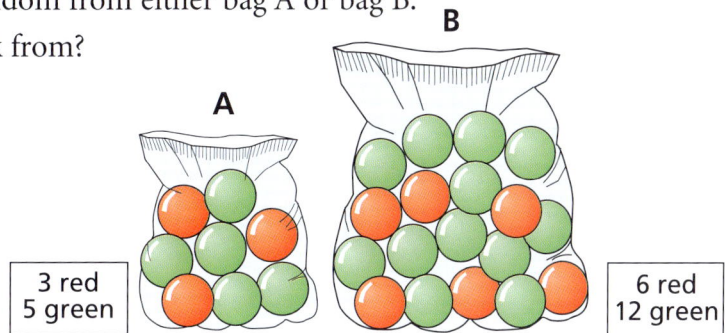

| 3 red |
| 5 green |

| 6 red |
| 12 green |

*F7 Dilesh likes green sweets but not red ones.
He can pick a sweet from either bag C or bag D.

Which bag should he pick from?

Why?

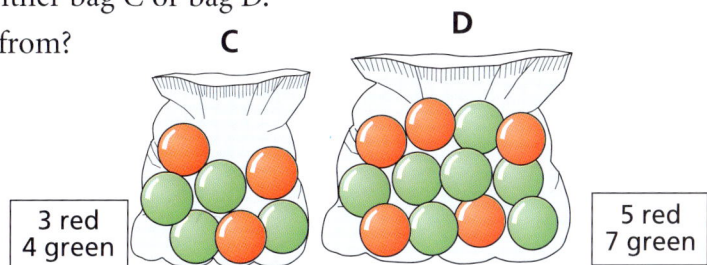

| 3 red |
| 4 green |

| 5 red |
| 7 green |

What progress have you made?

I understand the probability scale.

1 (a) Draw a probability scale.
What number goes at each end?

(b) What can you say about something whose probability is 0?

(c) What can you say about something whose probability is 1?

(d) Mark with an arrow on your scale the probability that a coin lands tails.

I can work out a probability using equally likely outcomes.

2 What is the probability of getting red on each of these spinners?

(a)   (b)

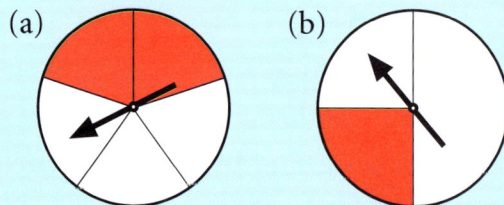

3 A box contains 80 raffle tickets, numbered from 1 to 80.
Zara has four tickets: 51, 52, 53, 54.
What is the probability that one of her numbers will be drawn?

I can simplify fractions.

4 Write each of these fractions as simply as possible.

(a) $\frac{18}{30}$ (b) $\frac{25}{45}$ (c) $\frac{16}{40}$

④ Symmetry

This work will help you

◆ recognise rotation symmetry
◆ draw patterns with rotation symmetry
◆ find all the different symmetries in a pattern

A What is symmetrical about these shapes?

B Rotation symmetry

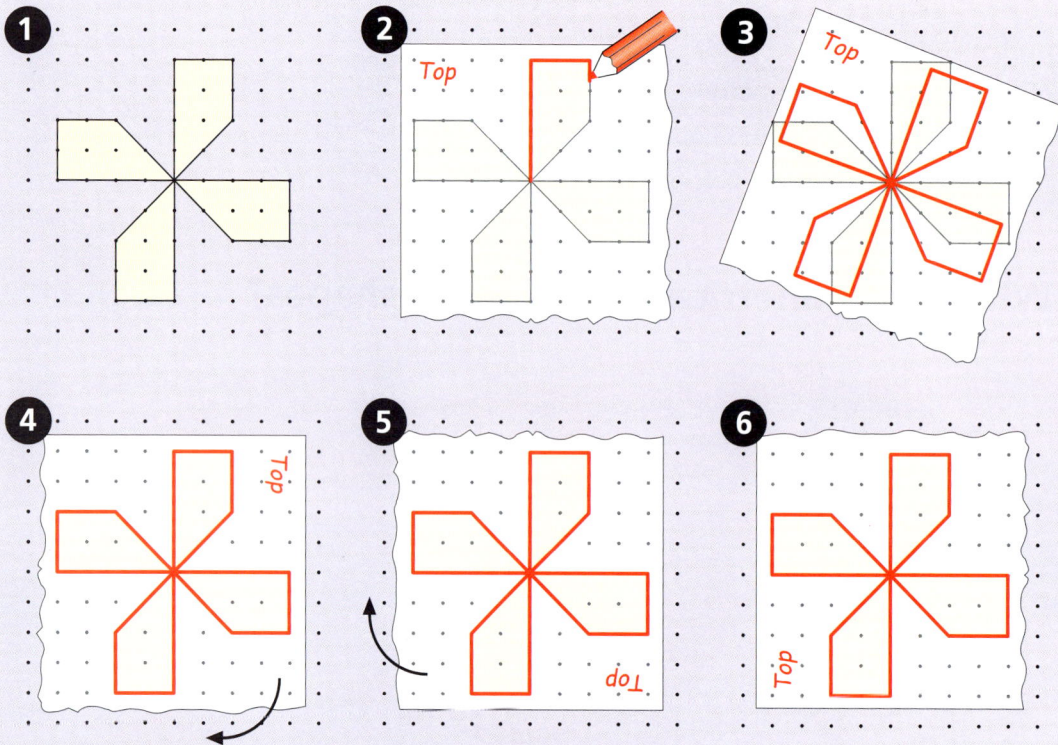

There are **four** positions where the tracing fits the pattern, the starting position and three more.

We say the pattern has **rotation symmetry of order 4**.
The centre of the pattern is called the **centre of rotation symmetry**.

*The number of times the tracing fits the shape is the **order** of rotation symmetry.*

A tracing of this shape will fit over the shape in only one position.
Strictly speaking, the shape has rotation symmetry of order 1, but there is no single centre of rotation symmetry.
We usually say the shape has **no rotation symmetry**.

B1 You need sheet 117.

Write down the order of rotation symmetry of each design.
Mark the centre of rotation with a dot (unless the order is 1).

C Making designs

C1 Make a design with rotation symmetry of order 4 like this.

1

Copy this on to square dotty paper.

The large dot will be the centre of rotation symmetry.

2

Draw a guide line from the centre of rotation symmetry.

3

Trace the shape and the line.

4 Rotate the tracing 90°.
Make a copy of the shape on the dotty paper.

90°

5 Rotate the tracing 90° twice more and copy the shape each time.

C2 On sheet 120, complete each design so it has rotation symmetry of order 4.
Do it without using tracing paper. Then check by tracing.

C3 Copy and complete each pattern so it has rotation symmetry of order 4.

(a)

(b)

(c)

Do not shade more squares than you need to.

C4 Make a design with rotation symmetry of order 3 like this.

1

Make sure your paper is the right way up!

Copy this on to triangular dotty paper.

The large dot is the centre of rotation symmetry.

2

Trace the shape.

3

120°

Rotate the tracing 120°

4

Make a copy of the shape on the dotty paper.

5

Rotate the tracing 120° once more and copy the shape on to the dotty paper again.

C5 On sheet 121, complete each design so it has rotation symmetry of order 3.

C6 Copy and complete each pattern so it has rotation symmetry of order 2.

(a)

(b)

(c)

Do not shade more squares than you need to.

*C7** Make a design with rotation symmetry of order 6.

D Rotation and reflection symmetry

Some patterns and shapes have
rotation symmetry **and**
reflection symmetry.

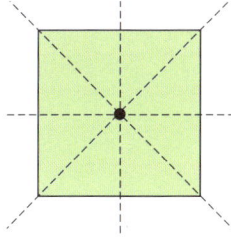

A square has four lines
of reflection symmetry and
rotation symmetry of order 4.

D1 Copy the shapes below.
For each shape, draw all the lines of symmetry. If there is a centre of rotation,
mark it and write the order of rotation symmetry under the shape.

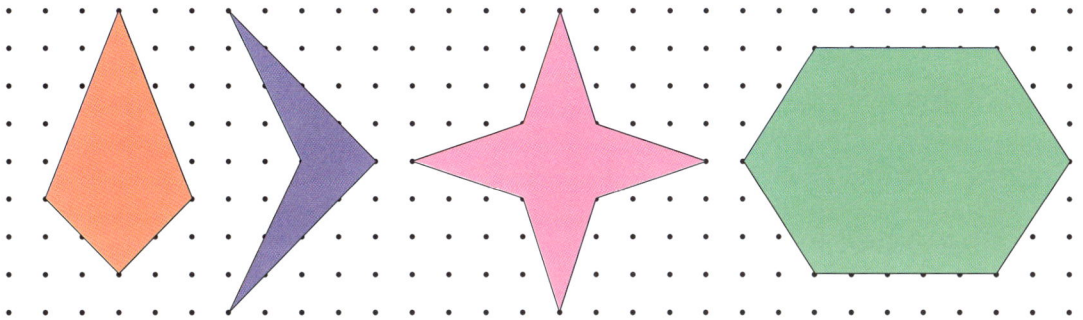

D2 For each design on sheet 122, draw all the lines of symmetry.
If there is a centre of rotation, mark it and write the
order of rotation symmetry under the design.

D3 Four squares are shaded on
this 4 by 4 grid.

(a) What is its order
of rotation symmetry?

(b) Does it have reflection symmetry?

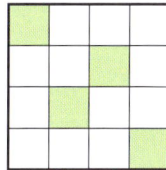

D4 Find eight different ways of shading four squares on a 4 by 4 grid to
make a pattern with rotation symmetry of order 2 or more.

What is the order of rotation symmetry of each pattern?
Show any lines of symmetry on your patterns.

D5 On a 3 by 3 grid, shade four squares to make a pattern with

(a) rotation symmetry (order 2 or more) and reflection symmetry

(b) rotation symmetry (order 2 or more) but no reflection symmetry

(c) reflection symmetry but no rotation symmetry (that is, order 1)

(d) no rotation symmetry or reflection symmetry

E Pentominoes

A pentomino is a shape made from
five squares touching edge to edge.

This pentomino has no rotation symmetry
and one line of reflection symmetry.

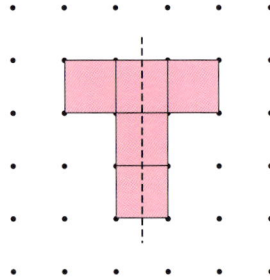

E1 Find a different pentomino with no rotation symmetry and one line of symmetry.

E2 Draw a pentomino with

(a) no rotation symmetry and no lines of symmetry

(b) four lines of symmetry and rotation symmetry of order 4

(c) rotation symmetry of order 2 and no lines of symmetry

(d) two lines of symmetry and rotation symmetry of order 2

E3 This shape is made from
two pentominoes.

They do not overlap.

It has rotation symmetry of
order 2 but no lines of symmetry.

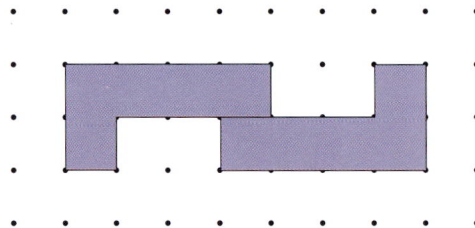

(a) With these two pentominoes and with no overlapping,

(i) make a different shape with rotation symmetry of order 2 but
no reflection symmetry

(ii) make a shape with a line of symmetry but no rotation symmetry
(you can flip over a pentomino)

(iii) make a shape with two lines of symmetry and rotation symmetry of order 2

(b) With four of these pentominoes and with no overlapping, make
a design with rotation symmetry of order 4.

Does your design have any lines of symmetry?

E4 Choose one of the pentominoes you drew in E1 or E2.

With two or more copies of your pentomino, try to make a design with

(a) reflection symmetry but no rotation symmetry

(b) rotation symmetry but no reflection symmetry

(c) reflection symmetry and rotation symmetry of order 2 or more

What progress have you made?

Statement

I know when shapes have rotation symmetry or reflection symmetry.

Evidence

1 Which of these shapes have

(a) rotation symmetry but no reflection symmetry

(b) reflection symmetry but no rotation symmetry

(c) rotation and reflection symmetry

I can find centres and orders of rotation symmetry and lines of symmetry.

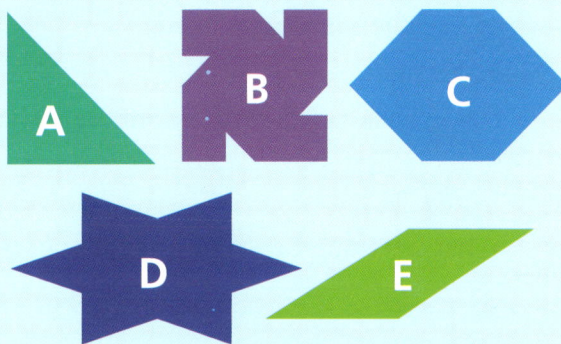

2 (a) Sketch these patterns, mark the centres of rotation and, next to each sketch, write its order of rotation symmetry.

(b) Show all lines of symmetry on your diagrams.

I can draw shapes with given symmetry.

3 On a 4 by 4 grid of squares, shade eight squares to make a pattern with rotation symmetry of order 4 but no reflection symmetry.

⑤ Fractions

This work will help you
◆ calculate a fraction of a number
◆ write one number as a fraction of another

A Revising fractions

A1 Sheila says this square is split into 3 parts,
so $\frac{1}{3}$ of the square is shaded.

Is she right?

If not, what fraction of the square is shaded?

A2 What fraction of each of these shapes is shaded?

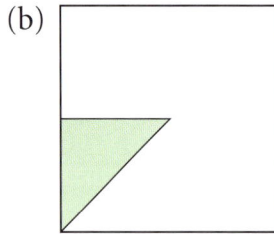

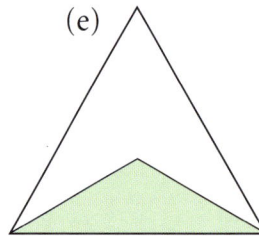

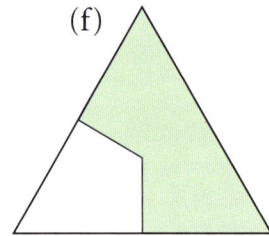

(a)　　　　　　(b)　　　　　　(c)

(d)　　　　　　(e)　　　　　　(f)

A3 Work these out.

(a) $\frac{1}{2}$ of 30　　(b) $\frac{1}{4}$ of 20　　(c) $\frac{1}{3}$ of 12　　(d) $\frac{1}{4}$ of 12

(e) $\frac{1}{4}$ of 24　　(f) $\frac{1}{3}$ of 18　　(g) $\frac{1}{5}$ of 10　　(h) $\frac{1}{5}$ of 40

(i) $\frac{1}{3}$ of 27　　(j) $\frac{1}{5}$ of 35　　(k) $\frac{1}{8}$ of 24　　(l) $\frac{1}{8}$ of 40

A4 Work these out.

(a) $\frac{1}{2}$ of 50 kilograms　　(b) $\frac{1}{3}$ of 24 centimetres　　(c) $\frac{1}{5}$ of 100 grams

(d) $\frac{1}{4}$ of 36 litres　　(e) $\frac{1}{8}$ of 56 kilograms　　(f) $\frac{1}{6}$ of 72 hectares

How do I work out $\frac{3}{5}$ of 20?

○○○○○○○○○○○○○○○○○○○○

First work out $\frac{1}{5}$ of 20.

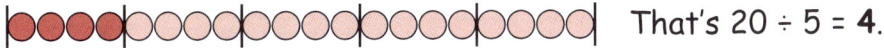

●●●●|○○○○|○○○○|○○○○|○○○○| That's 20 ÷ 5 = **4**.

Then multiply by 3.

●●●●|●●●●|●●●●|○○○○|○○○○| That's 4 × 3 = **12**.

A5 Work these out.

    (a) $\frac{2}{5}$ of 10   (b) $\frac{2}{3}$ of 12   (c) $\frac{3}{4}$ of 12   (d) $\frac{2}{5}$ of 15

    (e) $\frac{3}{4}$ of 20   (f) $\frac{4}{5}$ of 40   (g) $\frac{5}{6}$ of 18   (h) $\frac{3}{8}$ of 16

A6 There are 30 pupils in class 8W.
$\frac{2}{5}$ of them are away on a school trip.

How many pupils are away?

A7 Which would you rather have,

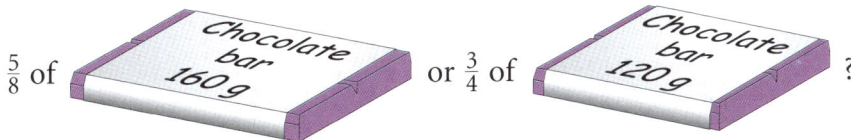

$\frac{5}{8}$ of   Chocolate bar 160 g   or $\frac{3}{4}$ of   Chocolate bar 120 g   ?

A8 Which would you rather have,

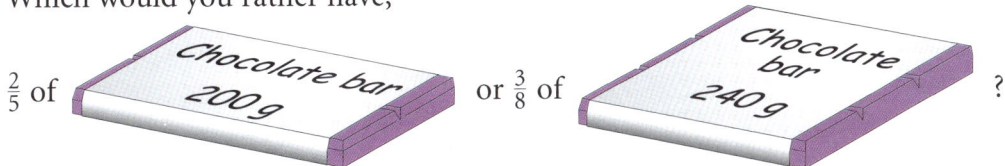

$\frac{2}{5}$ of   Chocolate bar 200 g   or $\frac{3}{8}$ of   Chocolate bar 240 g   ?

A9 (a) Work out $\frac{1}{3}$ of 237.

    (b) Now work out $\frac{2}{3}$ of 237.

A10 Work these out.

    (a) $\frac{3}{4}$ of 768   (b) $\frac{2}{5}$ of 785   (c) $\frac{3}{10}$ of 680   (d) $\frac{2}{3}$ of 405

    (e) $\frac{5}{8}$ of 176   (f) $\frac{5}{6}$ of 648   (g) $\frac{3}{8}$ of 600   (h) $\frac{4}{5}$ of 770

A11 Work these out.

    (a) $\frac{3}{10}$ of 130 litres   (b) $\frac{5}{8}$ of 192 centimetres   (c) $\frac{7}{10}$ of 250 grams

B Pie charts

A **pie chart** shows something split up into parts.

This pie chart shows what Sashi does with her pocket money.

She spends $\frac{1}{2}$ of her money on clothes.

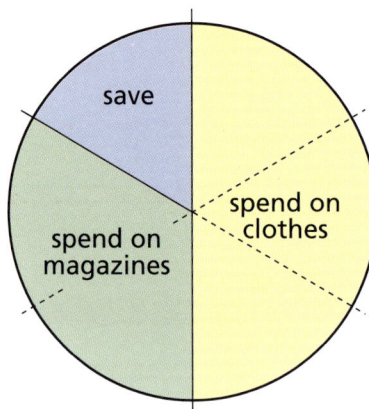

B1 (a) What fraction of her money does Sashi spend on magazines?

(b) What fraction does she save?

B2 Sashi gets £24 a month.
How much money does she

(a) save   (b) spend on clothes   (c) spend on magazines

B3 This pie chart shows what Grant does with his money.
What fraction does he spend on

(a) pet food   (b) magazines   (c) snacks

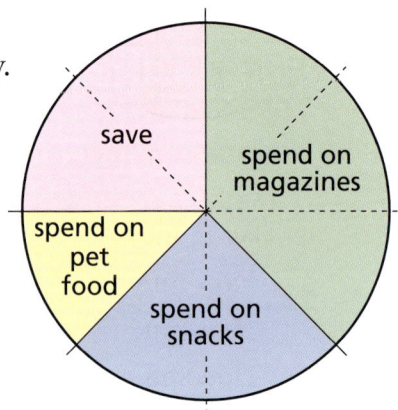

B4 Grant gets £16 pocket money in a month.
How much money does he spend on

(a) pet food   (b) magazines   (c) snacks

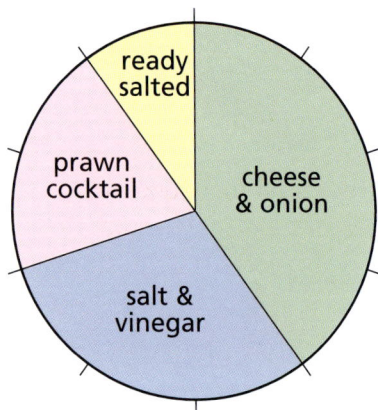

B5 Class 7H did a survey of favourite crisp flavours.
This pie chart shows the results.

(a) What fraction of the class liked ready salted best?

(b) What fraction liked salt and vinegar best?

(c) What fraction liked cheese and onion best?

B6 There are 30 pupils in class 7H.
How many pupils liked these best?

(a) ready salted   (b) salt and vinegar

(c) cheese and onion

B7 Class 7J did a survey of favourite ice cream flavours. The results are shown in this pie chart.

(a) What fraction of the class liked vanilla best?

(b) What fraction liked strawberry best?

(c) What fraction liked chocolate best?

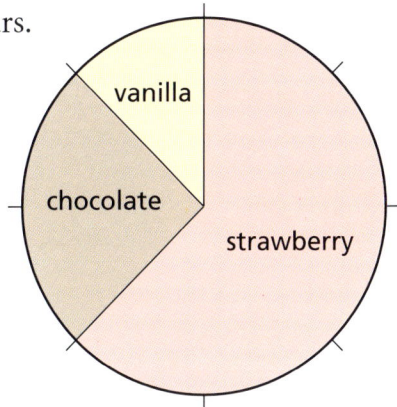

B8 There are 32 pupils in class 7J.
How many pupils liked these best?

(a) strawberry   (b) chocolate

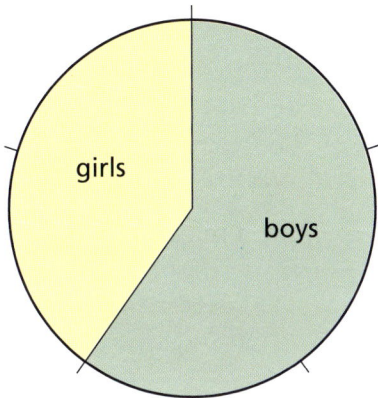

B9 This pie chart shows the proportions of boys and girls in class 8H.
There are 30 pupils altogether in the class.

How many of the pupils are boys?

B10 Class 8K has 35 pupils. The pie chart for this class looks the same as for class 8H.

How many girls are there in class 8K?

B11 This pie chart shows how Alice spends her pocket money. She gets £30 a month.

(a) How much does she save?

(b) How much does she spend on clothes?

(c) How much does she spend on other things?

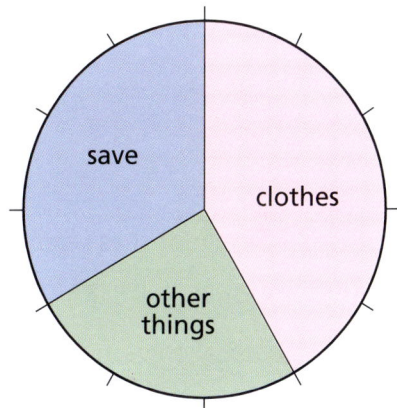

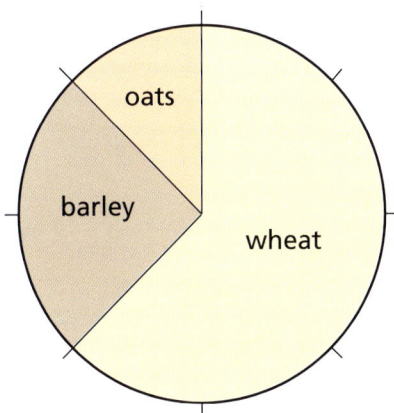

B12 Amos's farm covers 500 hectares.
(A hectare is a unit of area equal to $10\,000\,\text{m}^2$.)
This pie chart shows how the farm is planted.

How many hectares are planted with

(a) oats   (b) wheat   (c) barley

C Simplifying fractions

These diagrams show that $\frac{9}{12} = \frac{3}{4}$.

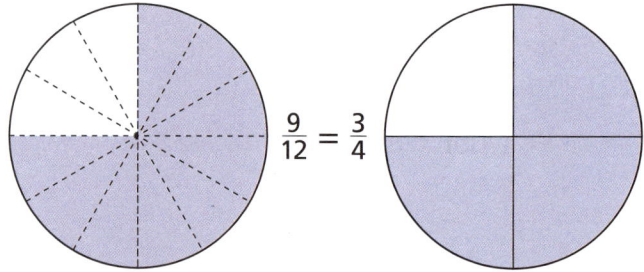

$$\frac{9}{12} = \frac{3}{4}$$

C1 What do these diagrams show?

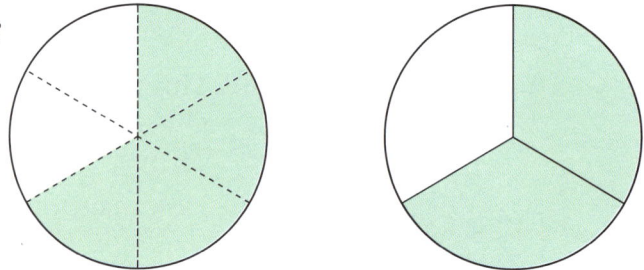

> You can simplify a fraction by dividing the numerator and denominator by the same number.
>
> For example,
> $$\frac{9}{12} \xrightarrow{\div 3} = \frac{3}{4}$$
> $\div 3$

C2 Simplify each of these fractions.

(a) $\frac{2}{4}$ (b) $\frac{2}{10}$ (c) $\frac{3}{9}$ (d) $\frac{6}{10}$ (e) $\frac{10}{15}$

C3 Write each of these fractions in the simplest possible way.

(a) $\frac{15}{20}$ (b) $\frac{12}{18}$ (c) $\frac{15}{24}$ (d) $\frac{12}{40}$ (e) $\frac{15}{60}$

C4 What fraction of this strip has been shaded?
Write it in its simplest form.

C5 What fraction of this row of beads is black?
Write the fraction in its simplest form.

C6 There are 6 cans here altogether.
2 of them have been opened.
So $\frac{2}{6}$ of the cans have been opened.

Write $\frac{2}{6}$ in its simplest form.

C7 What fraction of these cans have been opened?
Write the fraction in its simplest form.

C8 Write each of these fractions in its simplest form.

(a) The fraction of trees blown down

(b) The fraction of eggs broken

(c) The fraction of CD cases empty

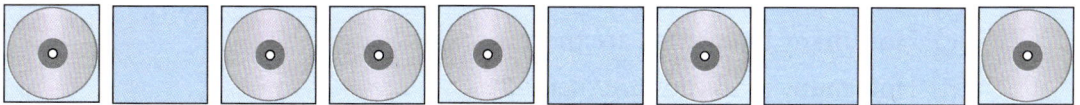

C9 There are 30 children in class 4S.
18 of them are absent with flu.

What fraction of the class is absent?
Write it in its simplest form.

C10 Jack has 40 stamps in his album.
25 are British, 10 are French and the rest American.

What fraction, in its simplest form, of his stamps are

(a) British   (b) French   (c) American

C11 What fraction of the area of this rectangle is shaded?
Write it as simply as you can.

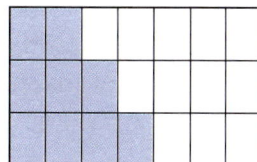

D Comparing parts

D1 In a model railway club, there are twice as many boys as girls.

(a) What fraction of the members are girls?

(b) What fraction of the members are boys?

D2 In a swimming pool, $\frac{3}{4}$ of the swimmers are women.

(a) What fraction of the swimmers are men?

(b) Copy and complete:

There are _____ times as many women in the pool as men.

D3 One tennis season, Sasha lost $\frac{1}{5}$ of the matches she played.

(a) What fraction of her matches did she win?

(b) Copy and complete:

She won _____ times as many matches as she lost.

D4 Kath has a bracelet made of red and blue beads.
There are 5 red beads for every blue bead.

(a) What fraction of the beads are blue?

(b) What fraction are red?

There are 42 beads in the bracelet.

(c) How many blue beads are there?

(d) How many red beads are there?

D5 Parvinder's bracelet has 6 red beads for every 2 green beads.
Copy and complete:

There are _____ times as many red beads as green beads.

D6 Nigel collects stamps.
He has 4 times as many foreign stamps as British stamps.
He has 200 stamps altogether.

(a) How many British stamps does he have?

(b) How many foreign stamps does he have?

D7 Dave is a nurse.
He works 2 night shifts for every 3 day shifts.
What fraction of his shifts are at night?

E Puzzles and problems

E1 You have these 'fraction cards'…   … and these number cards.

$\frac{1}{3}$ of $\frac{2}{3}$ of $\frac{2}{5}$ of $\frac{3}{4}$ of | 25 | 36 | 40 | 24 | 30 |

(a) Which pair of cards will give the result 8?

(b) Which pair gives the result 30?

(c) Which pair gives 27?

(d) Find two different pairs which each give 12.

(e) Find two different pairs which each give 10.

(f) Find two different pairs which each give 16.

E2 Knights have to pass through the four gates of Castle Dread.
At the first gate they must pay the gatekeeper $\frac{1}{2}$ of their money.
At the second they must pay $\frac{2}{3}$ of what they have left.
At the third they must pay $\frac{3}{4}$ of what they have left.
At the fourth they must pay $\frac{4}{5}$ of what they have left.

Sir Randolf has 120 gold pieces when he arrives
at the first gate.

How much does he have left when he leaves the fourth gate?

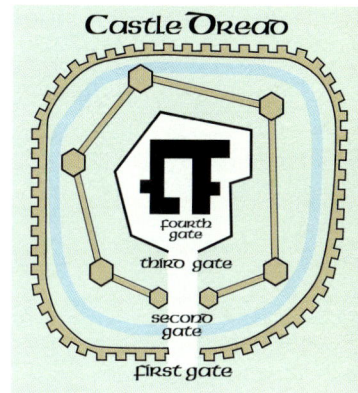

Castle Dread

E3 Copy and complete this table.

	12		
$\frac{1}{4}$ of	3		
$\frac{1}{6}$ of	2	6	
$\frac{2}{3}$ of			40

E4 How many different fractions can you make using pairs of digits
from this list?

1 2 3 4 6

For example, you can make $\frac{1}{2}$, $\frac{1}{3}$, $\frac{2}{3}$, …

Fractions which are equivalent do not count as different.
For example, $\frac{1}{2}$ and $\frac{2}{4}$ are counted as the same.

E5 $\frac{1}{4}$ of Jacob's trees were blown down in a storm.
Later a flood carried away $\frac{2}{3}$ of those that were left.
Afterwards there were only 8 trees still standing.

How many were there before the storm?

What progress have you made?

Statement

I can work out a fraction of a number.

Evidence

1 Work these out.

(a) $\frac{2}{3}$ of 27   (b) $\frac{3}{5}$ of 20

I can use fractions shown in pie charts.

2 This pie chart shows class 8W's favourite fruits.

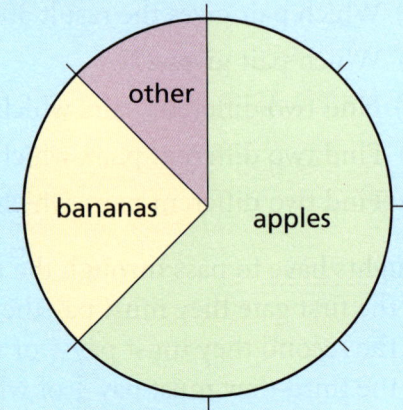

There are 32 pupils in class 8W.

(a) What fraction of the class like bananas best?

(b) How many pupils like bananas best?

I can simplify fractions.

3 Write each of these fractions in its simplest form.

(a) $\frac{21}{24}$ (b) $\frac{28}{40}$ (c) $\frac{18}{60}$

4 What fraction of this rectangle is green?

Write it as simply as you can.

⑥ Number grids

This is about number grids and algebra.
The work will help you

◆ solve problems and investigate patterns on a number grid
◆ simplify expressions
◆ use algebra to investigate rules

A Square grids

An introductory activity is described in the teacher's guide.

These number grids use the rules '+ 6' across (→) and '+ 2' down (↓).

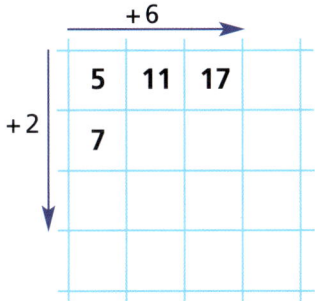

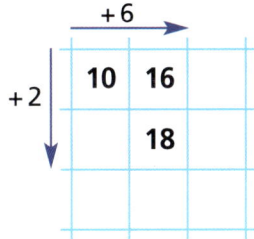

• Copy and complete these grids.

A1 (a) Draw three different sized square grids that use the rules '+ 6' across and '+ 2' down. Choose a different number for each top left corner and complete the grids.

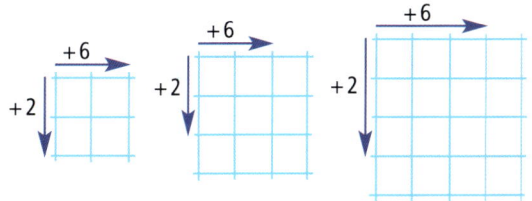

(b) For your grids, find a rule to go diagonally from one number to another. Make sure your rule works for all the grids. Explain how you found your rule.

(c) Use your rule to work out the numbers for the shaded squares in these grids.

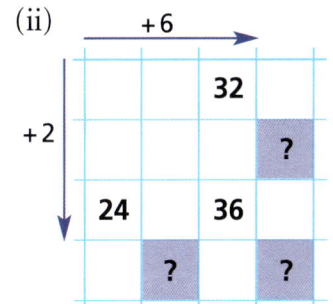

A2 (a) Copy and complete these number grids.

(i)

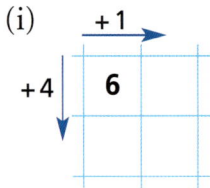

(ii)

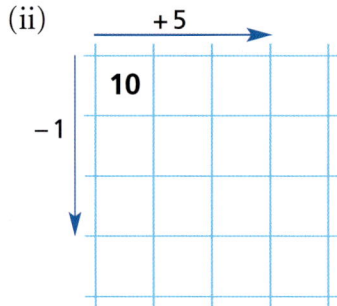

(iii)

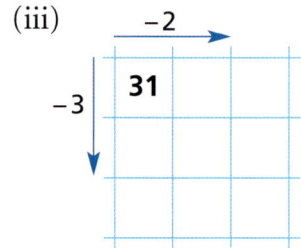

(b) For each grid,
find a rule to go diagonally (↘) from one number to another and
explain how you found your rule.

A3 Investigate your own number grids.

- Use only '+' or '−' in your rules.

- Choose your own numbers for the top left corner.

- Record your results in a table like the one below.

Across rule	Down rule	Diagonal rule

What is the link between the across, down and diagonal rules?

A4 What are the diagonal rules for these grids?

(a)

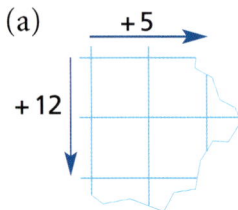

(b)

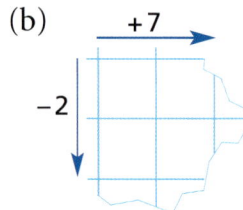

A5 Find some pairs of across and down rules that fit these grids.
What do you notice?

(a)

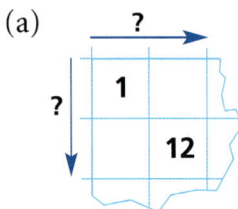

(b)

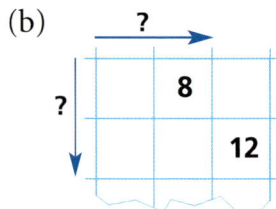

B Grid puzzles

B1 For each puzzle, work out the number in the shaded square.

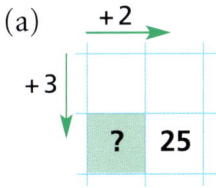

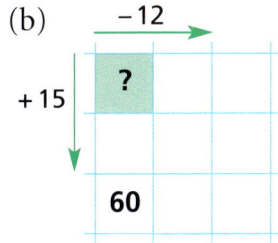

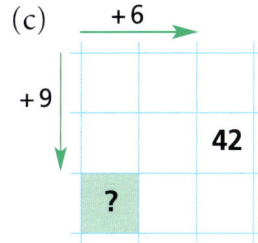

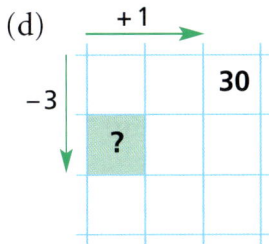

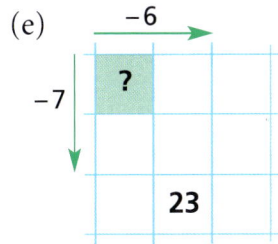

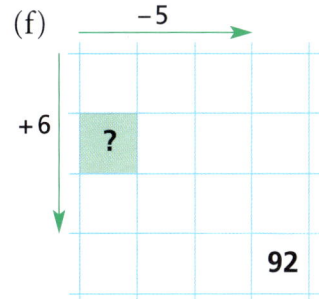

(a) +2 →, +3 ↓, ? 25

(b) −12 →, +15 ↓, ? , 60

(c) +6 →, +9 ↓, 42, ?

(d) +1 →, −3 ↓, 30, ?

(e) −6 →, −7 ↓, ? , 23

(f) −5 →, +6 ↓, ? , 92

B2 Work out the missing rules in these puzzles.

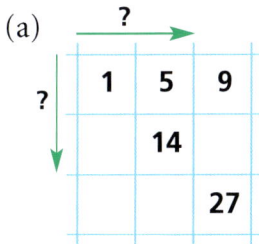

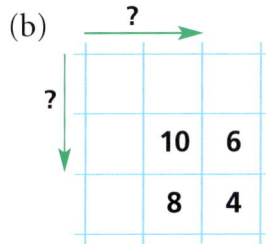

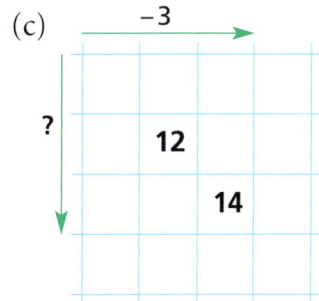

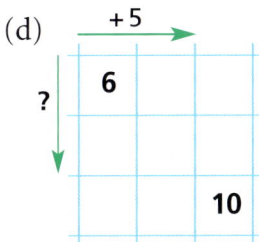

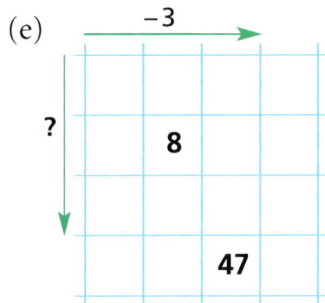

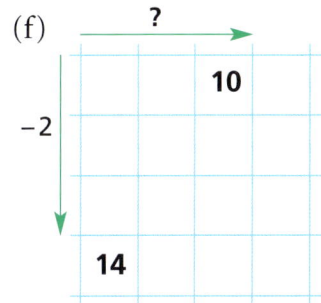

(a) ? →, ? ↓ : 1 5 9 / 14 / 27

(b) ? →, ? ↓ : 10 6 / 8 4

(c) −3 →, ? ↓ : 12 / 14

(d) +5 →, ? ↓ : 6 / 10

(e) −3 →, ? ↓ : 8 / 47

(f) ? →, −2 ↓ : 10 / 14

39

B3 Find the across and down rules for each of these number grid puzzles.

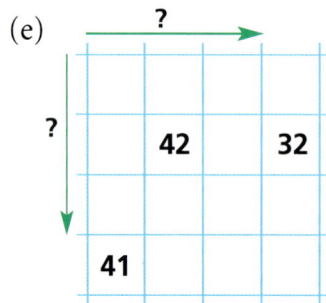

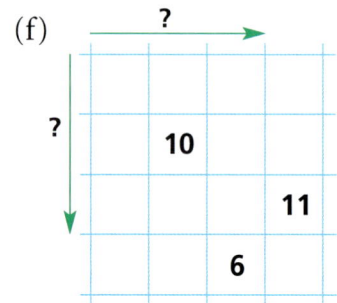

(a)

? →			
4			13
	15		
20			
28			

(down ?)

(b)

? →			
	13	27	
	4		

(down ?)

(c)

? →			
	40		
			30
	28		

(down ?)

(d)

? →			
		10	
		32	
47			

(down ?)

(e)

? →			
	42	32	
41			

(down ?)

(f)

? →			
	10		
			11
	6		

(down ?)

B4 (a) Which of the puzzles in B3 did you find most difficult to solve?

(b) Why do you think it was more difficult to solve than the others?

*B5 Find the missing rules in these puzzles.

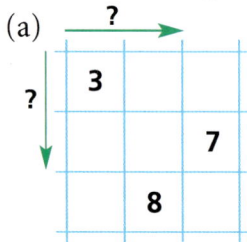

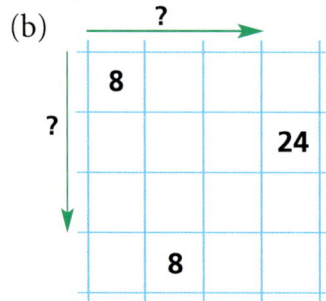

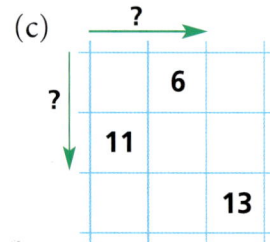

(a)

? →			
3			
	7		
8			

(down ?)

(b)

? →			
8			
		24	
	8		

(down ?)

(c)

? →			
		6	
11			
			13

(down ?)

*B6 (a) Write down pairs of rules that fit this grid.

(b) Find a link between the across rule and the down rule.

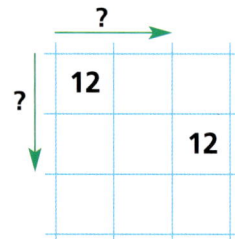

? →		
12		
	12	

(down ?)

40

C Algebra on grids

To find rules on grids, you can use algebra.
You can write n for the number in the top left square and
fill in the other squares.

+2

n	$n + 2$	$n + 4$
		$n + 9$
		$n + 14$

+5

> $n + 4 + 5$ is the same as $n + 9$
> for any number n.
>
> For example, $20 + 4 + 5 = 20 + 9$

- Copy and complete this grid.
- What is a rule to go from the number in the top left square
  to the number in the bottom right square?
- What is the number in the bottom right square
  when the number in the top left square is 12?
- What number in the top left square would
  give 100 in the bottom right square?
- What is a rule to go from the number in the top left square
  to the number in the bottom left square?

This grid uses the rules '– 2' and '+ 7'.
The letter h is used for the number in the top left square.

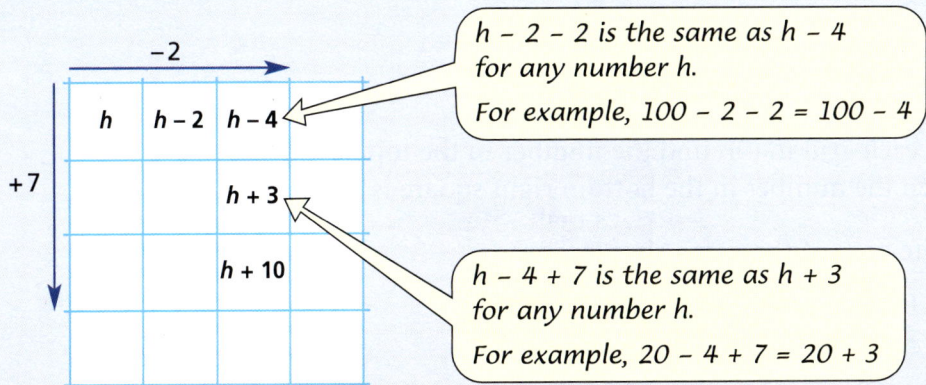

> $h - 2 - 2$ is the same as $h - 4$
> for any number h.
>
> For example, $100 - 2 - 2 = 100 - 4$

–2

h	$h - 2$	$h - 4$
		$h + 3$
		$h + 10$

+7

> $h - 4 + 7$ is the same as $h + 3$
> for any number h.
>
> For example, $20 - 4 + 7 = 20 + 3$

- Copy and complete this grid.

C1 Copy and complete these grids.

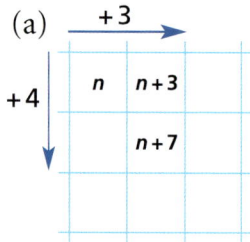

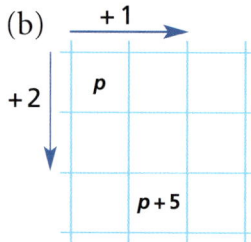

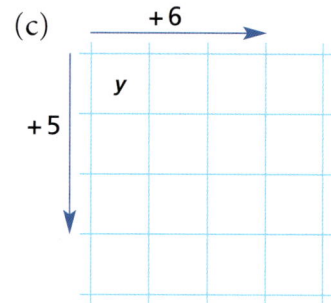

(a)
$+3 \rightarrow$

$+4 \downarrow$

n	$n+3$	
$n+7$		

(b)
$+1 \rightarrow$

$+2 \downarrow$

p		
	$p+5$	

(c)
$+6 \rightarrow$

$+5 \downarrow$

y		

C2 For each grid in C1, work out the number in the bottom right square when the number in the top left square is 100.

C3 Find rules for these grids.

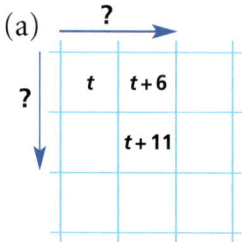

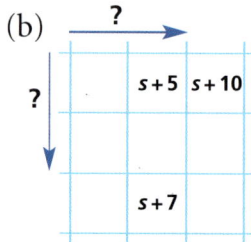

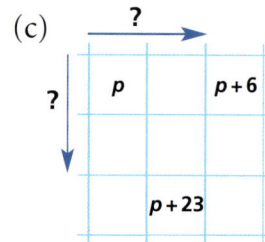

(a)
$? \rightarrow$

$? \downarrow$

t	$t+6$	
$t+11$		

(b)
$? \rightarrow$

$? \downarrow$

$s+5$	$s+10$	
$s+7$		

(c)
$? \rightarrow$

$? \downarrow$

p		$p+6$
		$p+23$

C4 Copy and complete these grids.

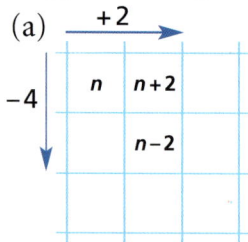

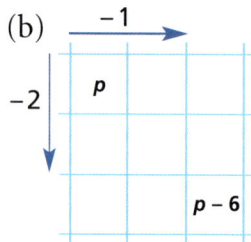

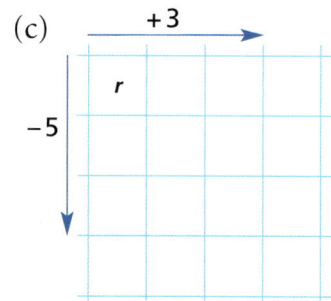

(a)
$+2 \rightarrow$

$-4 \downarrow$

n	$n+2$	
$n-2$		

(b)
$-1 \rightarrow$

$-2 \downarrow$

p		
	$p-6$	

(c)
$+3 \rightarrow$

$-5 \downarrow$

r		

C5 For each grid in C4, find the number in the top left square when the number in the bottom right square is 50.

C6 Write each of these in a simpler way.

(a) $f+3+5+3$ (b) $y+4+4+4$ (c) $x+2+1+2+1$

(d) $z-5-5$ (e) $p+4-3$ (f) $m+2-5$

(g) $q+2+2-1$ (h) $w-4-1-9$ (i) $h+1-8+5+7$

D Grid investigations

D1 Jo makes grids where the across and down rules add and take away the same number.

(a) Copy and complete Jo's grids.

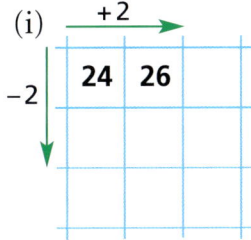

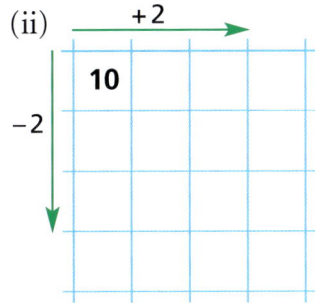

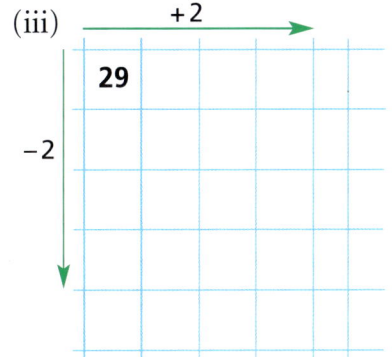

(i)

(ii)

(iii)

(b) Investigate other grids where the across and down rules add and take away the same number.

(c) What do you notice about these grids?

D2 Jo uses algebra to investigate her grids.

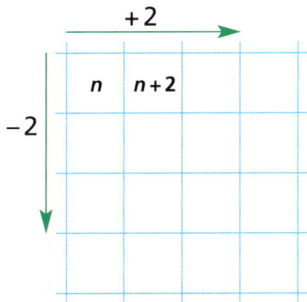

I completed this grid.
It shows the numbers in the top left and bottom right square will always be the same.

(a) Copy and complete Jo's grid.

(b) Explain why it shows the numbers in the top left and bottom right squares will always be the same.

(c) What else does it show?

D3 Suneet uses different numbers in his rules.
He adds the numbers in opposite corners on his grids.
This is one of his grids.

Calculations
Add opposite corners
10 + 40 = 50
37 + 13 =

Suneet's calculations

(a) Copy and complete Suneet's calculations.

(b) Make some more number grids that use the rules
'+ 9' and '+ 1', and add the opposite corners.

(c) What do you notice about the opposite corners totals
on your number grids? Can you explain this?

D4 Choose your own rules and make some number grids.
Investigate adding opposite corners on your grids.

D5 These grids are all the same size and use the rules '+ 2' and '+ 1'.

(a) Copy and complete the opposite corners table
for these grids.

(b) Draw some more grids like this and include
the results for your grids in the table.

(c) Find a rule that links the opposite corners total
and the top left number.

(d) What is the opposite corners total when
the number in the top left square is 100?

Opposite corners table	
Top left number	Opposite corners total
2	10
3	12
4	
10	

D6 Investigate opposite corners totals for your own sets of grids.

E Using algebra

Sue uses algebra to investigate her grids.

I use n for the top left number.

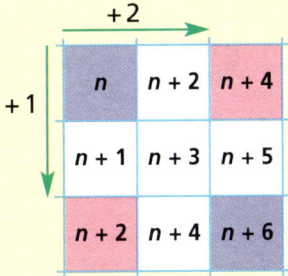

n	$n+2$	$n+4$
$n+1$	$n+3$	$n+5$
$n+2$	$n+4$	$n+6$

(+2 across the top, +1 down the side)

Adding opposite corners

blue corners: $n + n + 6$
$= 2n + 6$

pink corners: $n + 2 + n + 4$
$= n + n + 2 + 4$
$= 2n + 6$

$n + n + 6 = 2n + 6$ for any value of n.

So $n + n + 6$ and $2n + 6$ are called **equivalent expressions**.

The totals are both equivalent to $2n + 6$.
So I know that

• the totals will be equal no matter what n is

• to find the total I can use the rule 'multiply n by 2 and add 6'

$n + 2 + n + 4 = 2n + 6$ for any value of n.

So $n + 2 + n + 4$ and $2n + 6$ are also equivalent expressions.

For example, if the top left number is 50,
then the total will be $(50 \times 2) + 6 = 106$.

To check Sue's result, complete this grid and find the opposite corners total.

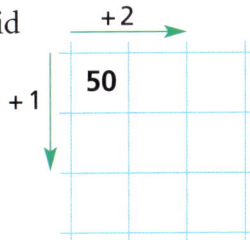

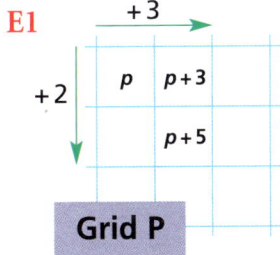

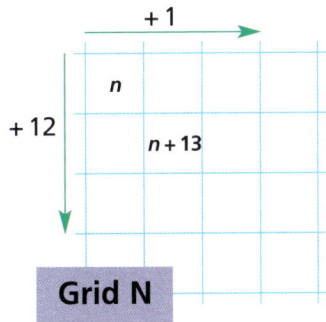

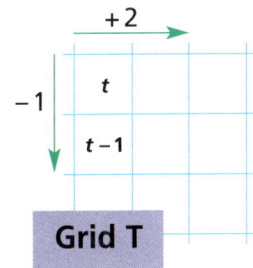

(grid with +2 across, +1 down, top left number 50)

E1

Grid P (+3 across, +2 down)

p	$p+3$	
	$p+5$	

Grid P

Grid N (+1 across, +12 down)

n		
$n+13$		

Grid N

Grid T (+2 across, −1 down)

t		
$t-1$		

Grid T

Do this for each grid.

(a) Copy and complete it.

(b) Find the total of each pair of opposite corners.

(c) Are the opposite corners totals equal?

(d) Find the opposite corners total if the top left number is 100.

E2 Find four pairs of equivalent expressions.

A $n + 5 + n + 1$

B $2n - 8$

C $n + n + 3 + n + 3$

D $n - 5 + n + 3$

E $3n + 6$

G $n - 6 + n - 2$

H $2n - 2$

F $2n + 4$

I $2n + 6$

E3 Explain the mistake this pupil has made.

When $n = 3$ $2n + 5 = (2 \times 3) + 5$
                          $= 11$

           $n + 8 = 3 + 8$

Not correct, Jake

                $= 11$

So $2n + 5$ and $n + 8$ are equivalent expressions.

E4 Write each of these in a simpler way.

(a) $p + p + 6$ (b) $y + 4 + y + 5$ (c) $q + 8 + q + q$

(d) $t + 1 + 3 + t + t$ (e) $x + 2 + x - 1$ (f) $r + r - 3 + r + 9$

(g) $w - 4 + w - 5$ (h) $j + 8 + j - 9$ (i) $h + 1 + h + h - 3$

E5 The diagonals of this number grid are shaded.

+4

+3

25	29	33	37
28	32	36	40
31	35	39	43
34	38	42	46

Investigate adding the numbers on the diagonals of number grids.
Use algebra to explain your conclusions.

What progress have you made?

Statement

I can solve number problems working forwards or backwards.

Evidence

1 Copy and complete this grid.

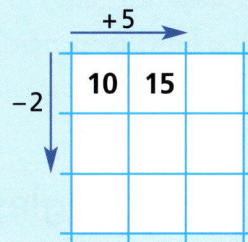

2 Work out the number in the pink square.

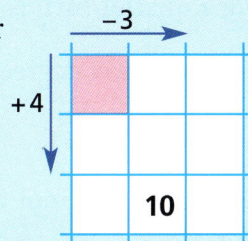

3 Work out the missing rules.

(a)

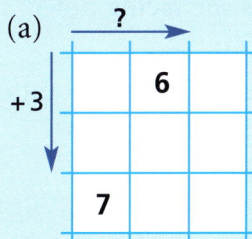

(b)

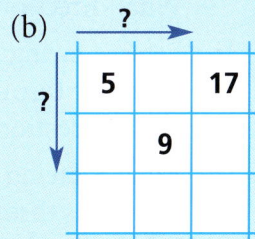

(c)

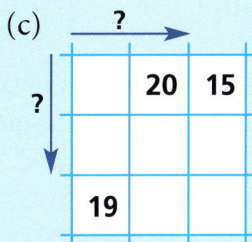

(d)

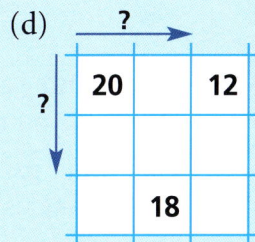

I can use algebra to investigate rules.

Your work in sections D and E gives evidence of this.

I can simplify expressions using addition and subtraction.

4 Write each of these in a simpler way.

(a) $n + 5 + 2$ (b) $p + 10 - 4$

(c) $y - 5 - 2$ (d) $t + 7 - 10$

(e) $h + 4 + h - 1$ (f) $v - 8 + v - 3 + v$

7 Perpendicular and parallel lines

This work will help you
 ◆ identify perpendicular and parallel lines
 ◆ draw perpendicular and parallel lines

A Right angles

Doing a quarter turn is turning through a right angle.

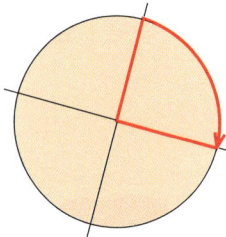

A1 How many degrees is a right angle?

A2 Make a sketch of the points of the compass (north, north-east, …).

 (a) Jenny is facing west.
 She turns through a right angle clockwise.
 What direction is she facing now?

 (b) Peter is facing south-east.
 He turns through a right angle anticlockwise.
 What direction is he facing now?

 (c) Amal is facing north-west.
 She turns through a right angle clockwise.
 What direction is she facing now?

A3 (a) Lines e and g are at right angles to one another.
 How can you tell this from the angles marked?

 (b) Find other pairs of lines that are
 at right angles to one another.

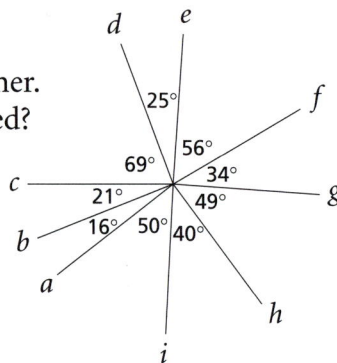

A4 A clock shows 11 o'clock.
 What time will it show when the hour hand has
 turned through a right angle clockwise?

A5 A clock shows twenty-five to nine.
 What time will it show when the minute hand has
 turned through a right angle clockwise?

A **set square** helps you draw accurate right angles.

Practise drawing some right angles with a set square.

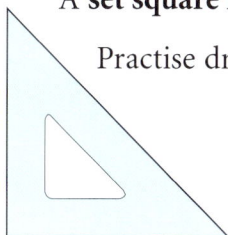

A6 A **rectangle** has a right angle at each of its four corners.

Follow these instructions to draw a rectangle 9 cm wide by 6 cm high.

1 Draw a line 9 cm long.

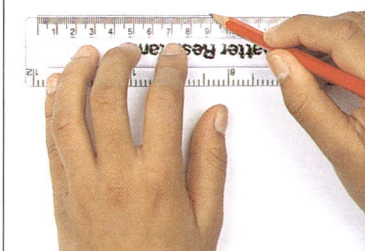

2 At one end, draw a line at right angles.

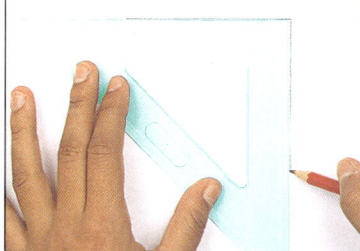

3 Do the same at the other end.

4 Put a mark 6 cm down each of these two lines.

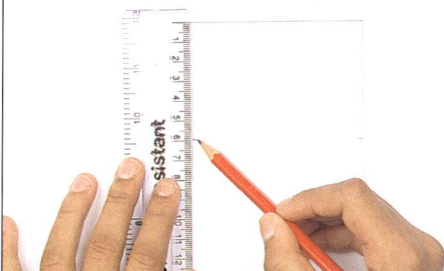

5 Join the marks.

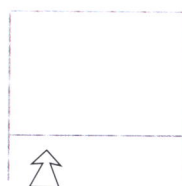

Check that this line is 9 cm long, like the first line.
Rub out the bits of line you don't need.

A7 This is a sketch of a rectangle. Draw the rectangle accurately on plain paper.

This means a right angle.

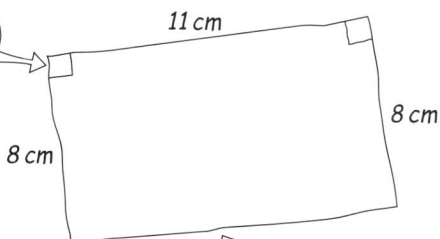

11 cm

8 cm

8 cm

Check this length.

A8 Draw this shape accurately.

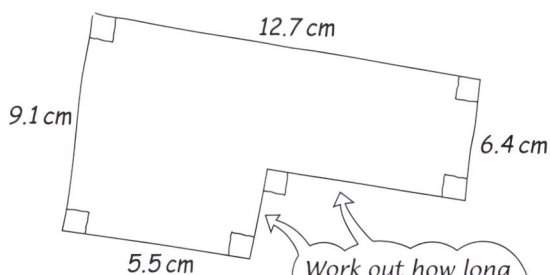

12.7 cm

9.1 cm

6.4 cm

5.5 cm

Work out how long these lines will be then check on your finished drawing.

A9 Draw a shape of your own with right angles at all its corners.

A10 Which red lines are at right angles to the black line?
Try to decide without a set square.
Then check with a set square.

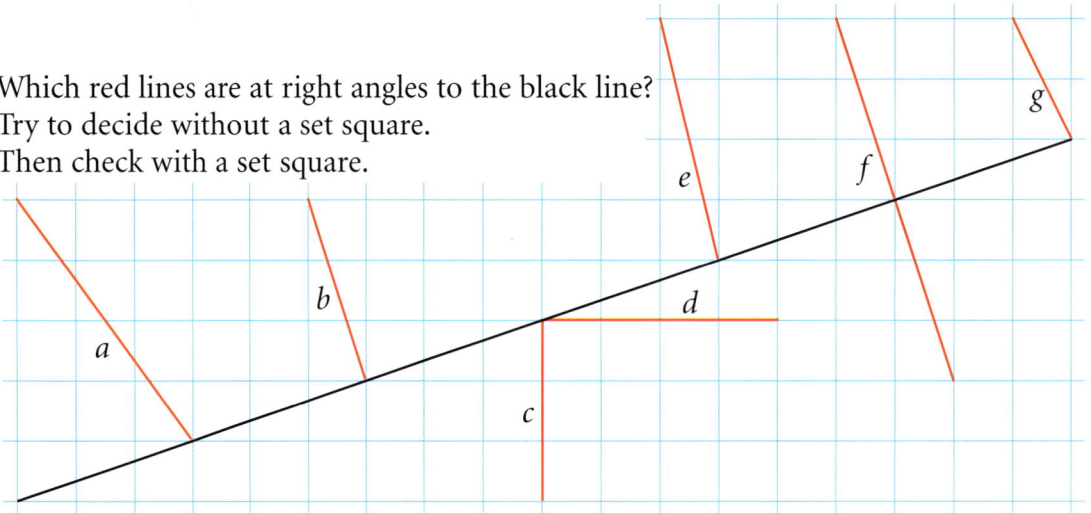

A11 Lines can be at right angles to one another
even if they are not touching.

Which red lines are at right angles to the black line?
Try to decide without a set square.
Then check with one.

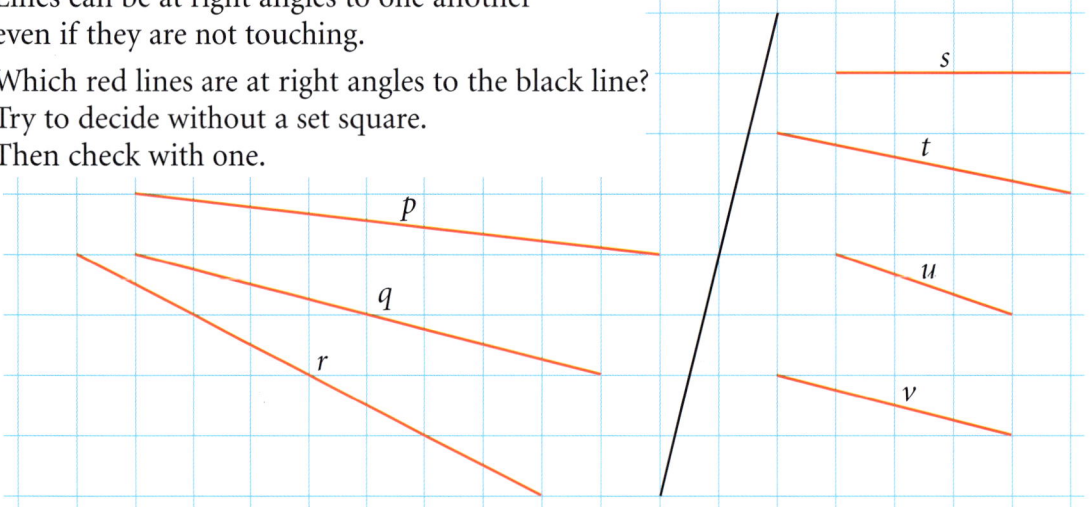

A12 Lines that are at right angles to one another
are called **perpendicular**.

Line *a* is perpendicular to line *b*.
Check this with a set square.

Find some more pairs of perpendicular lines.
Try to decide without a set square.
Then check with one.

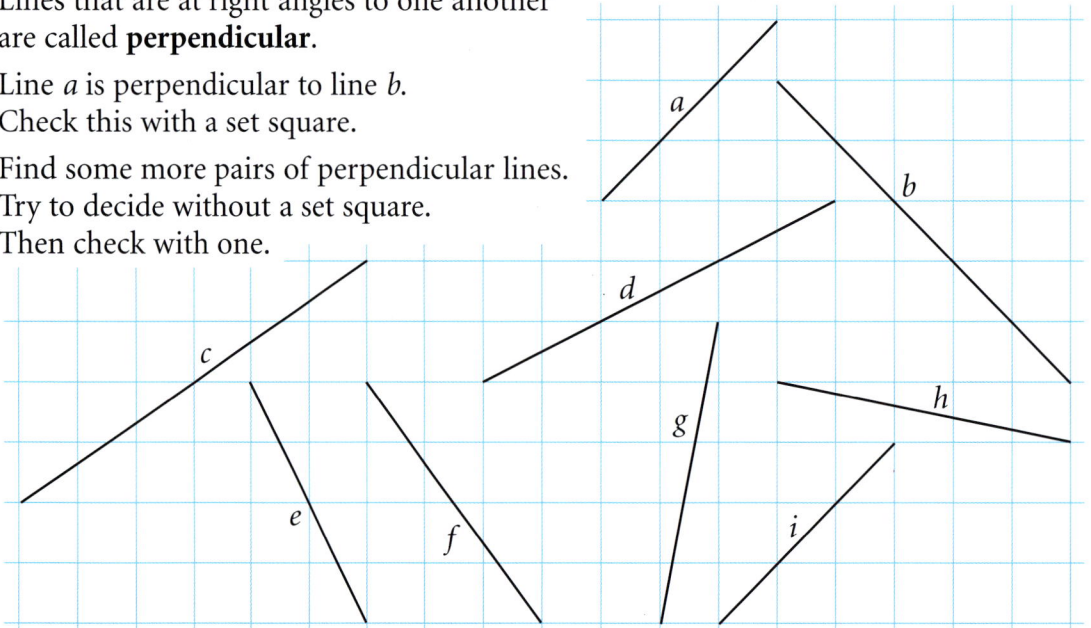

B The shortest route to a line

A house is at point H.
The line from A to B is a road.

A path has to be built from the house to the road.
The path needs to be as short as possible.

- What will the angle be between the path
  and the road?

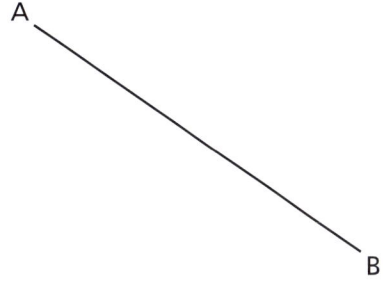

B1 Copy this diagram on to squared paper.

The pentagon ABCDE is a pond.
A swimmer is at point S.

(a) Draw in the shortest route from S
to line AB.
(Use a set square if you need to.)

Now draw the shortest route from S to
each of the other edges of the pond.

(b) Which of your routes should the
swimmer take if she wants to get out
of the pond as quickly as possible?

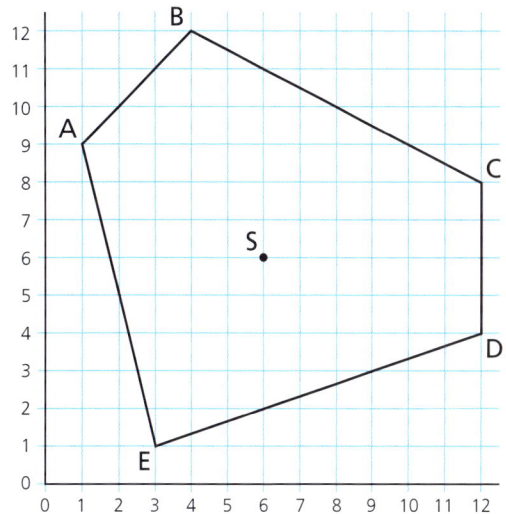

B2 Copy this diagram on to squared paper.

ABCD is a four-sided field.
The lines AB, BC, CD and DA are hedges.

(a) Mark this journey on your copy.

Alex starts at A.
She walks to hedge CD by
the shortest possible route.
From there she walks to hedge AB by
the shortest route.
Then she walks to hedge AD by
the shortest route.

(b) What are the coordinates of
the point she gets to?

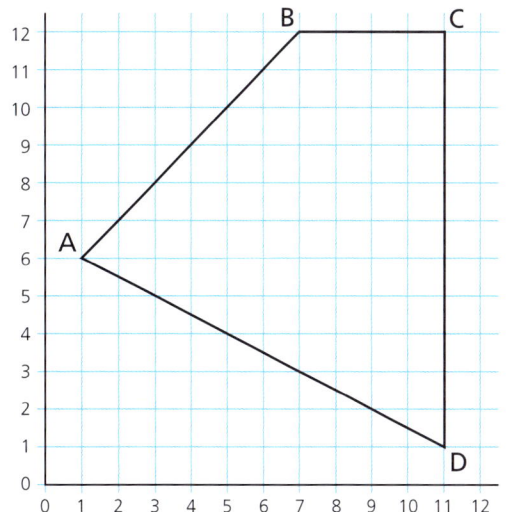

C Parallel lines

If you slide a line without turning it …

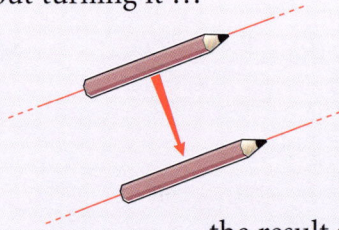

… the result is a line **parallel** to the first line.

Parallel lines go in the same direction, or have the same slope.
They don't meet, however far they go,
and they are always the same distance apart.

- How can you tell by counting grid squares
  whether line *a* is parallel to line *b*?

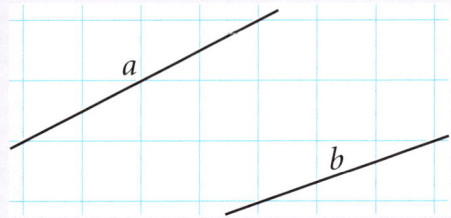

C1 Are these lines parallel to one another?

Explain your answer.

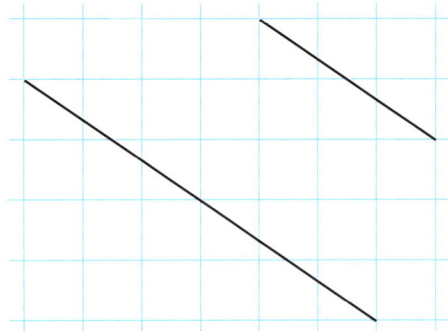

C2 Copy this on to squared paper.
Draw a line through P parallel to
line AB.

Draw another parallel line through Q.

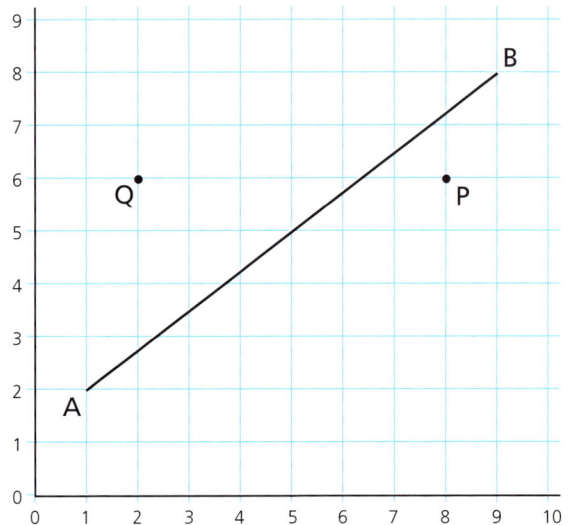

C3 Sort these into groups of lines that are parallel to one another.

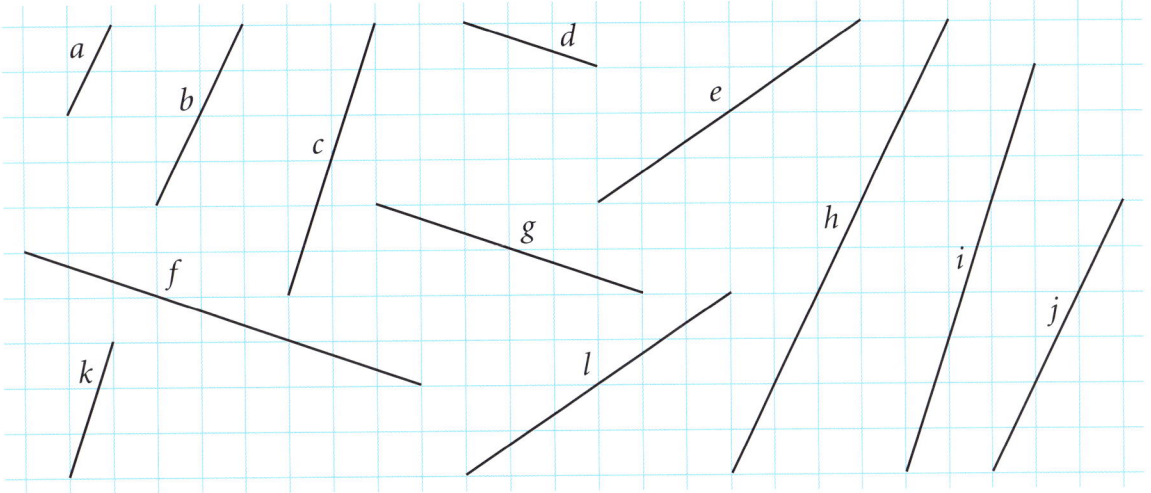

C4 Copy this diagram on to squared paper.

Lines AB and BC are two walls of a garden.
These are the clues to find a buried diamond.

> *Draw a line through P parallel to AB.*
> *Draw a line through Q parallel to BC.*
> *The diamond is where the lines meet.*

Follow the instructions to find
the coordinates of the diamond.

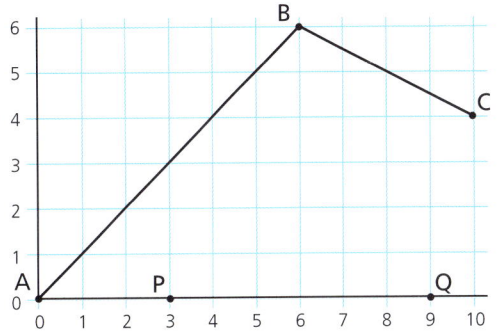

C5 On squared paper, draw axes
from 0 to 17 up and across.

Draw the castle walls as described
in this old document.

Draw where you would walk to
find the treasure.

What are the coordinates of
the place where it is buried?

Ye walls of ye castle form an irregular hexagon
with its vertices at these points.

A (1, 12)
B (11, 17)
C (15, 11)
D (10, 1)
E (7, 1)
F (1, 7)

To find ye treasure

Start at point D.
Walk parallel to wall EF until you get to wall AF.
Walk parallel to AB until you get to BC.
Walk parallel to AF until you get to CD.
Walk parallel to DE until you get to EF.
Ye treasure is buried there by the wall.

Try these methods for drawing or checking parallel lines.

1 Measuring along two lines that are perpendicular to your first line

Draw them using a set square.

Put a mark on each of them the same distance from your first line.

Join the marks.

2 The sliding set square method

Put an edge of the set square against your first line.

Put a ruler against a different edge of the set square.

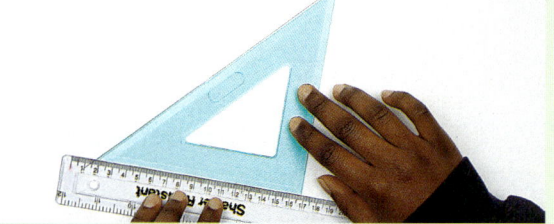

Hold the ruler tight and slide the set square along the ruler.

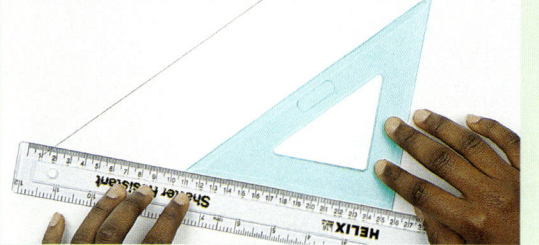

Draw the parallel line.

C6 Do this experiment.

1 Draw a pair of parallel lines (by any method).

2 Mark points 8 cm apart on one line and 4 cm apart on the other.

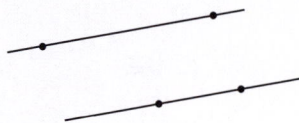

3 Join the points like this. Measure the lengths marked with arrows.

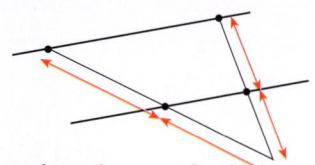

What do you find?

What happens if you mark points 12 cm apart and 4 cm apart?

Try other distances.

C7 Draw a pair of parallel lines.

Draw another pair, crossing the first pair at an angle.

Make them wider apart than the first pair.

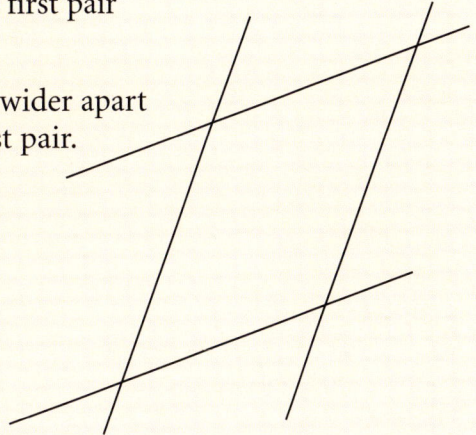

(a) Measure the sides and angles of the four-sided shape you have made. Write down what you notice.

(b) Does this four-sided shape have rotation symmetry (of order 2 or more)? If so, describe the symmetry.

(c) Does it have reflection symmetry? If so, describe it.

(d) Try to find out the name of this shape.

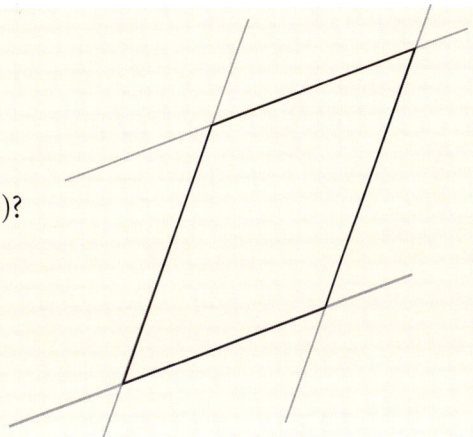

C8 Repeat all the stages of question C7, but draw the second pair of parallel lines the same distance apart as the first pair.

C9 Repeat all the stages of question C7, but draw the second pair of parallel lines at right angles to the first pair.

Parallel lines are good for drawing patterns.

Try using them in some designs of your own.

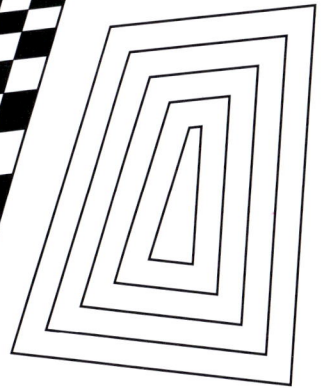

What progress have you made?

Evidence

I can find and draw perpendicular lines.

1 Which of these lines are at right angles to one another?

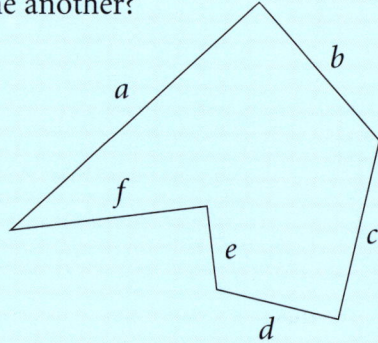

2 Draw this shape accurately on plain paper.

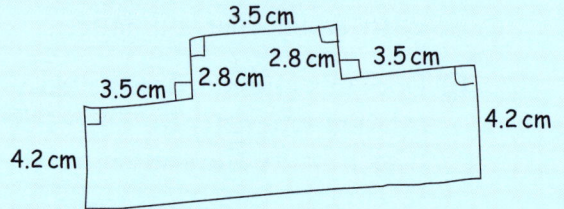

I can find and draw parallel lines.

3 Draw two parallel lines 4 cm apart.

4 Copy this diagram on to squared paper.

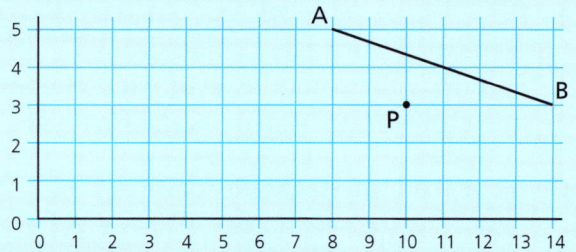

(a) Draw a line through point P, parallel to line AB.

(b) Draw three lines,

from (1, 4) to (2, 1)

from (2, 4) to (8, 1)

from (4, 4) to (7, 3)

Which of them is parallel to line AB?

Review 1

1 Write these times using the 24-hour clock.

   (a) 1:20 p.m.   (b) 5:45 a.m.   (c) 11:10 p.m.

2 Write these times using a.m. or p.m.

   (a) 0840   (b) 1525   (c) 1005

3 A film starts at 7:25 p.m. and finishes at 9:15 p.m. How long is it?

4 Gina wants to go to a concert. It starts at 20:15.
  She leaves home at 19:20.

  How long has she got before the concert starts?

5 A film lasts $2\frac{1}{4}$ hours. It starts at 8:25 p.m. When does it end?

6 (a) Leanne is at the Parade bus stop
      at 12:20 p.m. How long does she
      have to wait for a bus to Parkside?

   (b) John catches the bus at 2:50 p.m.
      at Lakeview. How long does it
      take him to get to Wyfield?

   (c) Raj is at the bus stop at Parkside
      at 1:05 p.m. How long does he have to wait for a bus to Yew Vale?

Shaldoo Buses			
Parade	1015	1245	1430
Station	1020	1250	1435
Lakeview	1035	1305	1450
Parkside	1042	1312	1457
Yew Vale	1050	1320	1505
Wyfield	1112	1342	1527

7 What is the probability that red will win on each of these fair spinners?

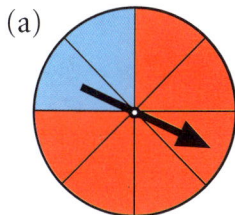

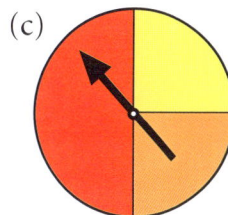

   (a)   (b)   (c)

8 What is the probability that
  red will **not** win on this spinner?

9 Simplify each of these fractions as far as possible.

   (a) $\frac{4}{8}$ (b) $\frac{5}{15}$ (c) $\frac{10}{12}$ (d) $\frac{30}{40}$ (e) $\frac{21}{36}$

10 Imagine these eight cards are turned over and shuffled.

| 3:15 p.m. | 10:00 a.m. | 2345 | 1330 | 1415 | 1630 | 0915 | 1215 |

You pick a card at random.
What is the probability that you will pick

(a) a time earlier than 12 noon   (b) a time later than 2 p.m.

11 Copy these shapes.

For each shape, draw all lines of symmetry and mark any centre of rotation.

Write the order of rotation symmetry under any shape with rotation symmetry.

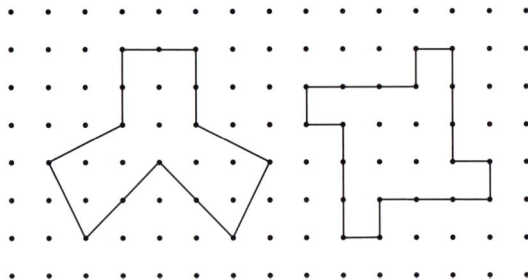

12 Copy this diagram on to squared paper.

(a) Mark the centre of rotation symmetry for the shape.

What are the coordinates of this point?

(b) What is the order of rotation symmetry of the shape?

(c) Which lines are parallel to AB?

(d) Which lines are perpendicular to AB?

(e) Mark two right angles on the shape.

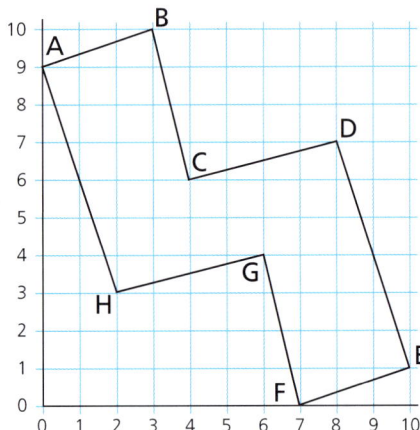

13 Work these out.

(a) $\frac{1}{4}$ of 24   (b) $\frac{2}{3}$ of 30   (c) $\frac{3}{5}$ of 10   (d) $\frac{3}{8}$ of 32   (e) $\frac{5}{7}$ of 21

14 Class 8T did a survey of favourite yoghurt flavours. The results are shown in this pie chart.

(a) What fraction of the class liked strawberry best?

(b) What fraction of the class liked raspberry best?

(c) There are 24 pupils in the class. How many pupils liked black cherry best?

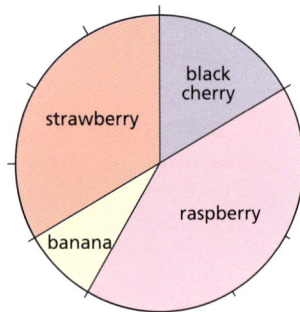

15 There are 12 eggs in a box but 8 of them are broken.

What fraction of the eggs are broken?
Write it in its simplest form.

16 Find the across and down rules for these number grids.

(a)

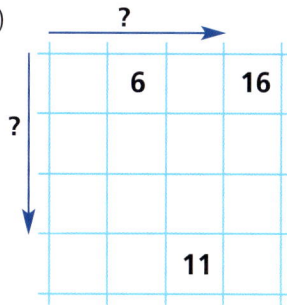

(b)

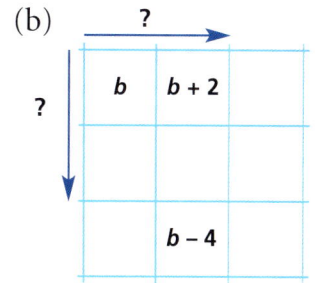

17 Copy and complete these grids.

(a)

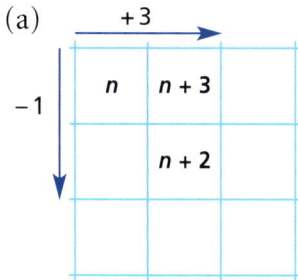

(b)

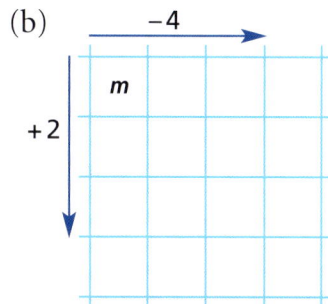

18 Write each of these in a simpler way.

(a) $h + 6 + 1$ (b) $k + 8 - 5$ (c) $m + 2 - 9$

(d) $w + 3 + w + 1$ (e) $n - 1 + n - 4$ (f) $x + 9 - 12 + x + x$

19 Copy this diagram on to squared paper.

(a) Draw a line through E parallel to CB. Draw a line through A parallel to CD.

What are the coordinates of the point where these lines meet? Label this point F.

(b) The hexagon ABCDEF is a bird table. A beetle is at the point X with coordinates (6, 6).

Draw in the shortest route from X to line CD.

Now draw the shortest route from X to each of the other edges of the bird table.

(c) Which of your routes should the beetle take if it wants to get off the bird table as quickly as possible?

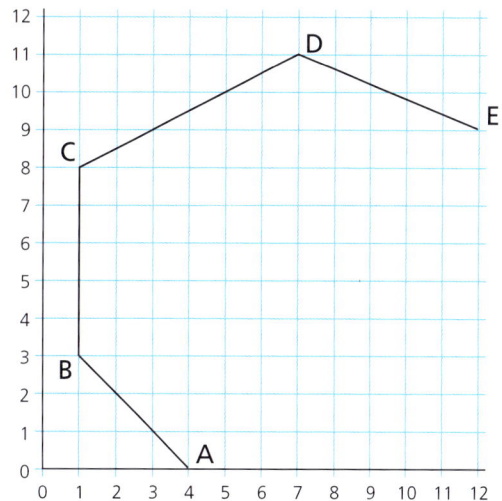

8 Comparisons

This work unit will help you

◆ understand median and range
◆ use them to make comparisons

A Comparing heights

For class or group discussion

- Do you think the girls here are taller or shorter than the boys?
  How do you decide?

- Look at each dot plot below.

  Would you say the girls are taller or shorter than the boys?
  How do you decide?

A

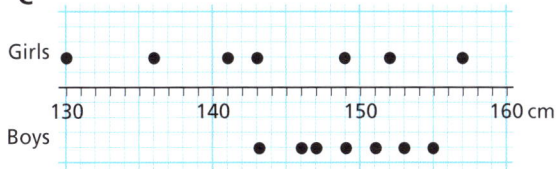

B

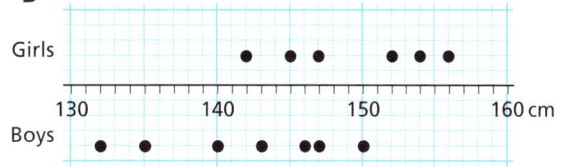

C

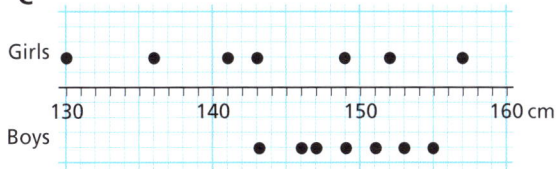

D

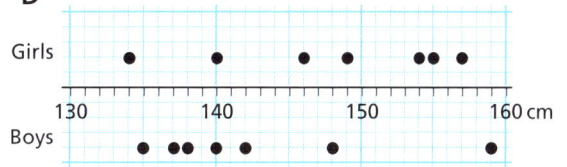

E

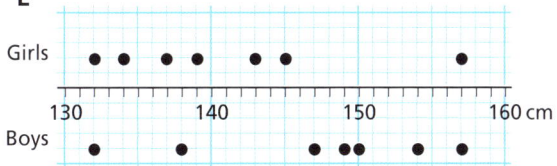

F

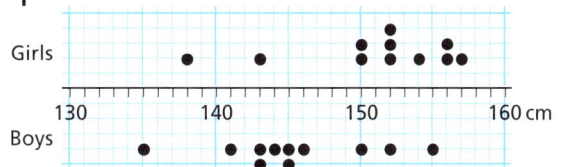

B Median

Here, the top dot plot shows seven girls' heights.
The middle girl's height is marked with an arrow (136 cm).
This is called the **median** height of the group.

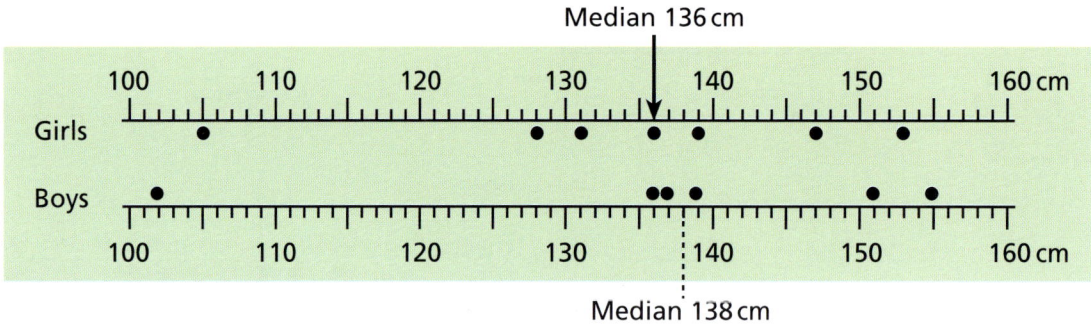
Median 136 cm

There are six boys' heights so there is no 'middle boy'.
But there is a middle **pair** of boys.

The median height is halfway between the heights of the middle pair.
So the median height is 138 cm.

The median is often used as an 'average' to compare two sets of data.
The median height of the boys is greater than the median height of the girls.

B1 What is the median height of each group shown below?

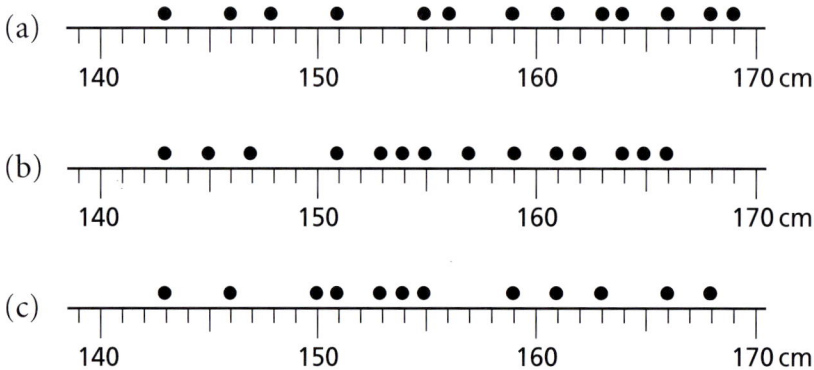

B2 In this group of girls there are two with height 155 cm.

(a) How many girls are there in the group?

(b) Find the dot that represents the middle girl.
Write down the median height.

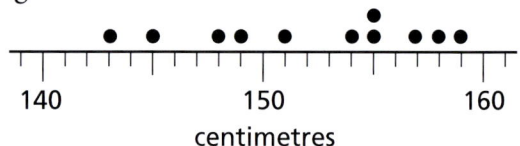

B3 For each of the dot plots on page 61,

    (a) find the median height of the girls

    (b) find the median height of the boys

    (c) use these results to write a statement comparing girls and boys

B4 What is the median height of each of these groups?

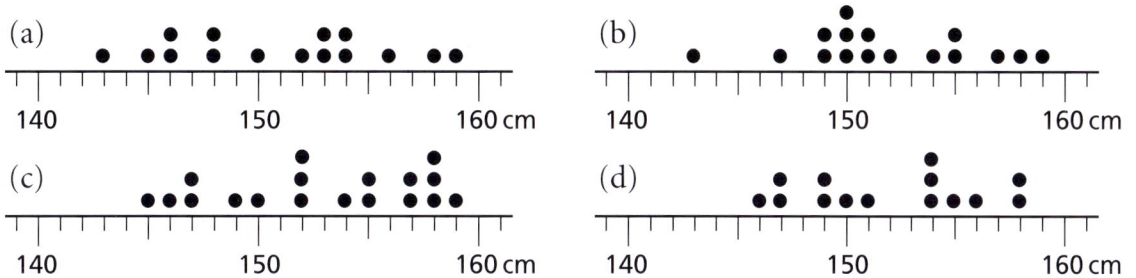

(a)

(b)

(c)

(d)

B5 (a) What is the median weight of the group of people shown here?

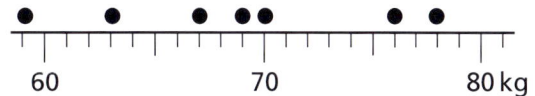

    (b) What would happen to the median weight if the heaviest person is replaced by someone even heavier?

    (c) What if the lightest person is replaced by someone even lighter?

    (d) What would happen to the median weight if, after Christmas dinner, everyone increased by 1 kg?

B6 Here are the weights, in kg, of the members of a seven-a-side football team:

        63, 54, 70, 65, 58, 52, 60

    (a) Write out these numbers in order of size, smallest first.

    (b) What is the median weight of the team?

> *Always* do this if you are finding a median and the numbers are not in order of size.

B7 Find the median of each of these sets of data.

    (a) 156 cm, 148 cm, 161 cm, 139 cm, 152 cm

    (b) 45 kg, 38 kg, 29 kg, 26 kg, 34 kg, 40 kg, 31 kg, 39 kg

B8 Here are the weights, in kg, of a group of baby boys and a group of baby girls.

Boys   3.2 2.2 1.9 2.8 1.6 2.7 2.2 3.4 1.9 3.0 2.9

Girls   2.7 3.0 3.1 1.4 2.6 2.6 3.5 2.6 2.8 2.1

Which group has the greater median weight?

C Range

The two groups shown here have the same median height.
But the girls' heights are more spread out than those of the boys.

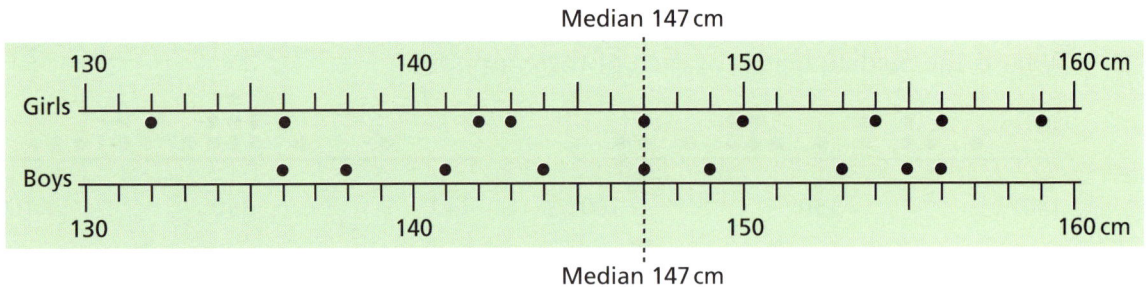

We use the **range** to measure the spread.
The range is the **difference between the largest and smallest**.

The range of the girls' heights is **27 cm** (159 − 132 = 27).

The range of the boys' heights is **20 cm** (156 − 136 = 20).

C1 (a) Work out the range of each group
of heights shown here.

(b) Which group has the greatest range?

(c) Which group has the smallest range?

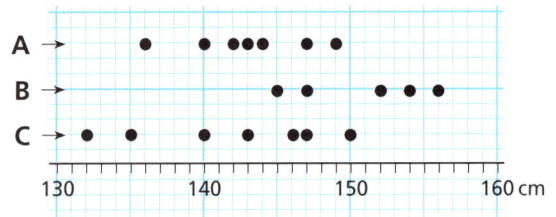

C2 The length of time between phoning for an ambulance and
the ambulance arriving is called the 'response time'.

An ambulance station recorded these response times over a period of one hour.

Time in minutes	10	8	11	6	13	10	4	6	10	7

(a) What was the longest response time?

(b) What was the shortest response time?

(c) Work out the range of the response times.

C3 This table shows information about the
weights of three herds of cows.

	Median	Range
Herd A	525 kg	65 kg
Herd B	545 kg	50 kg
Herd C	510 kg	35 kg

(a) Which herd is heaviest on the whole?

(b) In which herd are the weights most spread out?
How do you know from the table?

(c) In which herd are the weights least spread out?
How do you know?

C4 Two friends played a computer game.
They had five goes each. They got a score out of 100 on each go.

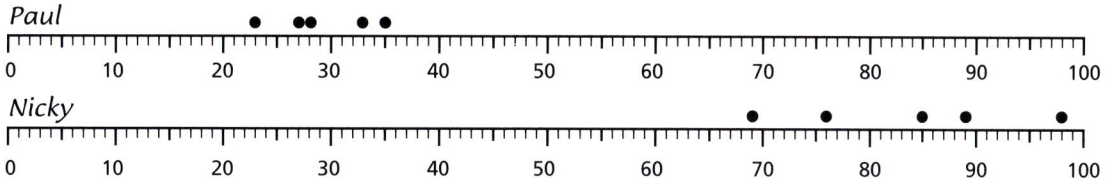

(a) Work out the median and range of Paul's scores.

(b) Work out the median and range of Nicky's scores.

Two other friends played the game.
These were the medians and ranges
of their scores.

	Median	Range
Martin	30	28
Carol	84	11

Use the information about **all four people** to copy and complete these sentences.

(c) _____ and _____ both had high scores,
but _____'s scores were the more spread out of the two.

(d) Nicky's scores and _____'s scores were both spread out,
but _____ had the higher scores of the two.

(e) _____ and _____ were both bad players
because they had _____ median scores.

(f) Paul was a consistent player because the range of his scores was _____.

C5 These trees grow on different sides of a hill.

(a) Find the median height and the range of the heights of each group.

(b) Write a couple of sentences comparing the groups.

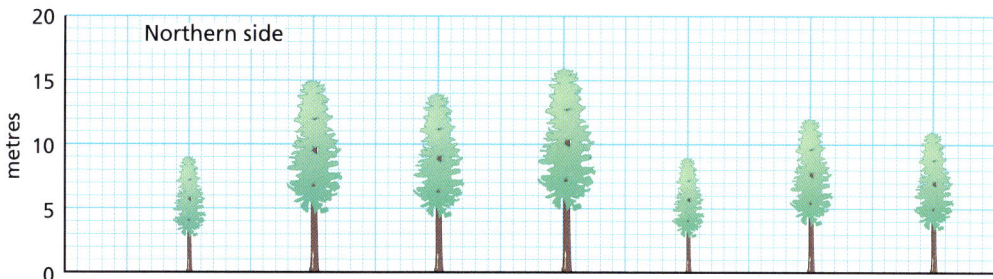

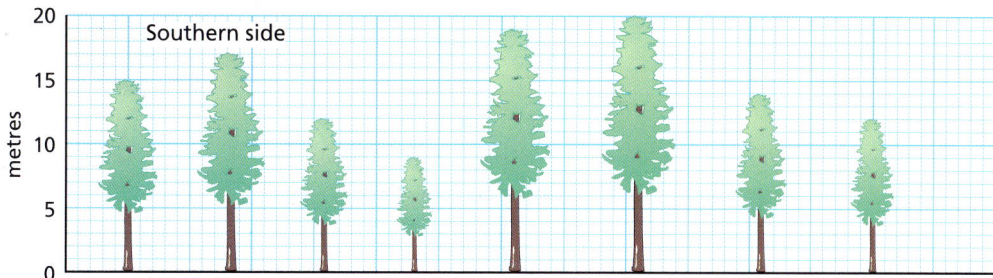

C6 Four machines in a factory fill packs with spaghetti.
Each pack should contain 500 g.

The owner operated the machines until each of them had filled nine packs.
She checked the weight of spaghetti in the packs and got these results.

Machine A   500 g   503 g   490 g   495 g   505 g   511 g   485 g   508 g   494 g

Machine B   499 g   496 g   501 g   499 g   497 g   498 g   497 g   499 g   497 g

Machine C   502 g   503 g   502 g   504 g   499 g   502 g   503 g   505 g   502 g

Machine D   499 g   518 g   512 g   521 g   508 g   524 g   514 g   505 g   514 g

(a) Work out the median and range of the weights for each machine.

(b) Which machine was consistent but generally underfilled the packs?

(c) Which was variable and generally overfilled the packs?

(d) Which was consistent and usually overfilled the packs?

(e) How would you describe the remaining machine?

(f) Which machine would the factory owner prefer, if it continued to work as it did in the test? Give a reason.

D How fast do you react?

For working in pairs

Cut out the reaction timer scale from sheet 141 and
stick it on to a ruler (or other wooden or plastic strip).

This is how you measure your reaction time.

- Your partner holds the reaction timer at the top.
- You have your thumb and finger ready at the zero mark.
- Your partner drops the reaction timer and you grip it as fast as you can.
  The scale tells you your reaction time in hundredths of a second.

Record the results of ten trials each. Use dot plots if you like.
Compare your results with those of your partner using **median** and **range**.

You could also compare your own reaction times using
your left hand and your right hand.

For the whole class

Collect the fastest or the median reaction time of every pupil.

Compare the reaction times of 12-year-olds with those of 13-year-olds.

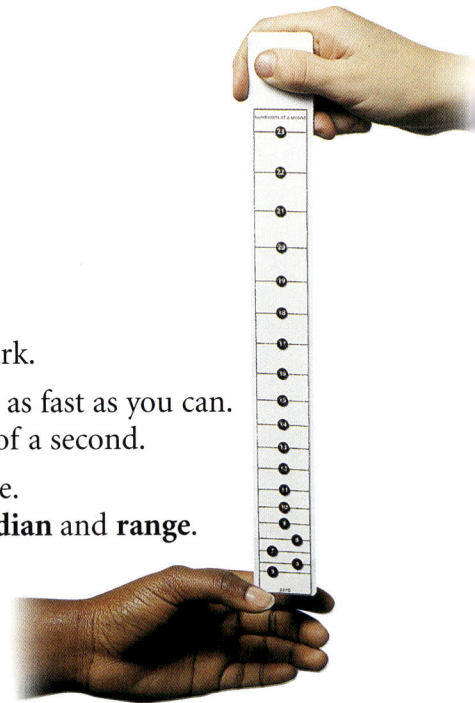

E Summarising data

The median and range can be used to help summarise a set of data.

The data on the right consists of Claire's reaction times (in hundredths of a second).

The median reaction time is 17 hundredths of a second.

The shortest time is 8 hundredths of a second.
The longest is 22 hundredths of a second.
The range is 22 − 8, which is 14 hundredths of a second.

Claire's reaction times, in hundredths of a second			
8	12	12	13
16	18	19	19
20	22		

This diagram summarises the data.
It shows the **smallest**, **largest**, **median** and **range**.

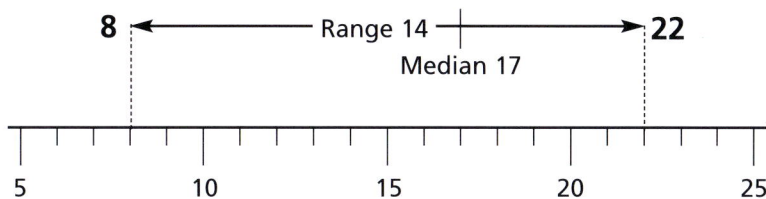

E1 Draw diagrams like the one above to summarise your reaction times and those of your partner.

Write about any differences you notice.

E2 (a) Here are the reaction times of different people.
Draw a summary diagram for each one.

(i) Janet, 42, a teacher

21, 15, 10, 22, 21, 16, 22, 13, 17, 20, 21

(ii) Linford, 25, a sprinter

13, 10, 14, 10, 9, 7, 13, 11, 11, 10, 7, 6, 9

(iii) Jules, 72, part-time computer games tester

11, 20, 9, 23, 13, 17, 18, 7, 9, 24

(b) Write about any differences you notice between Janet, Linford and Jules.

F Writing a report

On the opposite page is a report on a project by some pupils
who wanted to find out if boys could run faster than girls.

The report says clearly what questions the pupils were asking.

It then describes how the data was collected.

It tells us about any problems which the pupils had to
overcome when collecting the data.

The data is recorded very clearly.

The report shows how the data is used to help answer
the question the pupils started with.

These pupils have decided to draw a dot plot to
illustrate the data.

They find the medians and the ranges to help them compare
the two sets of data.

At the end of the report the pupils state their conclusion,
based on the data they have collected.

Questions for discussion

- If you were doing this project, what other practical
  problems could arise? How would you solve them?
- Do you agree with the conclusion these pupils have drawn
  from their data? If not, what would your conclusion be?

Can boys in our class run faster than the girls?   by Andrew, Farnaaz and Leo

We wanted to know if the boys in our class can run faster then the girls.
We know Sean is the fastest boy because he got picked for the school team!

How we got our data

We got every person in our class to run from one end of the playground to the other, and we timed them with a stopwatch. We did it in some PE lessons.

We had to find the best way of timing. The way we did it was like this.
One person started the race by moving their arm down when they said "Go!"
The person at the other end moved their arm down when the runner crossed the line.
The person with the stopwatch was halfway along so that they could see easily.

Data

| Boys' times (seconds) | 9.3 11.2 12.2 10.0 9.5 13.4 12.2 11.7 |
| | 13.5 12.8 14.1 10.7 14.3 14.0 |

| Girls' times (seconds) | 10.2 12.3 10.2 15.5 14.2 11.9 10.4 13.8 |
| | 13.3 9.9 12.1 11.7 13.4 10.8 13.5 10.2 |

Comparing the boys and girls

Dot plots of the boys' and girls' times

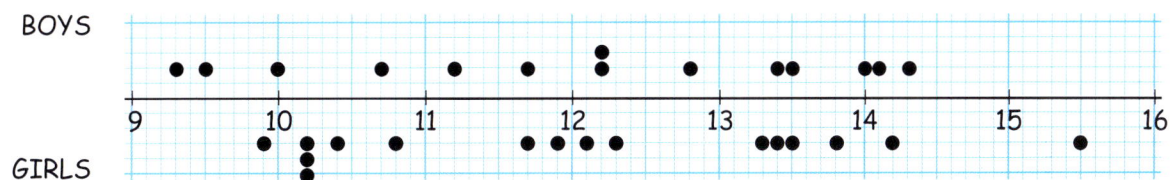

These diagrams show the medians, ranges and shortest and longest times.

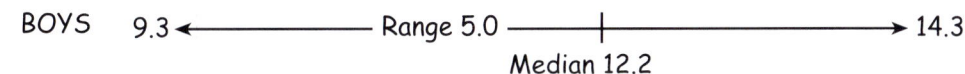

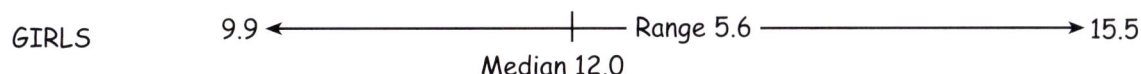

BOYS   9.3 ◄———————— Range 5.0 ———┼————————————→ 14.3
                                  Median 12.2

GIRLS   9.9 ◄———————————┼—— Range 5.6 ———————————→ 15.5
                           Median 12.0

Conclusion

The two fastest runners were boys, the slowest was a girl.
Using the median for comparison, the girls were faster but only slightly.
The girls' times were a little more spread out than the boys'.

G Projects

Here are some ideas for projects that involve collecting data and making comparisons.

The Argon Factor   for the class working together

In the mental agility test you have one minute to memorise the shapes and numbers. 15 questions are then read out to you and you have 5 seconds to write down each answer. You will be scored out of 15.

In the memory test you have two minutes to remember the pictures and details of the four people. You then have 10 minutes to answer 20 questions on paper to see what you remember.

Start of the day and end of the day?   *Young people's memories and older people's?*

Handwriting size   for working in pairs or small groups

Ask a number of boys and a number of girls to write this sentence:

The quick brown fox jumps over the lazy dog.

Measure the length of the sentence in centimetres.
Compare the girls and the boys and write a report.

What progress have you made?

Statement	Evidence
I can summarise a set of data using the median and range.	1 Pat recorded his reaction times for each hand. The times in hundredths of a second were Left hand 18, 9, 20, 16, 23, 8, 22, 24, 15 Right hand 14, 12, 13, 17, 12, 14, 17, 14, 18, 12 Find the median time, and the range of times, for each hand. Compare the times for each hand.
I can carry out a project involving data collection and write a report on it.	Your project work and report should give evidence of this.

⑨ Hot and cold

This work will help you

◆ calculate with money

◆ make decisions based on a variety of facts

This activity is described in the teacher's guide.

You need sheet 146 or sheet 147.

⑩ Inputs and outputs

This work will help you
- ◆ work out the value of algebraic expressions
- ◆ find equivalent expressions

A Input and output machines

This is an 'add 3' number machine.

If you feed in 7, out comes 10.

We can use a diagram like this.

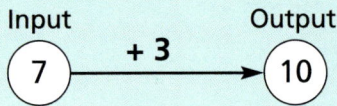

We can link machines together …

… and use a diagram like this.

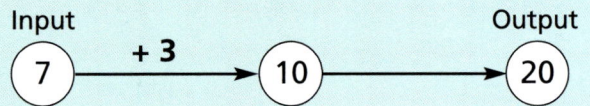

A1 What is the output for each of these machines?

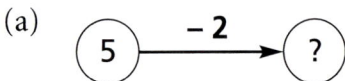

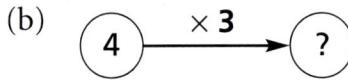

(a)
$$5 \xrightarrow{-2} ?$$

(b)
$$4 \xrightarrow{\times 3} ?$$

A2 Here is the number 7 going through a chain of two machines.

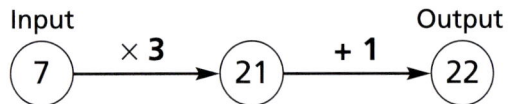

$$7 \xrightarrow{\times 3} 21 \xrightarrow{+1} 22$$

Find the output for each of these inputs.

(a) 4   (b) 5   (c) 0   (d) 12

A3 Copy and complete these diagrams.

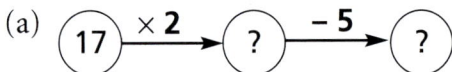

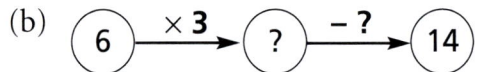

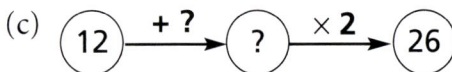

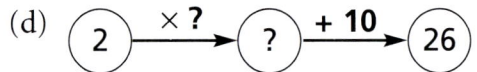

(a)
$$17 \xrightarrow{\times 2} ? \xrightarrow{-5} ?$$

(b)
$$6 \xrightarrow{\times 3} ? \xrightarrow{-?} 14$$

(c)
$$12 \xrightarrow{+?} ? \xrightarrow{\times 2} 26$$

(d)
$$2 \xrightarrow{\times ?} ? \xrightarrow{+10} 26$$

A4 Copy and complete each table.

(a)

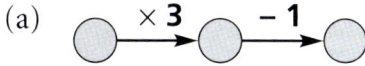

Input		Output
2	→	...
4	→	...
...	→	20
...	→	29

(b)

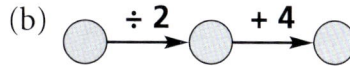

Input		Output
6	→	...
16	→	...
...	→	4
...	→	$5\frac{1}{2}$

(c)

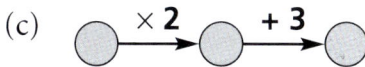

Input		Output
9	→	...
4	→	...
...	→	13
...	→	17

(d)

Input		Output
1	→	...
5	→	...
...	→	36
...	→	$13\frac{1}{2}$

*A5 Copy and complete each table.

(a)

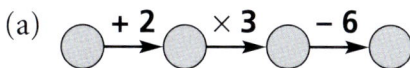

Input		Output
2	→	...
8	→	...
10	→	...
...	→	15
...	→	99
...	→	1.5

(b)

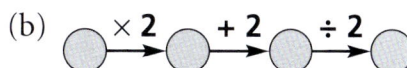

Input		Output
1	→	...
5	→	...
39	→	...
...	→	10
...	→	$8\frac{1}{2}$
...	→	100

*A6 (a) Look at the diagram in question A5(a).

Can you find a shorter chain that will give the same output for each input?
(It must work for *every* input and output.)

(b) Can you find a shorter chain to replace the chain in question A5(b)?

B Shorthand rules

We can use a letter to stand for any input number.
For example,

Input   Output

a $\xrightarrow{\times 4}$ $4a$ $\xrightarrow{+5}$ $4a + 5$

> We write
> $a \times 4$ or $4 \times a$
> as $4a$.

We can write the rule for this diagram in shorthand as $a \rightarrow 4a + 5$

We can use any letter we like.
For example,

c $\xrightarrow{+5}$ $c + 5$ $\xrightarrow{\times 4}$ $4(c + 5)$

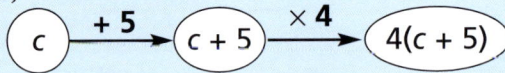

> We write
> $(c + 5) \times 4$
> as $4(c + 5)$.

The rule for this diagram can be written as $c \rightarrow 4(c + 5)$

B1 (a) Copy and complete this arrow diagram.

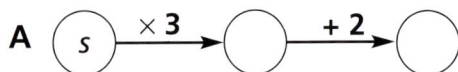

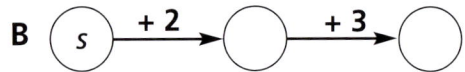

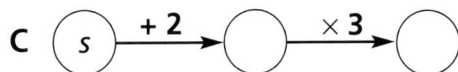

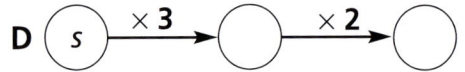

b $\xrightarrow{\times 3}$ $\bigcirc$ $\xrightarrow{-2}$ $\bigcirc$

(b) Which of these shorthand rules is correct for the diagram?

| $b \rightarrow b - 6$ | $b \rightarrow 3(b - 2)$ | $b \rightarrow 3b - 2$ | $b \rightarrow 2(b - 3)$ | $b \rightarrow 2b - 3$ |

B2 For each of these, copy and complete the arrow diagram.
Then match the diagram to the correct rule.

(a) p $\xrightarrow{\times 3}$ $\bigcirc$ $\xrightarrow{+4}$ $\bigcirc$

(b) p $\xrightarrow{+4}$ $\bigcirc$ $\xrightarrow{\times 3}$ $\bigcirc$

Rules

$p \rightarrow p + 12$	$p \rightarrow 3p + 4$
$p \rightarrow 4p + 3$	$p \rightarrow 4p \times 3$
$p \rightarrow 4(p + 3)$	$p \rightarrow 3(p + 4)$

B3 Look at this shorthand rule: $s \rightarrow 3(s + 2)$.

Which of these arrow diagrams is correct for the rule?
Copy and complete this diagram.

A s $\xrightarrow{\times 3}$ $\bigcirc$ $\xrightarrow{+2}$ $\bigcirc$

B s $\xrightarrow{+2}$ $\bigcirc$ $\xrightarrow{+3}$ $\bigcirc$

C s $\xrightarrow{+2}$ $\bigcirc$ $\xrightarrow{\times 3}$ $\bigcirc$

D s $\xrightarrow{\times 3}$ $\bigcirc$ $\xrightarrow{\times 2}$ $\bigcirc$

B4 Copy and complete these arrow diagrams.
For each of them, write a shorthand rule.

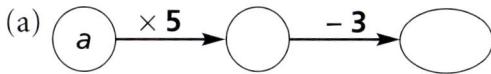

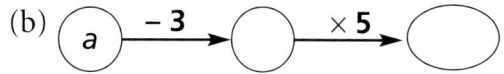

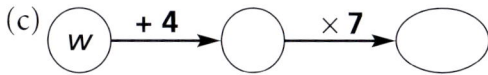

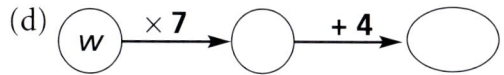

(a) a $\xrightarrow{\times 5}$ ◯ $\xrightarrow{-3}$ ◯

(b) a $\xrightarrow{-3}$ ◯ $\xrightarrow{\times 5}$ ◯

(c) w $\xrightarrow{+4}$ ◯ $\xrightarrow{\times 7}$ ◯

(d) w $\xrightarrow{\times 7}$ ◯ $\xrightarrow{+4}$ ◯

B5 Draw arrow diagrams for each of these rules.

(a) $s \rightarrow 2s + 1$　　　　　　(b) $t \rightarrow 3(t - 9)$

(c) $w \rightarrow 5w - 7$　　　　　　(d) $x \rightarrow 6(x + 7)$

(e) $y \rightarrow 7y + 3$　　　　　　(f) $z \rightarrow 2(z + 5)$

For each rule, work out the output when the input is 100.

B6 This is Masood's homework.
He has not done very well!

Do it correctly for him.

Complete each of these, and write down the rule.

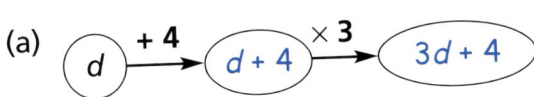

(a) d $\xrightarrow{+4}$ $d + 4$ $\xrightarrow{\times 3}$ $3d + 4$

　　　　　$d \rightarrow 3d + 4$　✗

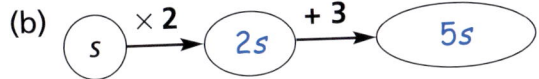

(b) s $\xrightarrow{\times 2}$ $2s$ $\xrightarrow{+3}$ $5s$

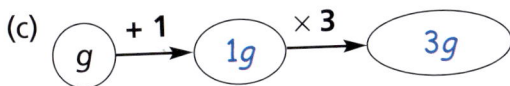

　　　　　$s \rightarrow 5s$　✗

(c) g $\xrightarrow{+1}$ $1g$ $\xrightarrow{\times 3}$ $3g$

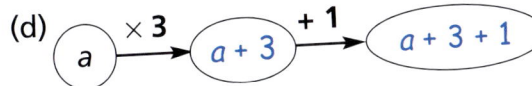

　　　　　$g \rightarrow 3g$　✗

(d) a $\xrightarrow{\times 3}$ $a + 3$ $\xrightarrow{+1}$ $a + 3 + 1$

　　　　　$a \rightarrow a + 4$　✗

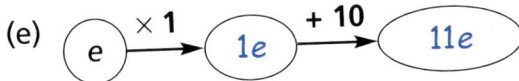

(e) e $\xrightarrow{\times 1}$ $1e$ $\xrightarrow{+10}$ $11e$

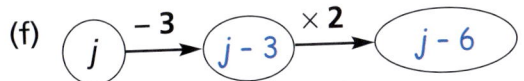

　　　　　$e \rightarrow 11e$　✗

(f) j $\xrightarrow{-3}$ $j - 3$ $\xrightarrow{\times 2}$ $j - 6$

　　　　　$j \rightarrow j - 6$　✗

C Evaluating expressions

The arrow diagram for the rule $p \to 5p - 3$ is

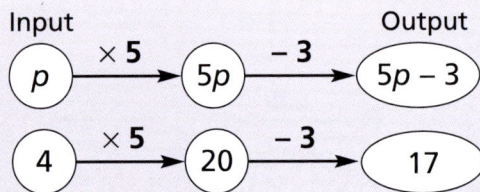

When the input is 4, the output is 17.

We can write this as   When $p = 4$, $5p - 3 = 17$
             or $4 \to 17$

C1 Work out the value of $3a + 7$ when $a = 3$.

C2 When $b = 5$, work out the value of
   (a) $2b - 1$ (b) $2(b - 1)$ (c) $6b - 4$ (d) $6(b - 4)$

C3 Work out the value of $4(c + 5)$ when
   (a) $c = 2$ (b) $c = 3$ (c) $c = 4$ (d) $c = 10$

C4 For the rule $c \to 4c + 5$, copy and complete
   (a) $2 \to \ldots$ (b) $3 \to \ldots$ (c) $4 \to \ldots$ (d) $10 \to \ldots$

C5 Match each rule with one or more pairs of values from the box.

(a) $p \to p + 3$	(b) $r \to 5r - 1$
(c) $s \to 2(s + 1)$	(d) $w \to w - 5$
(e) $h \to 3h + 3$	(f) $k \to 5(k - 3)$

$1 \to 4$	$2 \to 9$
$3 \to 0$	$4 \to 5$
$5 \to 0$	$5 \to 12$

C6 Find three different rules which fit $1 \to 6$.

Cover up

Cut out the 8 rectangular pieces on sheet 148.

Put the pieces on the board so that each piece covers two squares that fit the rule.

For example, $m \to m + 6$ may cover $4 \to 10$ and $6 \to 12$, or it may cover $6 \to 12$ and $0 \to 6$ and so on.

You can put the pieces this way ▭ or this way ▯.

- 4, 5 or 6 pieces on the board: excellent!
- 7 or 8 pieces on the board: brilliant!

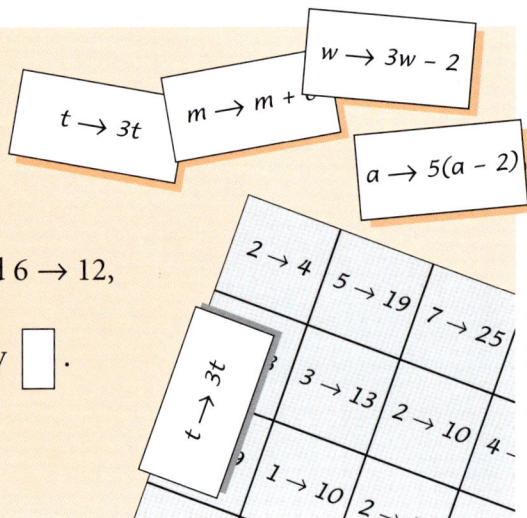

D Different rules?

- Can you match each rule with an arrow diagram?

$n \to 2n + 10$

$n \to n + 10$

$n \to n + 1 + 9$

$n \to 2(n + 5)$

- Match each rule with as many number pairs below as you can.

$10 \to 30$ $3 \to 16$ $1 \to 11$

$0 \to 10$ $1 \to 12$ $2 \to 12$

$10 \to 20$

$4 \to 18$ $5 \to 15$

$n \to 3n + 6$ $n \to 5n - 5$ $n \to 5(n - 1)$ $n \to 3(n + 2)$

- Copy and complete this table for each of the rules.

$n \longrightarrow \ldots$

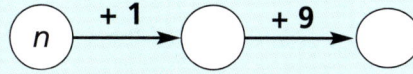

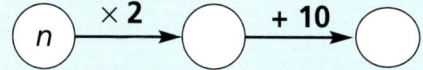

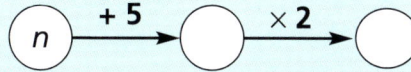

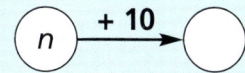

$1 \longrightarrow \ldots$

$2 \longrightarrow \ldots$

$3 \longrightarrow \ldots$

$4 \longrightarrow \ldots$

$5 \longrightarrow \ldots$

$6 \longrightarrow \ldots$

E Equivalent expressions

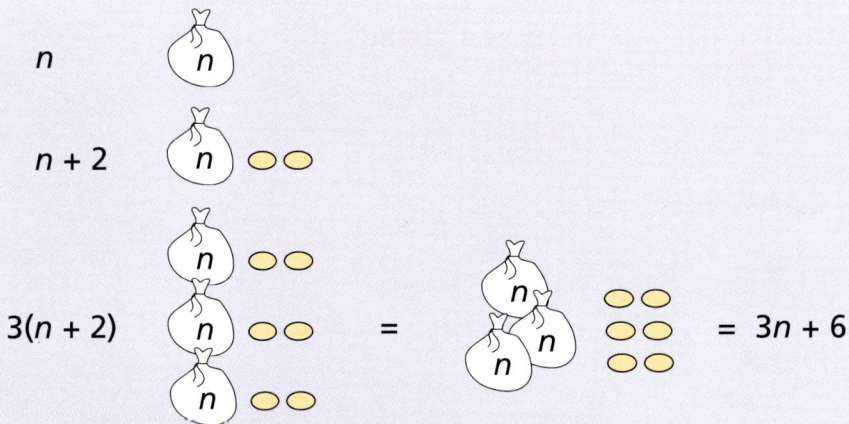

n

$n + 2$

$3(n + 2)$ $=$ $= 3n + 6$

$3(n + 2)$ and $3n + 6$ are **equivalent expressions**.

They have the same value, whatever the value of n.

E1 There are three pairs of equivalent expressions here.
Pair them up, and find the odd one left over.

$2(x + 4)$ $2(x + 16)$ $2x + 4$ $2(x + 8)$ $2x + 16$ $2(x + 2)$ $2x + 8$

E2 There are three pairs of equivalent expressions here.
Pair them up, and find the odd one left over.

$3a + 18$ $3(a - 2)$ $3a - 6$ $3(a + 6)$ $3a - 18$ $3(a - 6)$ $3a - 2$

E3 Find an equivalent expression for each of these.

(a) $3(x + 5)$ (b) $7(b + 3)$ (c) $5(c + 4)$ (d) $4(d + 1)$

(e) $12(e + 2)$ (f) $3(w - 2)$ (g) $4(a - 3)$ (h) $70(m - 1)$

(i) $6(2 + f)$ (j) $3(y - 9)$ (k) $8(5 + k)$ (l) $6(n - 2)$

E4 Find what is missing in each statement.

(a) $2a + 10 = \heartsuit(a + 5)$ (b) $2(a - 6) = 2a - \bullet$

(c) $4a - 12 = 4(a - \blacktriangle)$ (d) $3(a + 7) = \blacktriangledown a + 21$

(e) $5a - 20 = \blacksquare(a - \blacklozenge)$ (f) $\heartsuit a + 14 = 7(a + \blacklozenge)$

(g) $2(\heartsuit + \blacklozenge) = 12 + 2p$ (h) $4a - 32 = \blacksquare(\blacklozenge - 8)$

Expression snap *a game for two players*

Each player needs a set of 'Expression snap' cards on sheet 149.

Players take it in turns to turn over one of their cards on to their pile.

If the card turned over is equivalent to one on top of another pile, the first player to say 'SNAP' takes all the cards in the matching piles.

A wrong 'snap' means you lose the cards in your pile.

The first player to run out of cards loses.

F Number tricks

*F1 (a) Follow these instructions with some different numbers.

(b) Describe what happens each time.

> *Think of a number.*
> - *Add 2.*
> - *Multiply by 5.*
> - *Take away 10.*
> - *Divide by 5.*

(c) Copy and complete this diagram.

> *Think of a number.* n
> $\downarrow$
> - *Add 2.* $n + 2$
> $\downarrow$
> - *Multiply by 5.*   ......
> = ...
> - *Take away 10.* $\downarrow$
> ......
> - *Divide by 5.* $\downarrow$
> ......

> Use brackets here.

> Write an equivalent expression here that does not use brackets.

> Write this expression as simply as you can.

(d) How does this show you always end up with the number first thought of?

*F2 Copy and complete the last two lines so you always end up with the number you first thought of.

> *Think of a number.*
> - *Subtract 1.*
> - *Multiply by 8.*
> - *Add ...*
> - *Divide by ...*

*F3 Make up your own set of instructions so you always end up with the number first thought of.

What progress have you made?

Statement	Evidence

I can use arrow diagrams.

1 Copy and complete this diagram.

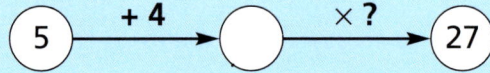

$$5 \xrightarrow{+4} \bigcirc \xrightarrow{\times\,?} 27$$

2 Copy and complete this table.

$$\bigcirc \longrightarrow \bigcirc \xrightarrow{-4} \bigcirc$$

Input	Output
3	...
10	...
5	...
...	36

I can find shorthand rules.

3 Copy and complete these.

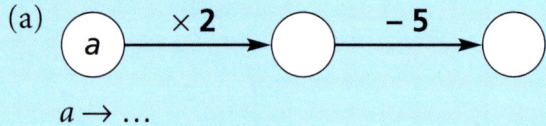

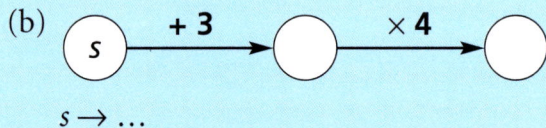

(a)
$$a \xrightarrow{\times\,2} \bigcirc \xrightarrow{-5} \bigcirc$$

$a \to$ ...

(b)
$$s \xrightarrow{+3} \bigcirc \xrightarrow{\times\,4} \bigcirc$$

$s \to$ ...

4 Draw an arrow diagram for $y \to 3y + 6$.

I can work out the value of expressions.

5 If $m = 5$, work out the value of

(a) $3m + 4$ (b) $3(m + 4)$

(c) $6(m - 2)$ (d) $6m - 2$

6 For the rule $y \to 3(y - 1)$,
copy and complete these.

(a) $6 \to$ ...   (b) $1 \to$ ...

I can find equivalent expressions.

7 Find expressions equivalent to

(a) $4(x - 3)$ (b) $5(s + 1)$

(c) $2(b + 9)$ (d) $6(k - 4)$

⑪ Fractions and decimals

This is about how fractions and decimals are related to one another.
The work will help you

- ◆ identify equivalent fractions
- ◆ relate decimals to hundredths, tenths and other fractions
- ◆ compare the sizes of fractions and decimals
- ◆ do simple calculations with decimals mentally

A Putting fractions on a fraction ruler

> What fractions can we label?

> What other fractions could we mark on the two scales at the bottom?

> How can we tell from the numbers that two fractions are equal?

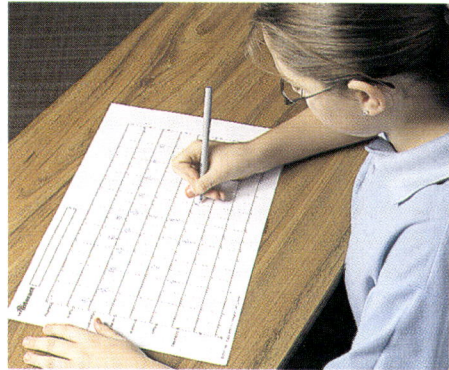

B Comparing fractions

Use the fraction ruler sheet to help answer these questions.

B1 Write two fractions equivalent to $\frac{1}{10}$.

B2 For each of these write one equivalent fraction.

(a) $\frac{1}{4}$ (b) $\frac{3}{5}$ (c) $\frac{15}{20}$ (d) $\frac{65}{100}$

B3 Which is larger, $\frac{3}{4}$ or $\frac{4}{5}$?

B4 Write these fractions in order of size, starting with the smallest.

$\frac{7}{10}, \quad \frac{1}{2}, \quad \frac{3}{5}, \quad \frac{1}{20}$

B5 How many twentieths are there in a fifth?

B6 Using your answer to B5, copy and complete these.

(a) $\frac{2}{5} = \frac{}{20}$ (b) $\frac{}{5} = \frac{12}{20}$ (c) $\frac{4}{5} = \frac{}{20}$ (d) $\frac{1}{5} = \frac{}{20}$

B7 How many hundredths are there in a twentieth?

B8 Using your answer to B7, copy and complete these.

(a) $\frac{7}{20} = \frac{}{100}$ (b) $\frac{}{20} = \frac{15}{100}$ (c) $\frac{4}{20} = \frac{}{100}$ (d) $\frac{11}{20} = \frac{}{100}$

B9 Copy and complete these.

(a) $\frac{1}{2} = \frac{}{20}$ (b) $\frac{3}{5} = \frac{}{10}$ (c) $\frac{}{10} = \frac{8}{20}$ (d) $\frac{7}{10} = \frac{}{100}$

(e) $\frac{3}{4} = \frac{15}{}$ (f) $\frac{30}{100} = \frac{6}{}$ (g) $\frac{18}{20} = \frac{90}{}$ (h) $\frac{3}{} = \frac{60}{100}$

B10 Write one equivalent fraction for each of these.
(You may not have marked them on your sheet.)

(a) $\frac{11}{20}$ (b) $\frac{15}{100}$ (c) $\frac{38}{100}$ (d) $\frac{2}{50}$

B11 If you didn't have a fraction ruler, how would you convince someone that $\frac{2}{5}$ is bigger than $\frac{1}{4}$?

Now hide the fraction ruler and do these.

B12 Write down three fractions equivalent to $\frac{1}{2}$.

B13 For each of these write one equivalent fraction.

(a) $\frac{3}{4}$ (b) $\frac{2}{5}$ (c) $\frac{5}{20}$ (d) $\frac{30}{100}$

B14 Which is larger, $\frac{2}{5}$ or $\frac{1}{2}$?

B15 Write these fractions in order of size, starting with the smallest.

$$\frac{9}{10}, \quad \frac{3}{4}, \quad \frac{20}{100}$$

B16 How many twentieths are there in a tenth?

B17 Using your answer to B16, copy and complete these.

(a) $\frac{2}{10} = \frac{}{20}$ (b) $\frac{}{10} = \frac{12}{20}$ (c) $\frac{7}{10} = \frac{}{20}$ (d) $\frac{9}{10} = \frac{}{20}$

B18 Copy and complete these.

(a) $\frac{1}{2} = \frac{}{4}$ (b) $\frac{1}{5} = \frac{}{10}$ (c) $\frac{2}{5} = \frac{}{20}$ (d) $\frac{2}{10} = \frac{}{100}$

(e) $\frac{1}{2} = \frac{5}{}$ (f) $\frac{1}{4} = \frac{5}{}$ (g) $\frac{2}{5} = \frac{4}{}$ (h) $\frac{15}{100} = \frac{3}{}$

Now uncover your fraction ruler and check whether your answers make sense.

C Putting decimals on the fraction ruler

How do we use decimals to write tenths?

How do we use decimals to write hundredths?

How do we write other fractions as decimals?

D Decimals and fractions

Use the fraction ruler sheet to help answer these questions.

D1 Mark these with arrows on the **decimals** scale.
Label each arrow with the value.
   (a) 0.72   (b) 0.57   (c) 0.85   (d) 0.04

D2 Mark and label the number halfway between
   (a) 0.8 and 0.9   (b) 0.1 and 0.2   (c) 0.7 and 0.8

D3 What number is halfway between
   (a) 0.3 and 0.4   (b) 0.2 and 0.3   (c) 0.5 and 0.6

D4 Write each of these as a fraction in two different ways.
   (a) 0.8   (b) 0.55   (c) 0.15   (d) 0.9

D5 Write each of these as a decimal.
   (a) $\frac{6}{10}$ (b) $\frac{9}{10}$ (c) $\frac{2}{10}$ (d) $\frac{7}{10}$

D6 How many tenths are there in a fifth?

D7 Use your answer to D6 to write these as decimals.
   (a) $\frac{3}{5}$ (b) $\frac{1}{5}$ (c) $\frac{2}{5}$ (d) $\frac{4}{5}$

D8 Write each of these as a decimal.
   (a) $\frac{80}{100}$ (b) $\frac{35}{100}$ (c) $\frac{48}{100}$ (d) $\frac{9}{100}$

D9 Write these numbers in order, smallest first.

0.54, 0.6, 0.45, 0.05, 0.5

D10 Write each of these in hundredths, then as a decimal.

(a) $\frac{7}{20}$ (b) $\frac{1}{20}$ (c) $\frac{9}{20}$ (d) $\frac{11}{20}$

D11 Write each of these as a decimal.

(a) $\frac{1}{10}$ (b) $\frac{19}{20}$ (c) $\frac{90}{100}$ (d) $\frac{6}{20}$

(e) $\frac{92}{100}$ (f) $\frac{1}{5}$ (g) $\frac{3}{4}$ (h) $\frac{7}{100}$

D12 Write each of these as a fraction.

(a) 0.47   (b) 0.99   (c) 0.02   (d) 0.77

D13 Write these numbers in order, smallest first.

0.12, $\frac{1}{2}$, 0.7, 0.04

D14 Write these numbers in order, smallest first.

$\frac{62}{100}$, 0.71, 0.8, $\frac{3}{4}$, 0.09

D15 Which is nearer to $\frac{3}{4}$?

(a) 0.71 or 0.77   (b) $\frac{1}{2}$ or 0.79   (c) 0.69 or $\frac{4}{5}$

D16 *0.28 is bigger than 0.7 because 28 is bigger than 7.*

Is he correct? Explain your answer.

If you filled in a twenty-fifths scale or a fiftieths scale on your fraction ruler, try to do questions D17 to D20 without looking at it.

D17 How many hundredths are there in a fiftieth?

D18 Write each of these in hundredths, then as a decimal.

(a) $\frac{3}{50}$ (b) $\frac{49}{50}$ (c) $\frac{17}{50}$ (d) $\frac{33}{50}$

D19 How many hundredths are there in a twenty-fifth?

D20 Write each of these in hundredths, then as a decimal.

(a) $\frac{11}{25}$ (b) $\frac{2}{25}$ (c) $\frac{24}{25}$ (d) $\frac{19}{25}$

Now hide the fraction ruler and do these.

D21 What number is halfway between
    (a) 0.6 and 0.7   (b) 0.4 and 0.5   (c) 0.9 and 1

D22 Write each of these as a decimal.
    (a) $\frac{7}{10}$ (b) $\frac{65}{100}$ (c) $\frac{3}{5}$ (d) $\frac{1}{4}$

D23 Write each of these as a fraction.
    (a) 0.92   (b) 0.43   (c) 0.29   (d) 0.61

D24 Write each of these as a fraction in two different ways.
    (a) 0.6   (b) 0.5   (c) 0.75   (d) 0.45

D25 Write these numbers in order, smallest first.
    0.34, 0.6, 0.08, 0.91

Now uncover your fraction ruler and check whether your answers make sense.

D26 This is part of another fraction ruler.
It is set out differently from yours.

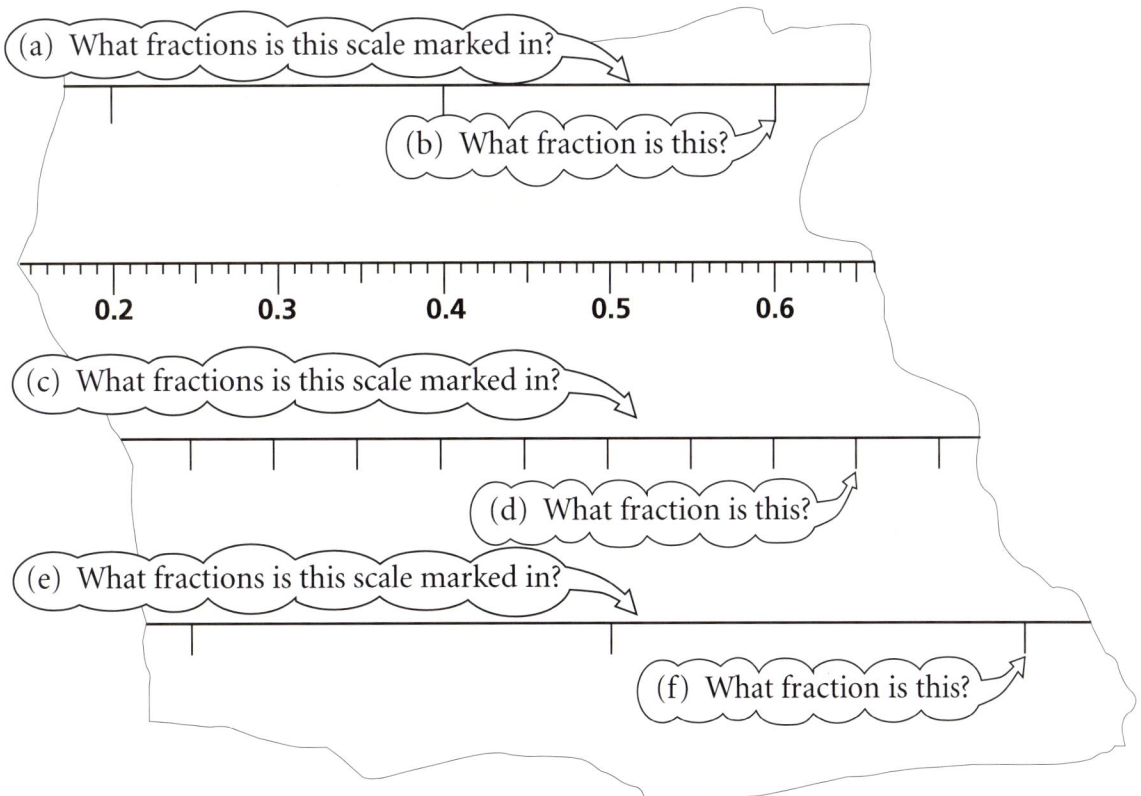

(a) What fractions is this scale marked in?

(b) What fraction is this?

0.2   0.3   0.4   0.5   0.6

(c) What fractions is this scale marked in?

(d) What fraction is this?

(e) What fractions is this scale marked in?

(f) What fraction is this?

E Mixed numbers

'Mixed numbers' are numbers like $2\frac{1}{2}$ (two-and-a-half).
They are a 'mixture' of a whole number and a fraction.
$2\frac{1}{2}$ can be written as a decimal, 2.5.

E1 Write these as decimals.

(a) $2\frac{3}{4}$ (b) $1\frac{3}{5}$ (c) $5\frac{9}{10}$ (d) $10\frac{1}{2}$

E2 Write these as mixed numbers.

(a) 8.25   (b) 7.2   (c) 9.4   (d) 3.85

E3 Write these in order of size, starting with the smallest.

$$2\frac{13}{20}, \quad 2\frac{1}{4}, \quad 2\frac{3}{4}, \quad 2\frac{1}{5}, \quad 2\frac{9}{10}$$

E4 How would you explain to someone that there are 9 quarters in $2\frac{1}{4}$?

E5 How many fifths are there in each of these?

(a) $3\frac{1}{5}$ (b) $4\frac{3}{5}$ (c) $10\frac{1}{5}$ (d) $8\frac{4}{5}$

E6 Work these out, writing your answers as mixed numbers.

(a) $\frac{4}{5}+\frac{4}{5}$ (b) $\frac{2}{3}+\frac{2}{3}$ (c) $\frac{3}{5}+\frac{3}{5}$ (d) $\frac{3}{4}+\frac{3}{4}+\frac{3}{4}$ (e) $\frac{7}{10}+\frac{7}{10}+\frac{7}{10}$

E7 Copy these, putting in the missing numbers.

(a) $5\times\frac{3}{4}=\frac{\ }{4}$ (b) $4\times\frac{4}{5}=\frac{\ }{5}$ (c) $9\times\frac{7}{10}=\frac{\ }{10}$ (d) $5\times\frac{5}{8}=\frac{\ }{8}$

E8 Write your answers to E7 as mixed numbers.

E9 Work these out, giving your answers as mixed numbers.

(a) $6\times\frac{2}{5}$ (b) $11\times\frac{2}{3}$ (c) $8\times\frac{3}{5}$ (d) $7\times\frac{3}{8}$ (e) $9\times\frac{9}{10}$

F Up to two decimal places

Do this section without a calculator.

F1 What is the length of each pin, in cm?

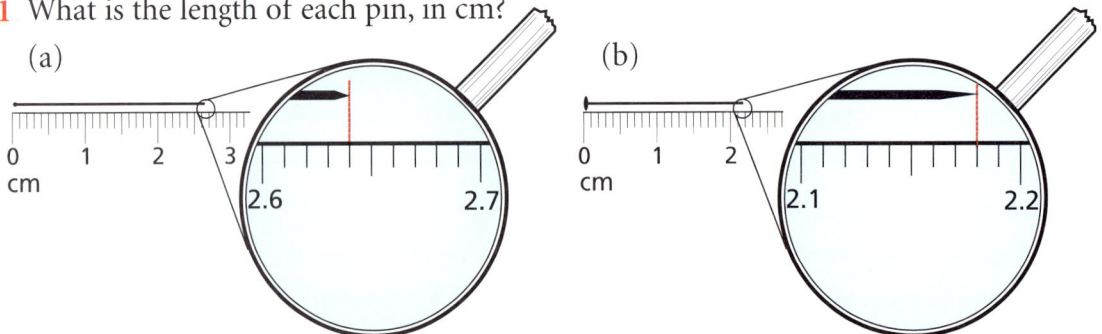

(a)

(b)

F2 What number does each arrow point to?

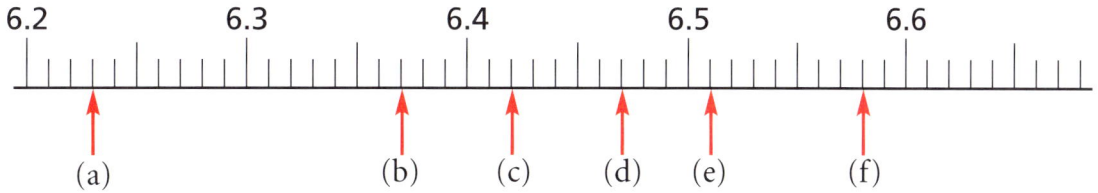

F3 (a) What number is halfway between 8.2 and 8.3?

(b) What number is halfway between 4.9 and 5.0?

(c) What number is halfway between 2.4 and 2.5?

(d) What number is halfway between 6.0 and 6.1?

(e) What number is halfway between 3.8 and 3.9?

(f) What number is halfway between 10.0 and 10.1?

F4 Which of the numbers in the box are between 2.3 and 2.5?

2.35   2.55   2.4
2.25   2.04

F5 Which of these numbers are between 5 and 5.2?

0.51   5.17   5.03
5.1   5.21

F6 Write each list in order of size, smallest first.

(a) 5.32, 5.84, 6, 5.09, 5.76

(b) 3.2, 3.07, 2.8, 3.19, 3.5

(c) 0.6, 0.15, 1.07, 1.1, 0.45

F7 Spell a word by arranging the numbers in order, smallest first.

A	D	O	L	I	S	H	Y
0.36	0.2	0.08	0.1	0.16	0.41	0.03	0.4

F8 Spell another word by arranging these numbers in order.

J	A	B	O	N	E	L	E	Y
1.57	1.96	2.05	1.6	1.3	1.14	2.26	2.4	1.8

F9 The figure 5 in this number stands for 5 tenths, or 0.5. What do these figures stand for?

(a) the 7   (b) the 2   (c) the 3

(d) the 1   (e) the 8

F10 Do these in your head.
- (a) Add 10 to 2713.58.
- (b) Add 1000 to 2713.58.
- (c) Add 0.1 to 2713.58.
- (d) Add 1 to 2713.58.
- (e) Add 0.01 to 2713.58.
- (f) Add 100 to 2713.58.

F11 What do these figures stand for?
- (a) the 7 in 16.72
- (b) the 3 in 4.03
- (c) the 6 in 2364.81
- (d) the 8 in 735.82
- (e) the 4 in 320.04
- (f) the 5 in 13.58

F12 Do these in your head.
- (a) 45.6 + 1
- (b) 45.6 + 10
- (c) 45.6 + 0.1
- (d) 7.34 + 0.1
- (e) 7.34 + 0.01
- (f) 7.34 + 1
- (g) 28.74 + 1
- (h) 28.74 + 0.1
- (i) 28.74 + 0.01

F13 Jason started with the number 463.86.
He subtracted something and ended up with 403.86.
What number did he subtract?

F14 Pam started with 248.71.
She subtracted a number and ended up with 248.01.
What number did she subtract?

F15 Grant started with 54.73.
He subtracted a number and ended up with 54.7.
What did he subtract?

You can describe the number 3.29 as
3 units + 2 tenths + 9 hundredths
or 3 units + 29 hundredths
or 329 hundredths.

F16 Describe 5.58 in three different ways.

F17 Describe 1.08 in two different ways.

F18 Describe 7.51 in three different ways.

F19 Describe 0.42 in two different ways.

F20 Write each of these as a decimal number.
- (a) 4 units + 84 hundredths
- (b) 9 units + 1 hundredth
- (c) 7 tenths + 9 hundredths
- (d) 226 hundredths

G Decimals of a metre

A metre is divided into 100 **centimetres**.
Each centimetre is one hundredth of a metre.

A height in metres and centimetres can be written in metres as a decimal.
For example, 2 metres and 46 centimetres can be written as 2.46 metres.

G1 Write these in metres.

 (a) 6 metres and 75 centimetres

 (b) 5 metres and 32 centimetres

 (c) 2 metres and 4 centimetres

 (d) 10 metres and 11 centimetres

 (e) 8 metres and 20 centimetres

G2 Write these in metres.

 (a) 248 cm   (b) 503 cm   (c) 22 cm   (d) 630 cm

G3 Write these in metres and centimetres.

 (a) 1.98 m   (b) 4.06 m   (c) 9.8 m   (d) 10.1 m

G4 Write these in metres and centimetres.

 (a) 622 cm   (b) 330 cm   (c) 1001 cm   (d) 408 cm

G5 Write these in centimetres.

 (a) 0.4 m   (b) 8.2 m   (c) 7.05 m   (d) 0.05 m

G6 Put these lengths in order, smallest first.

 2.4 m,   2.11 m,   2.09 m,   232 cm

G7 Put these lengths in order, smallest first.

 0.5 m,   0.32 m,   0.07 m,   40 cm

G8 This table gives the results of a jumping contest.

Name	1st jump	2nd jump	3rd jump
Singh	3.92 m	4.36 m	4.5 m
Barker	4.2 m	4.13 m	3.87 m
Church	4.18 m	4.4 m	4.12 m

 (a) How long was Barker's longest jump?

 (b) Whose 1st jump was longest of the three contestants?

 (c) Whose 2nd jump was longest of the three contestants?

 (d) What was the length of the longest jump of all?

G9 Katy had a ribbon 4.32 m long.
She cut off 20 cm.
How long was it now?

G10 Barrie had a rope 10.46 m long.
He cut some off and then it was only 10.16 m long.
How many centimetres did he cut off?

G11 Anuj was 1.59 m tall.
He grew 8 centimetres.
How tall was he now?

G12 Michael had a sunflower.
He measured it and it was 1.86 m tall.
A week later it was 2.04 m tall.
How many centimetres had it grown?

G13 Measuring tapes are marked in different ways.
What measurements do these arrows point to?
Give all your answers **in metres as decimals**.

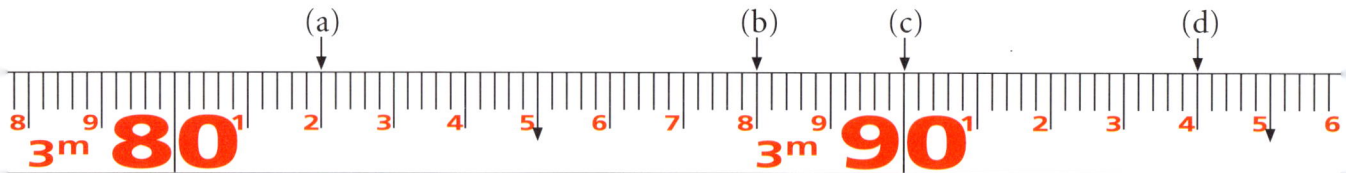

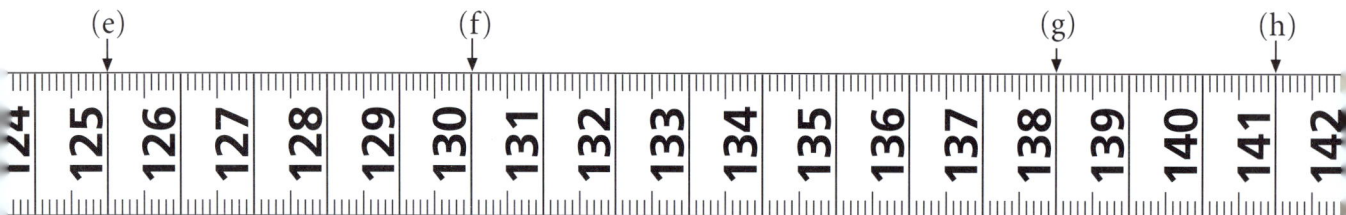

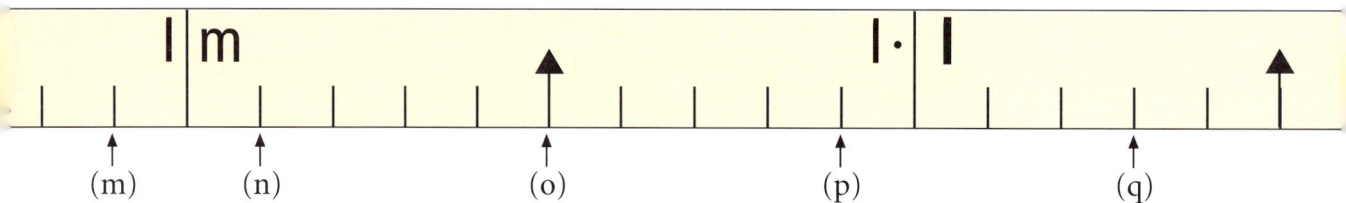

What progress have you made?

Statement	Evidence

I can work out equivalent fractions.

1 For each of these, write one equivalent fraction.

(a) $\frac{1}{5}$ (b) $\frac{6}{20}$ (c) $\frac{45}{100}$ (d) $\frac{8}{10}$

I can put fractions in order of size.

2 Which is larger, $\frac{3}{5}$ or $\frac{3}{4}$?

3 Write these in order of size, starting with the smallest.

$$\frac{7}{10}, \quad \frac{15}{20}, \quad \frac{1}{2}, \quad \frac{3}{5}$$

I can write decimals as fractions.

4 Write these as fractions.

(a) 0.4   (b) 0.35   (c) 0.71   (d) 0.03

I can write fractions as decimals.

5 Write these as decimals.

(a) $\frac{2}{5}$ (b) $\frac{3}{20}$ (c) $\frac{9}{100}$ (d) $\frac{7}{50}$

I can use mixed numbers.

6 Write these as decimals.

(a) $3\frac{2}{5}$ (b) $10\frac{1}{4}$ (c) $9\frac{9}{10}$ (d) $1\frac{1}{20}$

7 Write these as mixed numbers.

(a) 4.2   (b) 9.75   (c) 3.05   (d) 4.55

I can work with two places of decimals.

8 What number does each arrow point to?

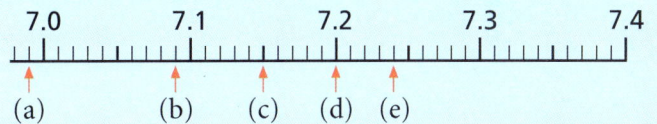

9 Do these in your head.

(a) 7.82 + 0.1   (b) 4.26 + 0.01

(c) 6.92 + 1   (d) 22.91 + 0.01

I can work with decimals of a metre and centimetres.

10 Tom had a piece of cable 2.42 m long. He cut 10 cm off it.

How long was it then?

⑫ Investigations

This work is about investigating mathematics for yourself.

A Crossing points

On the opposite page is Chris's report on an investigation.

Say what the investigation is about.

First Chris tells us what the investigation is about.

Say what you do.
Be systematic.

Then she tells us how she is going to start.
She is going to be **systematic**.

What does this mean?

Show your working.
Say what you find out.

Next she tells us what she found out.

State any decisions you make.

Chris tells us about a decision she makes.

Why do you think she decided to concentrate on the maximum number?

Write your results in a table.

She makes a table of her results.
This will make it easier to spot any patterns.

Can you see any pattern in these numbers?

<u>Crossing points</u>   Report by Chris Sparrow, 8T

I am investigating how many crossing points there
are with different numbers of straight lines.

I am going to start with 2 lines, then 3, then 4 and so on,
and see how many crossing points I get.

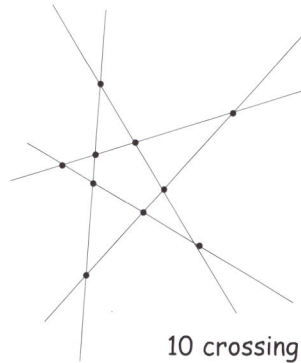

Then I am going to see if there is a pattern in
the numbers.

Crossing point

<u>2 lines</u>

With 2 lines you get 1 crossing point, or
none if the lines are parallel.

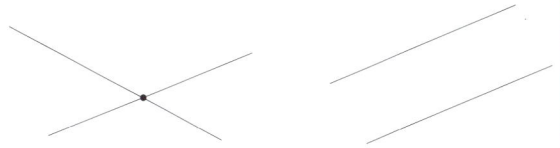

<u>3 lines</u>

With 3 lines you can get 0, 1, 2 or 3 crossing points.

From now on I am going to find the <u>maximum</u> number of
crossing points.

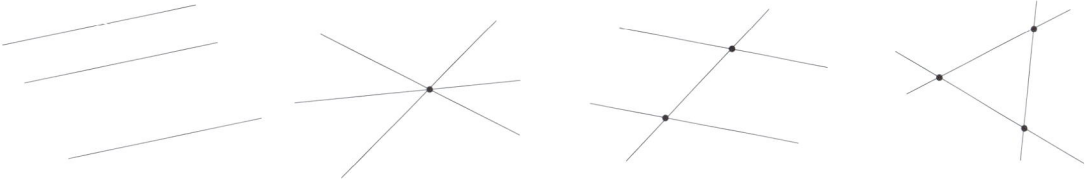

<u>4 lines</u>   <u>5 lines</u>

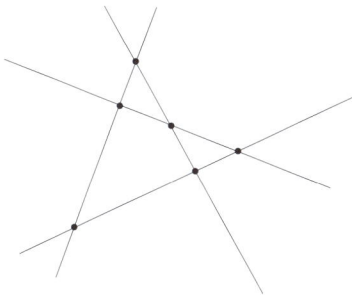

6 crossing points   10 crossing points

Number of lines	2	3	4	5
Maximum number of crossing points	1	3	6	10

Write about any patterns you see.

Chris notices a pattern in the table and writes about it.

Make a prediction …

She makes a prediction …

… and check it.

… and goes on to check it.

Write about anything interesting you notice.

She notices something interesting and writes about it.

Summarise your findings. Explain them if you can.

Chris tells us her main conclusion.

Chris has not tried to explain why her rule is true. Can you explain why it is true?

If possible, extend your investigation.

She is going to extend her investigation.

Carry out this further investigation yourself.

Number of lines	2	3	4	5
Maximum number of crossing points	1	3	6	10

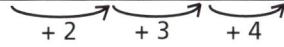

+ 2   + 3   + 4

I have noticed that the gap between these numbers goes up by 1 each time.

I predict that with 6 lines there will be 15 crossing points.

6 lines

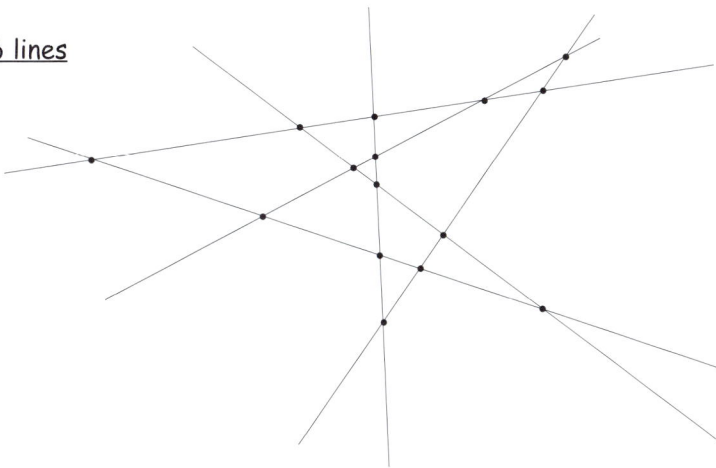

There are 15 crossing points, as predicted.

I have also noticed that each line has 5 crossing points on it.
When there were 5 lines, each one had 4 crossing points on it, and so on.

As you increase the number of lines, the maximum number of crossing points goes up by 1 more each time.

I am going to investigate the number of closed spaces you get.

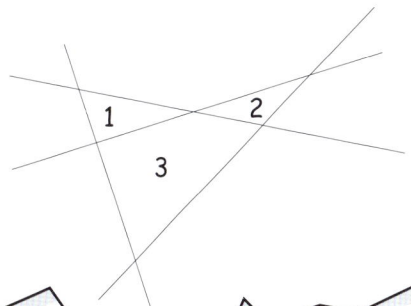

1   2
3

B Some ideas

B1 Round table

Five people sit at a round table.

- Arrange them round the table in a different way so that nobody sits next to a person they sat next to before.
- How many ways can they be arranged like this?
- Investigate for different numbers of people.

B2 Nine lines

Nine straight lines can be drawn so they form different numbers of squares.

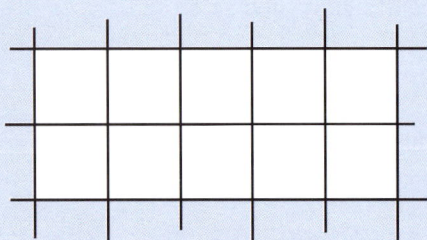

10 squares

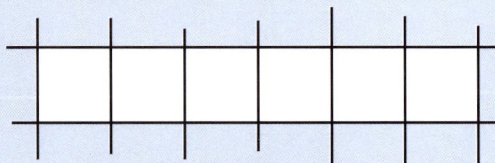

6 squares

- What other number of squares can you make with nine lines?
- Investigate for other numbers of lines.

B3 Swapover

'Swapover' is a puzzle on grids like this ▢▢/▢ or this ▢▢▢▢▢▢ etc.

- Start with two equal lines of counters like this.

- Swap the counters over so they are like this.

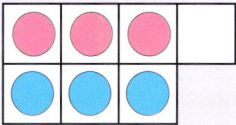

> A counter can move into an empty space horizontally, vertically or diagonally.

How many moves did you need?

- Can you do it in fewer than 9 moves?
  What is the least number of moves needed to swap these counters over?
- Investigate the number of moves for different sized grids.

B4 Cutting a cake

Sam has a square cake and a long straight knife.

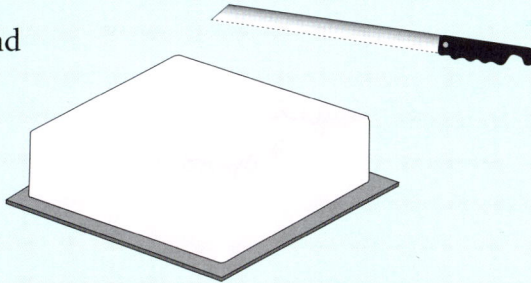

With three cuts, he cuts the cake into 5 pieces.

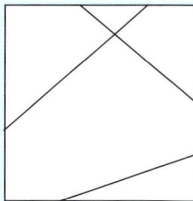

- What other numbers of pieces can you make with three cuts?
- Investigate for different numbers of cuts.

B5 Spots in a square

- Draw a square.

- Mark some spots inside the square.
  Make sure that no three spots are
  in a straight line.

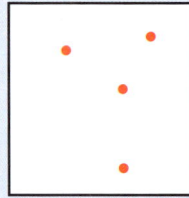

- Join up the spots to one another and to
  the corners of the square so that the inside
  of the square is split up into triangles.

- Count the triangles.

- Investigate.

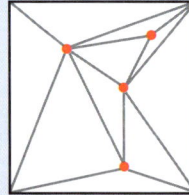

B6 Turn, turn, turn

To make a turning track

- Choose a set of whole numbers.
  (These tell you how far to move forward each time.)

- Decide if you are going to turn right or left after each move.

- Mark your starting position.

*This track repeats the
numbers 1, 2, 4 and turns
right after each move.*

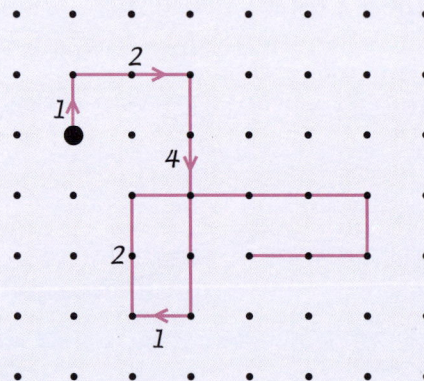

You must keep going using your numbers in order.
Always make a 90° turn after each move.

- Copy and continue the turning track above.
  Describe what happens.

- Investigate tracks made with different sets of three numbers.

- What happens if you try sets of two numbers? four numbers? and so on …

⓭ Think of a number

This is about 'think of a number' puzzles and equations.

The work will help you

- ◆ solve 'think of a number' puzzles by working backwards
- ◆ solve equations using inverses

A Number puzzles

> I think of a number.

> I multiply by 2.

> I add 1.

> I divide by 5.

> I subtract 3.

> The result is 4.

> What number did I think of?

I think of a number.
- I divide by 6.
- I add 7.
- I multiply by 13.

The result is 117.
What number did I think of?

I think of a number.
- I multiply by 10.
- I take away 5.
- I divide by 4.

The result is 7.
What number did I think of?

A1 To solve a puzzle, Pat has drawn an arrow diagram and reversed it.

Puzzle

I think of a number.
- *I take away 4.*
- *I multiply by 3.*

The result is 39.

What number did I think of?

Number thought of → **− 4** → ◯ → **× 3** → **39**

Reverse

? ← **?** ← **÷ 3** ← **39**

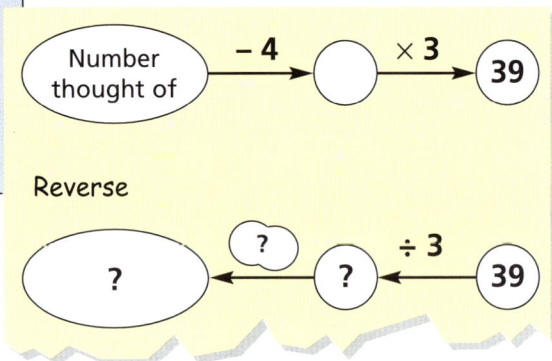

Copy and complete Pat's diagram and solve the puzzle.

A2 (a) Match each of these puzzles to an arrow diagram.

Puzzle 1

I think of a number.
- I multiply by 2.
- I add 1.

The result is 9.

What number did I think of?

Puzzle 2

I think of a number.
- I add 1.
- I multiply by 2.

The result is 9.

What number did I think of?

A Number thought of → **+ 1** → ◯ → **+ 2** → **9**

B Number thought of → **+ 1** → ◯ → **× 2** → **9**

C Number thought of → **× 2** → ◯ → **+ 1** → **9**

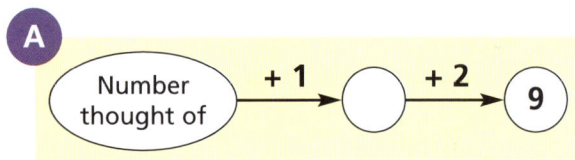

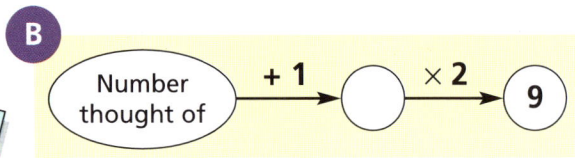

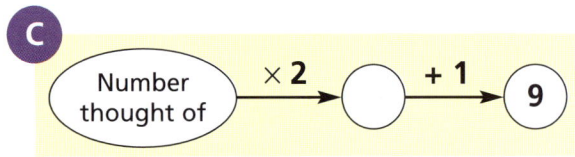

(b) Solve these puzzles by reversing their arrow diagrams.

A3 (a) Write a puzzle to match the arrow diagram below.

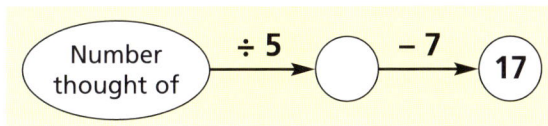

```
 ┌──────────┐   ÷ 5        − 7
 │  Number  │ ─────▶ ◯ ─────▶ (17)
 │thought of│
 └──────────┘
```

(b) Solve the puzzle by reversing the arrow diagram.

A4 Solve these puzzles using arrow diagrams.

(a)
> I think of a number.
> • I take away 5.
> • I multiply by 8.
>
> The result is 32.
>
> What number did I think of?

(b)
> I think of a number.
> • I multiply by 42.
> • I add 17.
>
> The result is 269.
>
> What number did I think of?

(c)
> I think of a number.
> • I add 6.
> • I divide by 7.
> • I take away 2.
>
> The result is 4.
>
> What number did I think of?

(d)
> I think of a number.
> • I multiply by 24.
> • I take away 3.
>
> The result is 9.
>
> What number did I think of?

(e)
> I think of a number.
> • I add 5.
> • I multiply by 20.
>
> The result is 350.
>
> What number did I think of?

A5 Jason makes up a number puzzle.

> I think of a number.
> • I add ✳
> • I multiply by ✳
> The result is 12.
> What number did I think of?

The number Jason thought of was 2.

What could the hidden numbers be in his puzzle?

A6 Make up some number puzzles of your own and ask someone else to solve them.

B Using letters

Here is a number puzzle.

> *I think of a number.*
> - *I add 3.*
> - *I multiply by 2.*
>
> *The result is 20.*
> *What number did I think of?*

We can use a letter to stand for the number thought of. The letter n is used here.

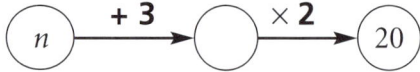

Brackets show that you work out '$n + 3$' first.

In the diagram we can show what happens to n.

$n \xrightarrow{+3} n + 3 \xrightarrow{\times 2} 2(n + 3)$

So this number puzzle can be written $\qquad 2(n + 3) = 20$

This is called an **equation**.

B1 (a) Match each arrow diagram with an equation.

A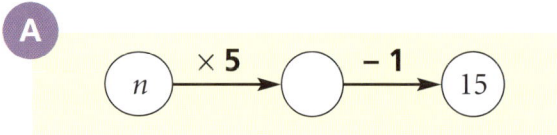

V $5(n + 1) = 15$

W $2(n + 1) = 15$

B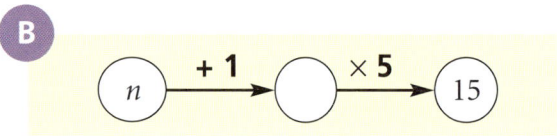

X $5(n - 1) = 15$

C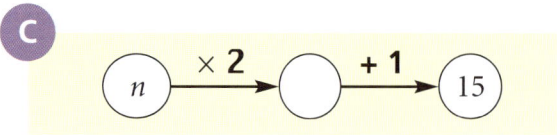

Y $2n + 1 = 15$

D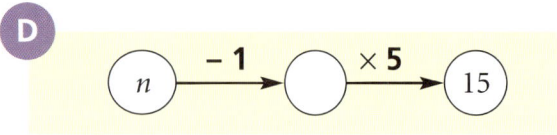

Z $5n - 1 = 15$

(b) Draw an arrow diagram for the unmatched equation.

B2 (a) Match each number puzzle with an equation.

Puzzle 1

I think of a number.
- I multiply by 4.
- I add 1.

The result is 8.
What number did I think of?

Puzzle 2

I think of a number.
- I multiply by 5.
- I take away 2.

The result is 8.
What number did I think of?

Puzzle 3

I think of a number.
- I add 1.
- I multiply by 4.

The result is 8.
What number did I think of?

Puzzle 4

I think of a number.
- I take away 5.
- I multiply by 2.

The result is 8.
What number did I think of?

A $5(m - 2) = 8$

B $4(x + 1) = 8$

C $5q - 2 = 8$

D $2(p - 5) = 8$

E $4y + 1 = 8$

(b) Write a puzzle for the unmatched equation.

B3 Write an equation for each of these number puzzles.
Use n to stand for the number each time.

(a)
I think of a number.
- I multiply by 3.
- I add 4.

The result is 108.
What number did I think of?

(b)
I think of a number.
- I multiply by 16.

The result is 52.
What number did I think of?

(c)
I think of a number.
- I take away 5.
- I multiply by 6.

The result is 42.
What number did I think of?

B4 Write an equation for each arrow diagram.

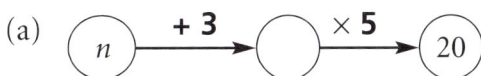

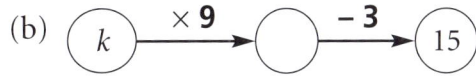

(a) n —— **+ 3** —→ ◯ —— **× 5** —→ 20

(b) k —— **× 9** —→ ◯ —— **− 3** —→ 15

B5 Draw an arrow diagram for each equation.

(a) $3n + 1 = 22$ (b) $6(n - 4) = 30$

C Solving equations

We can find the value of n in the equation $2(n-3) = 130$ using arrow diagrams.

2(n – 3) = 130

- Draw an arrow diagram for the equation.

n $\xrightarrow{-3}$ $\bigcirc$ $\xrightarrow{\times 2}$ 130

- Reverse it to find the value of n.

68 $\xleftarrow{+3}$ 65 $\xleftarrow{\div 2}$ 130

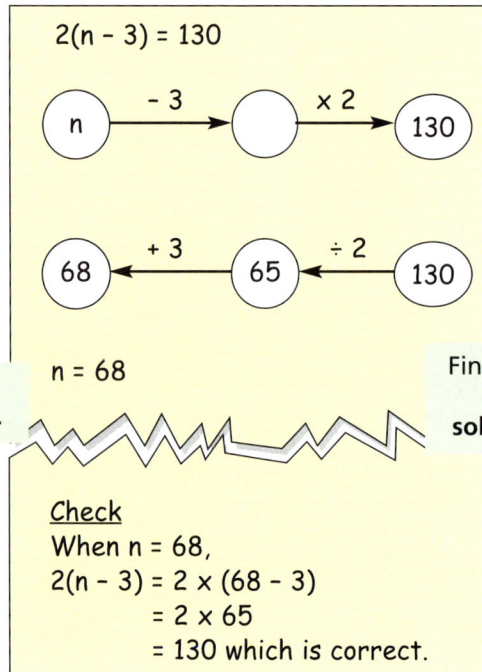

68 is called the **solution** of the equation.

$n = 68$

Finding the value of n is called **solving** the equation.

- Check the solution.

Check
When n = 68,
2(n – 3) = 2 × (68 – 3)
= 2 × 65
= 130 which is correct.

C1 Solve these equations, using arrow diagrams.
Check each solution.

(a) $7n - 5 = 93$ (b) $4(h + 1) = 104$ (c) $3(m - 5) = 48$

(d) $5x + 3 = 68$ (e) $8p - 5 = 123$ (f) $12(z + 6) = 132$

C2 Solve these equations.
Check each solution.

(a) $8m = 20$ (b) $4a - 5 = 9$ (c) $5n + 4 = 25$

(d) $10(p - 3) = 26$ (e) $7(x + 5) = 87.5$ (f) $5y - 3 = 60$

C3 Check that $n = 6$ is a solution to $2n + 4 = 16$.
Make up three different equations with $n = 6$ as a solution.

C4 Make up two different equations that have $y = 1.5$ as a solution.

*C5 Solve these equations.
Check each solution.

(a) $2(m - 5) + 9 = 45$ (b) $7(3q - 1) = 98$

(c) $4.5(p + 2.3) - 5.6 = 4.975$

D Quick solve

In the game 'Quick solve' you win points by solving equations.

One way to play 'Quick solve'

- Play in groups of three or four.
- Each group needs three sets of 12 different cards (36 cards in total) from sheet 159.
- Shuffle each set of cards.

  Put each set face down in a pile.

  You now have three piles of cards (1-point pile, 2-point pile and 3-point pile).

- At the start of the game, each player chooses a card from any pile and tries to solve the equation on the card.
- When a player thinks they have solved the equation, they take another card from any pile.
- Repeat until all the cards have been taken.
- Players check each other's solutions (sheet 160).

  A correct solution wins the number of points on the card.

  A point is lost for any incorrect solution.

- The player with the most points is the winner.

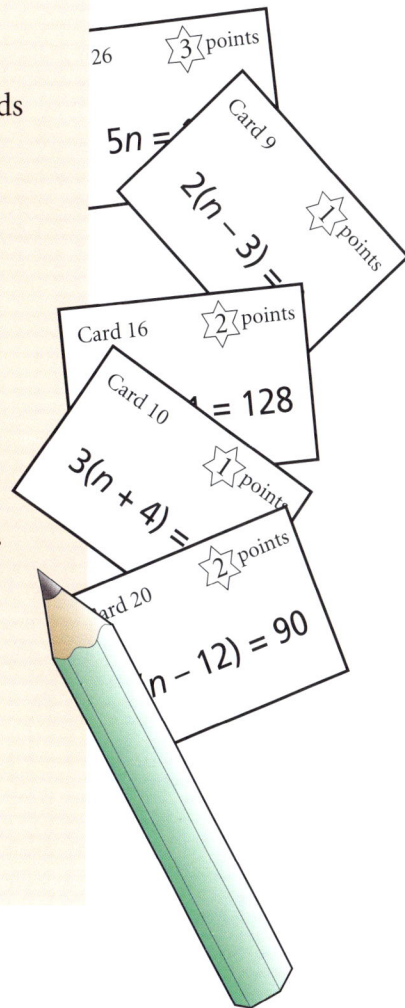

26   3 points

$5n =$

Card 9

$2(n - 3) =$ 1 points

Card 16   2 points

Card 10 $= 128$

$3(n + 4) =$ 1 point

Card 20   2 points

$(n - 12) = 90$

You could write your solutions in a table like this.

Card number	Solution	Correct?	Points
25	$n = 5$	Yes	Win 3
12	$n = 10$		Lose 1
	$n = 3$		

Play 'Quick solve'.

What progress have you made?

Statement

Evidence

I can solve 'think of a number'
puzzles using arrow diagrams.

1 Solve these puzzles using arrow diagrams.

(a)
> *I think of a number.*
> - *I multiply by 3.*
> - *I take away 5.*
>
> *The result is 82.*
> *What number did
> I think of?*

(b)
> *I think of a number.*
> - *I add 7.*
> - *I multiply by 4.*
>
> *The result is 38.*
> *What number did I
> think of?*

I can match arrow diagrams
and equations.

2 Match each arrow diagram with an
equation.

A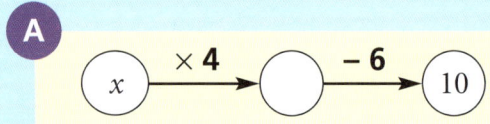

B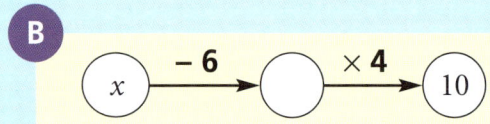

C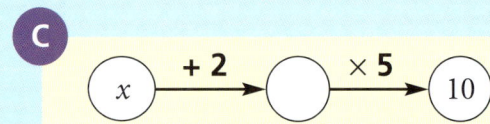

W $4(x - 6) = 10$

X $5x + 2 = 10$

Y $5(x + 2) = 10$

Z $4x - 6 = 10$

I can solve equations.

3 Solve these equations.

(a) $2z - 5 = 69$

(b) $3(p + 4) = 108$

(c) $4y - 7 = 15$

(d) $5(x + 3) = 21$

(e) $2.4q - 200 = 4$

⑭ Practical problems

This work will help you measure and estimate quantities.

Weighty problems   for a group of pupils

1 There are two stones.

   (a) Someone weighs the small stone.

   (b) **Without touching the large stone**, everyone in the group
      looks at it and estimates its weight.
      Each person writes down their estimate in secret.
      One person collects in the estimates.

   (c) Now someone weighs the large stone.
      Everyone compares their estimates with the weight of the stone.
      They record everybody's estimates and the real weight.

2 Now everyone looks at the set of objects.

   (a) **Without touching them**, everyone in the group decides
      what order of weight they should go in.
      Each person writes down their order in secret.

   (b) Now people can touch the objects.
      Without weighing them on the scales, each person
      writes the objects in order of weight again, in secret.
      One person collects in both sets of estimates.

   (c) Now someone weighs the objects.
      Each person compares their two orders of weight with the real order.

Beans   for pupils working individually

Estimate the number of beans in the jar.

Write down how you worked out your estimate
and any measurements that you made.

Cornflakes for pupils working individually

1 (a) Get a cereal bowl.
    Put into it enough cornflakes for a reasonable breakfast.
    Weigh this amount.

  (b) Weigh out the suggested portion size given on the box.
    How does this portion compare with your portion?

2 (a) Work out how many portions you can pour from
    the box if they are the recommended size.

  (b) How many portions can you pour from the box if
    they are your size?

3 (a) Work out the cost of the recommended portion.

  (b) Work out the cost of your own portion.

Getting better for pupils working individually

You have three bottles. Suppose each one is filled with medicine.

1 Look at these instructions.

```
Take one 5 ml spoonful
     3 times a day.
```

How long will each of the three bottles last?

2 How long will each bottle last with this prescription?

```
Take two 5 ml spoonfuls
     twice a day.
```

3 You are told to take two 5 ml spoonfuls 4 times a day for 20 days.
Would any of your three bottles be big enough?

15 Chocolate

This is about sharing.

The work will help you

◆ solve problems

◆ explain your reasoning to other people

• Where will you sit?

Review 2

1 When Wanda goes out to play hockey she allows the amounts of time in the box.

  (a) How long do these things take altogether?

  (b) If the hockey match starts at 2:00 p.m. what time should Wanda set off?

  (c) What time will she expect to get back home?

Drive to the game	$\frac{3}{4}$ hour
Change and warm up	$\frac{1}{4}$ hour
Play the game	$1\frac{1}{4}$ hour
Shower and change	$\frac{1}{2}$ hour
Drive home	$\frac{3}{4}$ hour

2 Copy this number line on to graph paper.

```
150    160    170    180    190    200    210    220 mm
```

  (a) Show these handspans (in mm) as dots on your number line.

169 174 201 219 183 214 205 155 208 166 211 179 164 172 214 203 175
204 216 209 161 205 173 207 214 169 211 208 162 174 167 209

  (b) What is the range of these handspans?

  (c) What is the median handspan?

  (d) What does your diagram tell you about the handspans that the range and median do not tell you?

3 Copy and complete these arrow diagrams.

  (a) ? —×2→ ? —+5→ 23

  (b) 2 —×?→ ? —+14→ 32

109

4 (a) Draw an arrow diagram like this and complete it to show the rule $s \rightarrow 4(s+2)$.

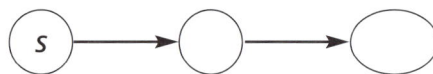

Do the same for these rules.

(b) $z \rightarrow 5z + 6$ (c) $w \rightarrow 3(w-9)$ (d) $p \rightarrow 4p - 7$ (e) $h \rightarrow 3(h+9)$

5 Write these in metres and centimetres.

(a) 3.2 m   (b) 5.16 m   (c) 1.8 m   (d) 4.09 m

6 Write these in metres using decimals.

(a) 1 m 7 cm   (b) 205 cm   (c) 280 cm   (d) 7 m 8 cm

7 Write each of these lengths in centimetres.

(a) 6.25 m   (b) 12.51 m   (c) 6.3 m   (d) 10.03 m

8 From these fractions and decimals find pairs that are equivalent and write them down.

$\frac{1}{2}$ 0.4   0.8   0.5 $\frac{2}{5}$

0.2   0.45 $\frac{1}{5}$ 0.25 $\frac{4}{5}$

9 Work out the value of these when $q = 7$.

(a) $4(q + 5)$ (b) $7q + 1.5$ (c) $2(q - 5)$ (d) $2q - 11$

10 Find the missing measurement, giving your answer in metres as a decimal.

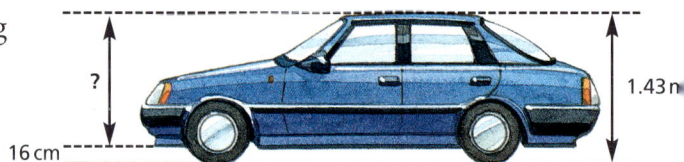

? 16 cm   1.43 m

11 80 seeds are planted in a seed tray. The diagram shows how long each seed takes to germinate (to begin to sprout).

This shows that 6 seeds started sprouting on the 9th day after planting.

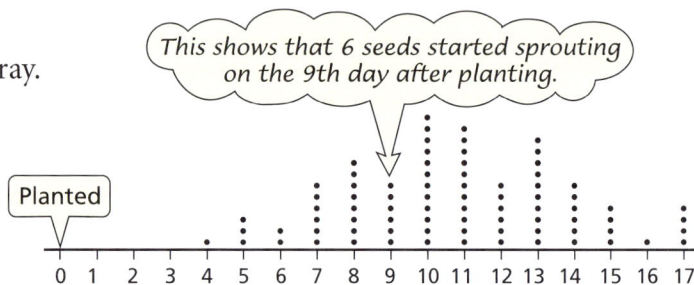

(a) What is the longest time taken to germinate?

(b) What is the range of germination times?

(c) What is the median germination time?

(d) The suppliers guarantee that $\frac{3}{4}$ of the seeds will start sprouting within 13 days of being planted.
How long does it actually take for $\frac{3}{4}$ of the seeds to start sprouting?

12 Write an equivalent expresssion without brackets for each of these.

(a) $4(p + 2)$ (b) $3(x - 7)$ (c) $5(d + 5)$ (d) $7(2 + t)$

13 Find what is missing in each statement.

(a) $2a + 8 = 2(a + \blacksquare)$ (b) $\blacklozenge b - 45 = 9(\blacktriangledown - 5)$ (c) $\bullet(s - 2) = 7s - \blacktriangledown$

14 What numbers do the arrows point to?

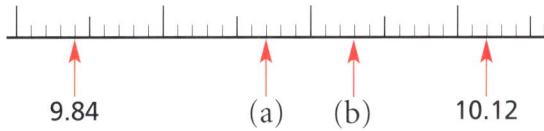

9.84   (a)   (b)   10.12

15 Look at these scales carefully.
What numbers do the arrows point to?
Give each answer as a decimal.

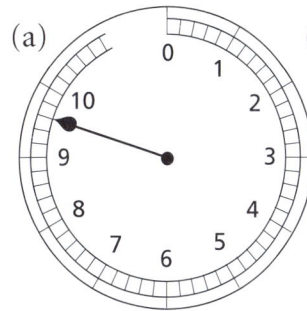

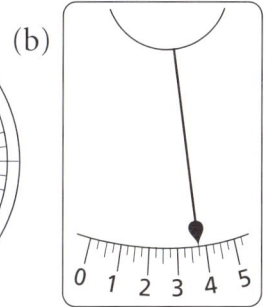

(a)   (b)

16 Write the total length in metres of each of these parcels.

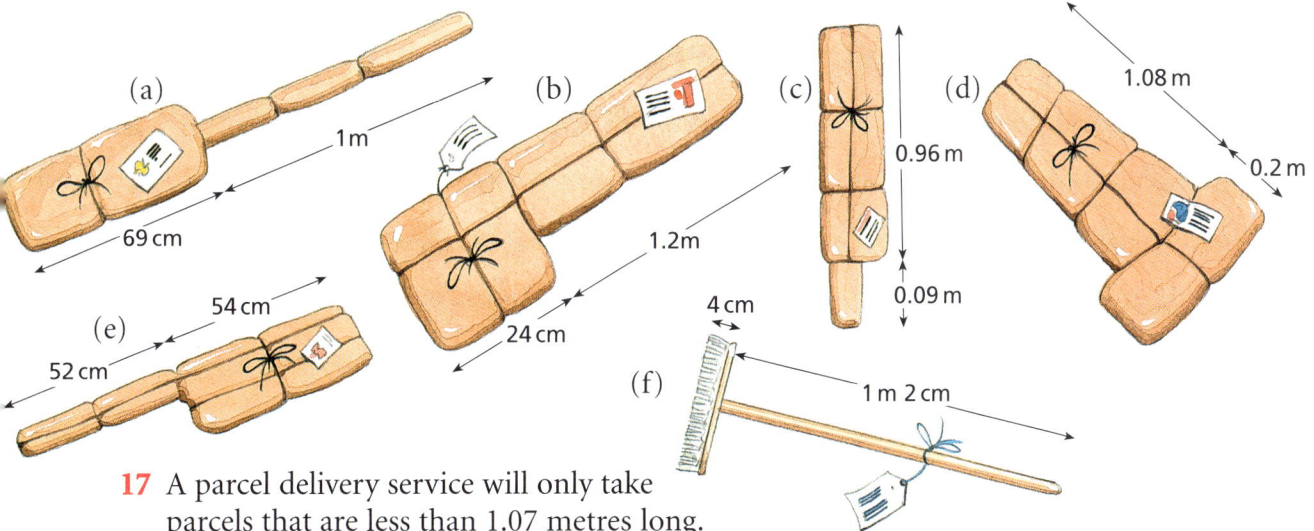

(a) 1m, 69 cm

(b) 1.2m, 24 cm

(c) 0.96 m, 0.09 m

(d) 1.08 m, 0.2 m

(e) 54 cm, 52 cm

(f) 4 cm, 1m 2 cm

17 A parcel delivery service will only take parcels that are less than 1.07 metres long.
Which of the parcels in question 16 will they take?

18 John stands on a block in the school play. This makes him seem 2.05 m tall.
Without the block he is 1.69 m tall. How high is the block in centimetres?

19 For each of these puzzles, write an equation using *n* for the number thought of. Then solve the equation.

(a)
I think of a number.
• *I multiply by 2.*
• *I add 9.*

The result is 23.
What number did I think of?

(b)
I think of a number.
• *I subtract 17.*
• *I multiply by 4.*

The result is 16.
What number did I think of?

(c)
I think of a number.
• *I multiply by 6.*
• *I subtract 15.*

The result is 0.
What number did I think of?

20 Solve these equations.

(a) $3z - 5 = 31$ (b) $4(p + 8) = 36$ (c) $5d - 25 = 4$ (d) $4(x - 7) = 6$

⑯ Multiplication and division

This work will help you

◆ multiply or divide by a two-digit number without a calculator

◆ find remainders and deal with them

A Multiples of ten

$$20 \times 30$$
$$= 2 \times 10 \times 3 \times 10$$
$$= 2 \times 3 \times 10 \times 10$$
$$= 6 \times 100$$
$$= 600$$

A1 Work these out.

(a) 20×40 (b) 30×30 (c) 40×30 (d) 50×3 (e) 70×20

(f) 50×40 (g) 20×50 (h) 9×70 (i) 60×80 (j) 50×80

A2 Work these out.

(a) 20×300 (b) 400×30 (c) 20×400 (d) 600×70 (e) 9×300

(f) 500×4 (g) 600×80 (h) 400×50 (i) 200×300 (j) 500×60

A3 Find the missing number in each calculation.

(a) $20 \times \blacksquare = 1200$ (b) $\blacksquare \times 60 = 3000$ (c) $20 \times \blacksquare = 18\,000$

(d) $\blacksquare \times 300 = 2400$ (e) $200 \times \blacksquare = 80\,000$ (f) $\blacksquare \times 600 = 3000$

B Table method

12×14

×	10	4
10	100	40
2	20	8

```
   100
+   40
+   20
+    8
   ___
   168
```

34

23

23 × 34

×	30	4
20	600	80
3	90	12

```
  600
+  80
+  90
+  12
  782
```

B1 Copy and complete this table and work out 13 × 12.

×	10	2
10		
3		

B2 Work out 14 × 15 by copying and completing this table.

×	10
10	

B3 Work out 16 × 23 by copying and completing this table.

×	20
10	

B4 Work out 24 × 35 by copying and completing this table.

×	30
20	

B5 Work out 43 × 64 by using a table.

B6 Work out 53 × 148 by copying and completing this table.

×	100	40	8
50			
3			

B7 Work out 362 × 47 by copying and completing this table.

×	40	7
300		
60		
2		

B8 Make up two multiplications of your own and work them out. You could check the answers with a calculator.

C Some ways of setting out multiplication

Here are two different ways in which people do 34×23.

Table method

×	20	3
30	600	90
4	80	12

$$
\begin{array}{r}
600 \\
+\ 90 \\
+\ 80 \\
+\ 12 \\
\hline
782
\end{array}
$$

'Long multiplication'

$$
\begin{array}{r}
34 \\
\times\ 23 \\
\hline
102 \\
+\ 680 \\
\hline
782
\end{array}
$$

34×3

34×20

Use whichever method you find easiest to do these.

C1 (a) 13×45 (b) 54×28 (c) 47×36 (d) 53×52

C2 (a) 33×75 (b) 81×36 (c) 66×54 (d) 123×32

D Lattice method

This pencil and paper method is called the lattice (or 'gelosia') method and is many hundreds of years old. It came from India and then spread to China.

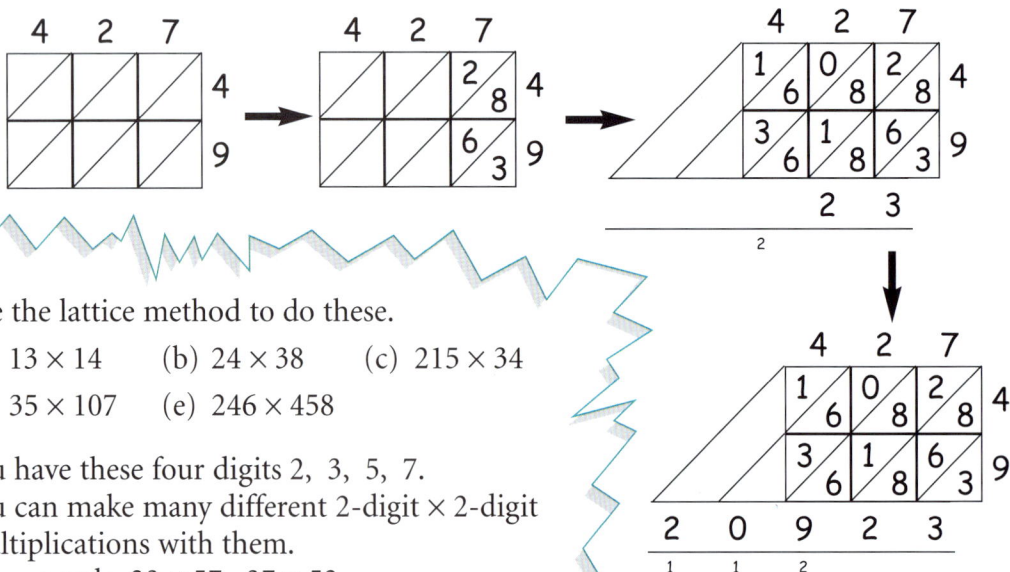

427×49

$427 \times 49 = 20\,923$

D1 Use the lattice method to do these.

(a) 13×14 (b) 24×38 (c) 215×34

(d) 35×107 (e) 246×458

D2 You have these four digits 2, 3, 5, 7.
You can make many different 2-digit × 2-digit multiplications with them.
For example, 23×57, 37×52, …

Which has the largest result?
Which has the smallest result?

E Division with no remainders

Sheena is working out 368 ÷ 23 without a calculator.

I think of 368 ÷ 23 as 'How many 23s in 368?'

```
                          368
     10 × 23          −  230
                          138
      5 × 23          −  115
                           23
      1 × 23          −   23
                            0

     so 368 ÷ 23 is 16
```

- How would you work out 325 ÷ 13 without a calculator?

Use any non-calculator method you like to do these.

E1 (a) 192 ÷ 32   (b) 328 ÷ 41   (c) 161 ÷ 23   (d) 440 ÷ 55

(e) 276 ÷ 23   (f) 224 ÷ 14   (g) 450 ÷ 25   (h) 1344 ÷ 64

E2 600 chairs are arranged in a hall, with 24 chairs in each row.
How many rows are there?

E3 Bob has 756 tulip bulbs. He can plant 36 bulbs in each large pot.
How many large pots does he need?

E4 A school with 896 pupils has 32 teachers.
How many pupils is this to each teacher?

E5 It costs £273 to take 39 pupils on a school trip.
How much should they each pay to cover the cost of the trip?

E6 A group of 14 people win £784 in a prize draw.
How much will they each get?

E7 A builder has to lay 3192 tiles on a floor with 42 tiles in each row.
How many rows will there be?

E8 A milk crate holds 18 bottles.
Make up a problem in words which leads to the calculation 594 ÷ 18.

E9 Make up problems in words which involve dividing by

(a) 25   (b) 32   (c) 72

Ask someone to solve your problems. Check their answers.

E10 Find the missing numbers in these.

(a) 47 × **?** = 987   (b) **?** × 59 = 1003   (c) **?** × 92 = 3496

115

F Division with remainders

Sheena is working out $819 \div 52$.

$$
\begin{array}{r}
819 \\
10 \times 52 \quad -520 \\
\hline
299 \\
4 \times 52 \quad -208 \\
\hline
91 \\
1 \times 52 \quad -52 \\
\end{array}
$$

What is the remainder?

F1 Work these out, and also give the remainders

    (a) $243 \div 20$ (b) $371 \div 32$ (c) $480 \div 25$ (d) $727 \div 44$

    (e) $605 \div 31$ (f) $678 \div 74$ (g) $999 \div 65$ (h) $1710 \div 64$

F2 For each calculation below turn the remainder into a letter using the rule
$1 = A$, $2 = B$, $3 = C$, …

Rearrange the letters to make a vegetable.

    $76 \div 37$ $373 \div 23$ $509 \div 39$ $256 \div 17$ $1001 \div 71$ $622 \div 27$ $364 \div 19$

F3 Make up a word puzzle like the one above for someone else to solve.

F4 How many of the numbers from 20 to 25 give odd-number remainders
when you divide 1000 by them?

F5 Cheese rolls are sold in packets of 18.
Abdul needs 300 cheese rolls for a picnic.

How many packets does he need to buy?
How many more rolls will he get than he needs?

F6 Karl is using beads to make necklaces.
Each necklace needs 46 beads.
He has 1000 beads.
How many necklaces can he make? How many beads are left over?

F7 A full coach can carry 56 passengers.
23 coaches are needed for a trip to a rock concert and there are 9 empty seats.
How many people go on the trip?

F8 Patrice has 1307 tomatoes, enough to fill 27 standard boxes with
some tomatoes left over.
How many tomatoes are there in a standard box?

F9 Suzannah is packing 1948 chocolates into cartons.
Each carton holds the same number.
She has enough chocolates to fill 59 cartons.
How many chocolates are left over?

F10 A swimmer takes 2 minutes and 35 seconds to swim 100 metres.
How long is this in seconds?

F11 A worker on a production line takes 47 seconds to assemble a kettle.
How long will she take to assemble 50 kettles?
Give your answer in minutes and seconds.

F12 It takes 14 minutes to mix one load of cement in a cement mixer.
How long will it take to mix 20 loads?
Give your answer in hours and minutes.

What progress have you made?

Statement	Evidence
I can do multiplications like 30×40 and 60×500.	**1** Work these out. (a) 30×40 (b) 60×500 (c) 800×30 (d) 200×600
I can multiply by a two-digit number without a calculator.	**2** Do these without a calculator. (a) 57×34 (b) 46×28 (c) 235×46 (d) 19×392
I can divide by a two-digit number without a calculator.	**3** Work these out. (a) $682 \div 31$ (b) $221 \div 17$ (c) $1007 \div 53$
I can find remainders.	**4** Work these out and give the remainders. (a) $351 \div 20$ (b) $999 \div 43$ (c) $780 \div 19$
I know how to deal with remainders. when I solve a problem.	**5** To do an investigation each pupil needs 16 cubes. There are 450 cubes. How many pupils can do the investigation?

⑰ Approximation

This is about rounding numbers to give a rough idea of their size. The work will help you

◆ round numbers to the nearest hundred or thousand

◆ round numbers to so many decimal places

A Numbers in the news

Trader fights $6m Sumitomo claim

By Melanie Tringham

YASUO Hamanaka, the former Sumitomo Corporation copper trader, is to fight a claim for $5·81m from his former employer in connection with $2·6 billion of unauthorised trades dating back to 1985.

GAFFE-prone Lord Irvine has proved a deep embarrassment to Tony Blair ever since he was elevated to the post of Britain's top lawman.

The Lord Chancellor has been the PM's mentor for years and helped Mr Blair get together with wife Cherie when he was boss of the chambers where they met. The Premier repaid him by putting him in charge of the legal profession on £135,000 a year.

And ever since the 57-year old peer has been accused of misusing taxpayers' money – particularly on his official House of Lords residence.

He has already splashed out up to £10,000 on two beds, £21,000 on carpets, £9,640 on a dining table, £59,211 on wallpaper, £51,000 on soft furnishings, £96,000 on furniture and £5,000 on blinds

● **£59,000 spent on wallpaper**

Lotto man's scrap wins him a million

A SECURITY guard who picked his lottery numbers from a scrap of paper he found on a pavement has won more than £1 million.

Scotsman Niven Mitchell, 58, pictured with wife Margaret, had a strange urge to pick up a piece of paper from the pavement outside a London Underground station.

He turned the phone number written on it into five lines of lottery numbers.

EVERY line was a winner. The jackpot line gave him £1,242,466, while the other four netted an extra £3,288

It might be old, but this 1920 Rolls-Royce has just 7,000 miles on its clock, reports **David Burgess-Wise**

'**B**ODY BY BREWSTER" sounds like a stage direction from *Arsenic and Old Lace*, and maybe playwright Joseph Kesselring was subconsciously influenced by a coachbuilder's plate when he chose the surname "Brewster" for the sweet little old ladies with poisonous habits in his corpse-strewn black comedy.

But there's nothing remotely macabre about the real-life body by Brewster adorning a remarkable 1920 Rolls-Royce that's just emerged from 66 years' concealment in San Francisco, having covered just 7,066 miles since its chassis was shipped out of London Docks aboard the SS Vasconia in April 1921, bound for the oldest and finest coachbuilder in the United States, Brewster & Company of New York.

Time traveller: the splendid Brewster-bodied Rolls-Royce has not turned a wheel since 1932, when its wealthy owner put it into storage with just 7,066 miles showing on the odometer (left).

A1 The amount in this headline is different from the amount in the story.

Why do you think this is?

Student wins £16 million on lottery

When 18-year-old student Jason Brodie from Kingardie bought a lottery ticket, he thought he might just win £10 to buy a CD. But it was a lucky day for him. Jason won £15,942,847 and is now the richest maths so much that he maths student in the college, and probably the richest in the country. Asked whether it would make any difference to him, Jason said he liked

A2 Make up a headline for each of these stories.

(a) A record-breaking crowd of 37,165 saw United win their first match of the year against their local rivals Munchester Wanderers.

(b) A dentist who retired this week calculated that he had extracted 24,819 teeth during his career. 'And I remember every one of them', he said.

(c) The Barsetshire Animal Hospital continues to treat more patients every year. During the past five years 1969 hedgehogs have been treated in the hospital.

(d) In the last 90 years the Cornhall fire brigade has rescued 369,206 cats from trees, according to a report sent to members of Cornhall City Council.

A3 Here are some headlines.

Make up a sentence which might be part of the story and which says what the exact number is.

(a) **Cyclist finishes 3600 mile trip**

(b) **8000 enter competition**

(c) **Space probe now 20 million miles from Earth**

(d) **Record 210,000 at concert**

B Rounding to the nearest hundred

B1 This number line is marked in **hundreds**.

1800 1900 2000 2100 2200 2300 2400 2500 2600 2700

Imagine where the number 2563 is.
Which is the nearest hundreds mark to 2563? (Is it 2500 or 2600?)

B2 Which is the nearest hundred to
    (a) 1937   (b) 1893   (c) 1827   (d) 2384   (e) 2052

B3 Round these numbers to the nearest hundred.
    (a) 549   (b) 1974   (c) 2074   (d) 13 058   (e) 54 266

B4 The number 2350 is exactly halfway between 2300 and 2400.
We round up and say the nearest hundred is 2400.

Which is the 'nearest' hundred to
    (a) 650   (b) 1350   (c) 1850   (d) 2450   (e) 24 950

B5 This table gives the depths of some of Europe's deepest caves.

(a) Write the names and depths in order, deepest first, to the nearest hundred feet.

Cave	Country	Depth in feet
Corchia	Italy	3118
Holloch	Switzerland	2713
Snieznej	Poland	2569
Jean Bernard	France	4258
Kacherlschact	Austria	2996
Cellagua	Spain	3182
Pierre St-Martin	France/Spain	4370

(b) Draw a diagram, like the one started here, to show the depths of the caves.

Drawn to the scale of the diagram, the Eiffel Tower gives an idea of the enormous depths of these caves.

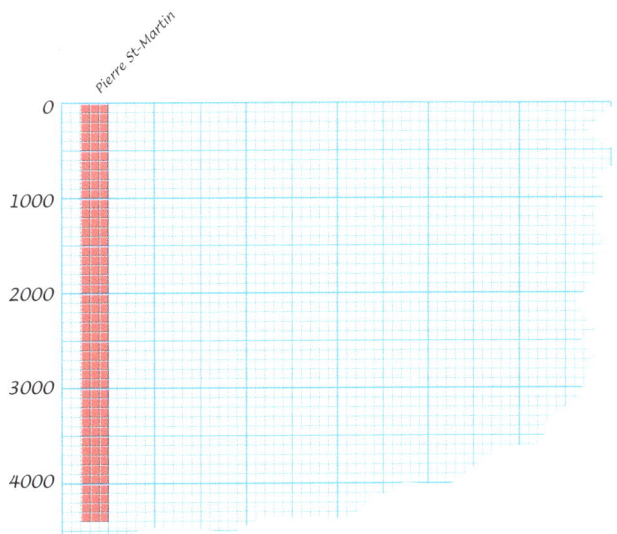

C Rounding to the nearest thousand

Worked example   Round 42 195 to the nearest thousand.

What is the thousands figure?	Which thousands is the number between?	Which is it nearest to?
42 195	**42** 000 **43** 000 ⊢——⊣————⊣——— 42 195	**42** 000

C1 Round these numbers to the nearest thousand.

(a) 5762   (b) 12 379   (c) 18 941   (d) 19 996   (e) 46 521

(f) 4828   (g) 74 509   (h) 285 612   (i) 842 319   (j) 740 061

C2 The table shows the top six League football teams in the 1995–96 season and the average gate (number of spectators per match).

Position	Team	Gate
1	Manchester Utd	55 081
2	Newcastle Utd	36 466
3	Arsenal	37 821
4	Liverpool	39 777
5	Aston Villa	36 027
6	Chelsea	27 001

(a) List the teams in order of the size of their gate, largest first.

(b) What happens if you round the numbers to the nearest thousand before putting them in order?

C3 The total attendances at Football League matches in England and Wales in 1996–97 are given in this table.

Rewrite the table with the numbers rounded to the nearest thousand.

Division	Attendance
Premier	10 804 762
1	6 931 539
2	3 195 223
3	1 851 639

C4 Work these out on a calculator.
Write your answer rounded to the nearest thousand.

(a) 425×74 (b) 75×92 (c) 568×237 (d) 368^2

(e) 432×963 (f) 811×56 (g) 431×231 (h) 99^2

D Rounding decimals

D1 This number line is marked every tenth (every 0.1).

```
1.8   1.9   2.0   2.1   2.2   2.3   2.4   2.5   2.6   2.7   2.8   2.9   3.0   3.1
 |     |     |     |     |     |     |     |     |     |     |     |     |     |
```

(a) Imagine where the the number 2.43 is.
Which marking is it closest to?

(b) Imagine where the the number 2.06 is.
Which marking is it closest to?

D2 Numbers rounded to the nearest 0.1 have
one digit to the right of the decimal point.
We say they are rounded to one decimal place (1 d.p.).

Round these numbers to one decimal place.

(a) 4.26　　(b) 7.31　　(c) 5.4377　　(d) 2.1804　　(e) 12.5052

D3 The number 2.75 is exactly halfway between 2.7 and 2.8.
We round up and say that it is 2.8 to one decimal place.

Round these to one decimal place.

(a) 1.65　　(b) 0.95　　(c) 4.352　　(d) 7.857　　(e) 10.8501

D4 This number line is marked every hundredth (every 0.01).

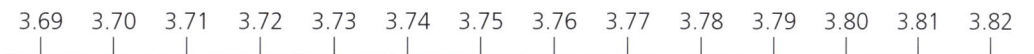

```
3.69  3.70  3.71  3.72  3.73  3.74  3.75  3.76  3.77  3.78  3.79  3.80  3.81  3.82
 |     |     |     |     |     |     |     |     |     |     |     |     |     |
```

(a) Imagine where the the number 3.737 is.
Which marking is it closest to?

(b) Imagine where the the number 3.793 is.
Which marking is it closest to?

(c) Imagine where the the number 3.8062 is.
Which marking is it closest to?

D5 We say numbers rounded to the nearest 0.01 are
rounded to two decimal places (2 d.p.).

Round these numbers to two decimal places.

(a) 3.574　　(b) 21.429　　(c) 14.038　　(d) 16.596　　(e) 20.5713

D6 When you are rounding to 2 d.p., a number like 7.365 is rounded up.
Round these to 2 d.p.

(a) 1.6253　　(b) 17.405　　(c) 9.0157　　(d) 11.4951　　(e) 19.0954

D7 Petra works out these lengths of silver wire
for a jewellery design.
Round the lengths to two decimal places.

Piece A 9.642369 cm
Piece B 4.105427 cm
Piece C 5.396781 cm

D8 Work these out on a calculator, giving each answer to 2 d.p.

    (a) 4.26×1.09 (b) 5.71×3.03 (c) 0.42×0.37 (d) $23 \div 7$ (e) $7 \div 13$

You use the same approach when rounding to three decimal places, as these examples show.

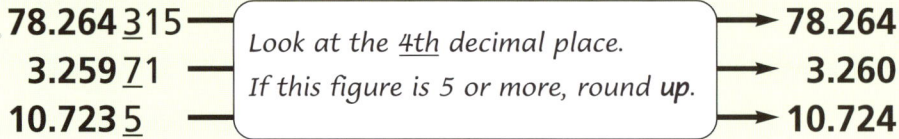

78.264<u>3</u>15	Look at the <u>4th</u> decimal place.	**78.264**
3.259<u>7</u>1	If this figure is 5 or more, round *up*.	**3.260**
10.723<u>5</u>		**10.724**

D9 Round these numbers to three decimal places.

    (a) 1.4774   (b) 3.2429   (c) 2.5038   (d) 2.7596   (e) 3.15814

    (f) 2.8605   (g) 6.1995   (h) 41.3669   (i) 0.0085   (j) 0.00409

D10 Round

    (a) 8.74521 to 1 d.p.   (b) 45.7043 to 2 d.p.   (c) 2.3078 to 2 d.p.

    (d) 3.4139 to 3 d.p.   (e) 67.05374 to 3 d.p.   (f) 0.00863 to 2 d.p.

D11 Work these out on a calculator, rounding the answers as shown.

    (a) 26.24×5.78 (2 d.p.)   (b) $30 \div 17$ (1 d.p.)   (c) 0.71×0.86 (3 d.p.)

    (d) $73 \div 43$ (1 d.p.)   (e) $6 \div 19$ (3 d.p.)   (f) 20.1×6.5 (1 d.p.)

What progress have you made?

Statement	Evidence
I can round numbers to the nearest ten, hundred or thousand.	**1** Round 7528 to the nearest ten.
	2 Round 13 806 to the nearest hundred.
	3 Round 24 089 to the nearest hundred.
	4 Round 13 806 to the nearest thousand.
	5 Round 417 852 to the nearest hundred.
	6 Round 417 852 to the nearest thousand.
I can round numbers to a given number of decimal places.	**7** Round 4.823 to one decimal place.
	8 Round 59.8967 to two decimal places.
	9 Round 8.05357 to three decimal places.

⑱ Decimal calculation

This work will help you calculate with decimals.

A One decimal place

Find two numbers in the loop that

- add to give 12
- subtract to give 2.7
- multiply to give 10
- divide to give 2.1

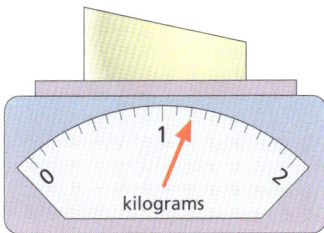

Do not use a calculator for this section.

A1 Work these out in your head.

(a) 4.2 + 3   (b) 1.5 + 2.5   (c) 3.7 + 0.2   (d) 1.4 + 2.7   (e) 8.9 + 2.3

(f) 3 − 0.5   (g) 7.6 − 1.5   (h) 4.9 − 3   (i) 2.3 − 1.4   (j) 2.2 − 0.7

A2 Work these out in your head.

(a) 1.2×3 (b) 1.5×4 (c) 2.7×2 (d) 3.2×5 (e) 1.3×4

(f) $1.5 \div 3$ (g) $4.8 \div 2$ (h) $3.2 \div 2$ (i) $1.2 \div 3$ (j) $6 \div 4$

A3

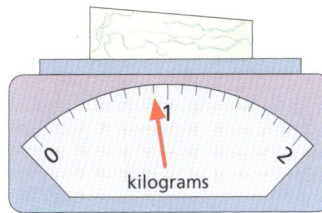

Cheddar   Stilton

(a) What is the weight of each piece of cheese?

(b) How much heavier is the Cheddar than the Stilton?

(c) Work out the total weight of the two pieces of cheese.

(d) What would be the weight of five pieces of Cheddar like this?

(e) What would be the weight of two pieces of Stilton like this?

(f) If the Stilton was cut into three equal pieces, how heavy would each piece be?

(g) If the Cheddar was cut into four equal pieces, how heavy would each piece be?

A4 Four of these calculations are wrong.
Find the wrong ones and do them correctly.

A $12.3 + 5.9$

```
   12.3
 +  5.9
 ------
   18.2
```

B 6.2×9

```
   6.2
 ×   9
 ------
 54.18
```

C $12.8 \div 8$

```
    1.1
 8)12.8
```

D 3.3×5

```
   3.3
 ×   5
 ------
  1.65
```

E $17 - 6.8$

```
  17.0
 - 6.8
 ------
  11.2
```

F $16.2 \div 3$

```
    5.4
 3)16.2
```

A5 Work these out.

(a) $2.3 + 14.9$ (b) $6.3 - 2.8$ (c) 5.6×3 (d) $7.5 \div 3$

(e) 4.3×7 (f) $32.6 + 19.2$ (g) $15.6 \div 6$ (h) 3.9×8

(i) 0.6×5 (j) 0.7×9 (k) $3.2 \div 8$ (l) $9.6 \div 4$

(m) $26 - 15.8$ (n) 2.4×7 (o) $19.8 \div 9$ (p) $42.5 \div 5$

A6 Write down two weights that have a total of 3.1 kg.

A7 Tim has five tins, each holding 1.5 litres of paint.
What is the total amount of paint?

A8 Mira wants to make eight curtains.
She needs 2.6 metres of material for each curtain.

How much material does she need altogether?

A9 A piece of wood 5.6 metres long is cut into four equal pieces.
How long is each piece?

A10 1.2 litres of orange juice is shared between six children.
How much juice do they each get?

A11 Three bags contain 28.5 kg of potatoes altogether.
The bags all weigh the same.

What is the weight of potatoes in one bag?

A12 Asad's truck can carry up to 200 kg.
He has seven boxes, each weighing 28.4 kg.

Can the truck carry all the boxes? Show your working.

A13 Here are two sets of cards.

Number cards

7.2   1.2   6   0.8   14.4   0.9

Operation cards

× 3   ÷ 6   + 1.5   ÷ 3   × 2   − 3.6

Calculations can be made from pairs of cards. For example.

0.8   × 2

gives a result of 1.6.

(a) Which number and operation cards make a calculation that gives 10.8?

(b) Find two cards that give

   (i) 1.2   (ii) 2.7   (iii) 2.3   (iv) 4.8

(c) Sort the cards into pairs that give 2.4 each time.

B Two decimal places

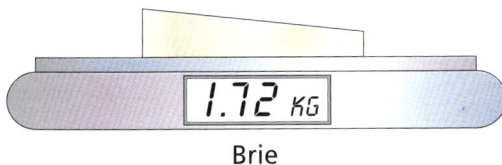

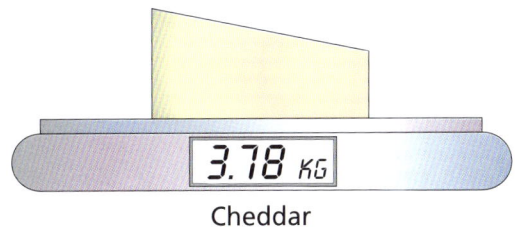

1.72 KG
Brie

3.78 KG
Cheddar

Do not use a calculator for this section.

B1 Work these out in your head.

   (a) 1.25 + 0.4   (b) 13.78 + 0.01   (c) 4.03 + 2   (d) 127.86 + 0.1
   (e) 1.53 + 0.47   (f) 2.59 + 0.01   (g) 14.95 − 1   (h) 2.65 − 0.1
   (i) 7.23 − 0.03   (j) 3.45 − 3.4   (k) 1 − 0.76   (l) 5.67 − 0.05

B2 Work out each missing number in your head.

   (a) 2.54 + ■ = 2.64   (b) 3.52 + ■ = 3.82   (c) ■ + 2.39 = 2.4
   (d) 16.82 − ■ = 11.82   (e) ■ − 0.01 = 18.91   (f) ■ − 0.1 = 7.35

B3 Two of these calculations are wrong.
Find the wrong ones and do them correctly.

   A   2.32 + 4.9   B   5.02 − 2.81   C   6.3 − 5.75   D   6.54 − 3.9

$$\begin{array}{r} 2.32 \\ +\ 4.9 \\ \hline 28.1 \end{array}$$
$$\begin{array}{r} 5.02 \\ -\ 2.81 \\ \hline 2.21 \end{array}$$
$$\begin{array}{r} 6.30 \\ -\ 5.75 \\ \hline 0.55 \end{array}$$
$$\begin{array}{r} 6.54 \\ -\ 3.9 \\ \hline 3.45 \end{array}$$

127

B4 Work these out.

(a) $6.24 + 3.89$ (b) $5.21 + 7.3$ (c) $823.65 + 45.7$ (d) $8.14 - 6.21$

(e) $131.27 - 12.8$ (f) $8.02 - 6.7$ (g) $5.6 - 1.23$ (h) $135.2 - 19.16$

B5 Copy and complete these calculations.

(a)
```
     .34
 + 16. 6
  22.10
```

(b)
```
    6.71
 -  0. 3
     .48
```

(c)
```
    5.0
 -  1. 1
     .41
```

(d)
```
    23.5
 -  1 .32
  106. 8
```

B6 Work these out.

(a) $6.32 + 5.1 + 2.9 + 14.82$ (b) $1.25 + 4.5 + 452.56 + 36.7$

B7 Work these out in your head.

(a) 0.01×5 (b) 2.01×3 (c) 0.04×6 (d) 0.13×4 (e) 0.08×7

B8 Work these out.

(a) 1.52×6 (b) 6.24×5 (c) 7.02×9 (d) 15.67×2 (e) 308.76×8

B9 Copy and complete these calculations.

(a)
```
   12. 6
 ×     4
  4 .44
```

(b)
```
    5. 6
 ×     3
  4 .1
```

(c)
```
     .5
 ×     9
  5. 4
```

(d)
```
    0. 2
 ×     8
 487.3
```

B10 Work these out.

(a) $2.68 \div 2$ (b) $14.52 \div 3$ (c) $23.64 \div 4$ (d) $1.89 \div 9$ (e) $50.54 \div 7$

B11 Here is how Jake worked out $1.3 \div 2$.
Explain why he wrote 1.3 as 1.30

```
   0.65
 2)1.30   ✓
```

B12 All of these calculations are wrong.
Do them correctly.

(a) $6.6 \div 4$ (b) $18.36 \div 9$ (c) 6.21×5 (d) $3.1 \div 5$

```
    1.62
 4)6.60
```

```
     2.4
 9)18.36
```

```
    6.21
 ×     5
  30.105
```

```
     6.2
 5)3.10
```

B13 Work these out.

(a) $5.3 \div 2$ (b) $25.06 \div 7$ (c) $14.7 \div 6$ (d) $6.1 \div 2$ (e) $23.1 \div 5$

B14 The table shows the lengths and widths of some kayaks.

	Length	Width
Corsica	3.04 m	0.62 m
Dancer Pro	3.50 m	0.61 m
Pirouette	3.02 m	0.58 m
Fly	2.69 m	0.61 m

(a) What is the total length of a Dancer Pro and a Fly?

(b) How much wider is a Dancer Pro than a Pirouette?

(c) How much space is needed to lay 5 Corsicas end to end?

(d) How much space is needed to lay 4 Pirouettes side by side?

Here are two sets of cards.

Number cards

| 18.8 | 2.4 | 6 |
| 23.2 | 5.44 | 2 |

Operation cards

| × 3 | ÷ 5 | ÷ 4 |
| + 3.6 | ÷ 8 | − 1.2 |

B15 (a) Which two cards make a calculation that gives 1.5?

(b) Find two cards that make

(i) 0.8 (ii) 0.75 (iii) 5.8 (iv) 16.32 (v) 0.48

(c) Which pair of cards gives the highest possible result?

(d) Which pair of cards gives the lowest possible result?

*****B16** Three cards can be arranged to make a chain that gives 4.6.

Final result
4.6

(a) Arrange these four cards to make a chain with a final result of

(i) 0.64 (ii) 0.7 (iii) 0.88

(b) (i) What is the largest possible final result with these four cards?

(ii) What is the smallest possible result?

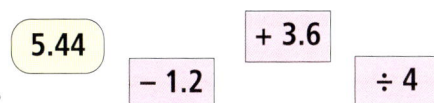

C Multiplying and dividing by 10, 100, 1000, …

When you multiply by 10, every digit moves **one place to the left**.

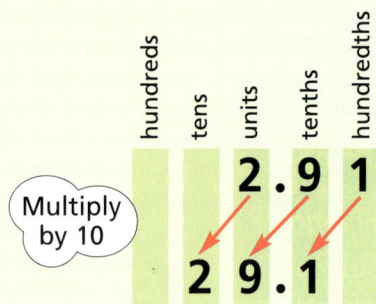

When you divide by 100, every digit moves **two places to the right**.

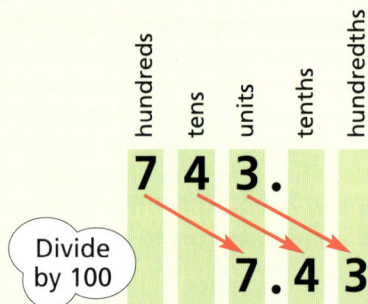

So 743 ÷ 100 = 7.43

Do not use a calculator for this section.

C1 Work these out.

(a) 47.1×10
(b) $47.1 \div 100$
(c) 3.83×100
(d) 1000×4.92

(e) $26.8 \div 10$
(f) $157 \div 1000$
(g) 0.01×1000
(h) $7.4 \div 100$

(i) 0.71×100
(j) $9 \div 10$
(k) 0.3×100
(l) $0.12 \div 10$

C2 Find the missing number in each of these calculations.

(a) $3.43 \times \blacksquare = 343$
(b) $\blacksquare \div 10 = 4.5$
(c) $\blacksquare \times 1000 = 2100$

(d) $56 \div \blacksquare = 0.56$
(e) $\blacksquare \times 10 = 15.4$
(f) $\blacksquare \div 100 = 0.12$

(g) $1.5 \times \blacksquare = 1500$
(h) $0.35 \div \blacksquare = 0.035$
(i) $\blacksquare \div 1000 = 0.0008$

C3 Copy and complete these chains.

(a) 3.2 → $\times 100$ → ☐ → $\div 10$ → ☐ → $\div 100$ → ☐

(b) 0.6 → $\times 1000$ → ☐ → $\div 100$ → ☐ → $\div 100$ → ☐

(c) 56 → $\div 1000$ → ☐ → $\div 10$ → ☐ → $\times 100$ → ☐

(d) ☐ → $\times 100$ → 423 → $\div 100$ → ☐ → $\div 100$ → ☐

(e) ☐ → $\div 100$ → ☐ → $\times 10$ → 3.09 → $\div 1000$ → ☐

130

D Metric units

Animal	Weight in g	Weight in kg	Length in mm	Length in cm	Length in m
Blue whale		130 000		3350	
Mandrill	45 000		950		
Tiger		300			2.8
Guinea pig	900		260		
Pygmy shrew		0.0015		3.6	
House mouse	12				0.064

D1

A	B	C	D
4.2 × 100	4.2 × 1000	4.2 ÷ 1000	4.2 ÷ 100

(a) Choose the correct calculation to change 4.2 kg to grams.

(b) Choose the correct calculation to change 4.2 cm to metres

D2 Change these weights to grams.

    (a) 1.234 kg   (b) 2.45 kg   (c) 1.5 kg   (d) 0.8 kg   (e) 0.06 kg

D3 Change these lengths to kilometres.

    (a) 23 900 m   (b) 124 800 m   (c) 560 m   (d) 9200 m   (e) 90 m

D4 Change these lengths to centimetres.

    (a) 78 mm   (b) 0.78 m   (c) 2 mm   (d) 45.1 m   (e) 0.098 m

D5 Change these lengths to metres.

    (a) 60 cm   (b) 2.35 km   (c) 4900 mm   (d) 0.09 km   (e) 5670 cm

D6 Put these weights in order, smallest first.

    300 g, 0.5 kg, 0.07 kg, 67 g, 892 g, 1.04 kg, 0.985 kg

Volumes of liquids are measured in **litres** or **millilitres**   1 litre = 1000 millilitres

D7 Change these volumes to millilitres.

    (a) 6 litres   (b) 3.612 litres (c) 15.2 litres (d) 8.07 litres (e) 0.02 litres

D8 Change these volumes to litres.

    (a) 4765 ml   (b) 6700 ml   (c) 900 ml   (d) 42 ml   (e) 7 ml

D9 1.5 litres of juice is shared equally between six people.
How many millilitres of juice does each person get?

D10 A shop sells Cheddar in 75 gram portions.
What is the weight of 100 portions in kilograms?

D11 A 7.8 metre ribbon is cut into four equal pieces.
How long is each piece in centimetres?

D12 Sue has a bottle that holds 0.2 litres of medicine.
She takes 5 ml of this medicine every day.

How long will her medicine last?

D13 A poplar tree grows 3 mm taller every day.
At this rate how long would it take to grow 7.5 metres?

E Buying food

Use a calculator for these questions.

E1 (a) Explain how you know without doing any calculation
that 2.3 kg of olives costs more than £13.00.

(b) Calculate the cost of 2.3 kg of olives.

E2 (a) Explain how you know without doing any calculation
that 0.8 kg of pepperoni costs less than £14.05.

(b) What is the cost of 0.8 kg of pepperoni?

E3 To the nearest penny, calculate the cost of

(a) 2.6 kg of pepperoni   (b) 1.6 kg of cheddar   (c) 0.3 kg of capers

(d) 1.2 kg of ham   (e) 0.4 kg of ham   (f) 1.5 kg of pepperoni

(g) 2.51 kg of capers   (h) 0.8 kg of cheddar   (i) 1.38 kg of ham

(j) 0.81 kg of salami   (k) 1.13 kg of olives   (l) 0.53 kg of pepperoni

F Unit cost

2kg
£3.70

1.5kg
£1.80

2.4kg
£3.76

How much does 1 kg cost?

Use a calculator for these questions.

F1 For each bag, calculate the cost of 1 kg.

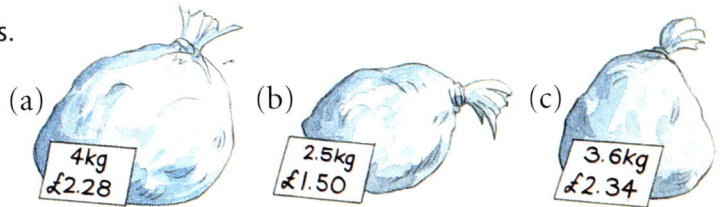

(a) 4kg £2.28

(b) 2.5kg £1.50

(c) 3.6kg £2.34

F2 2.5 kg of grapes cost £5.75. Calculate the cost of 1 kg of grapes.

F3 Calculate the unit cost for each of these, to the nearest penny.
Write the answer as '… per litre' or '… per kg', etc.

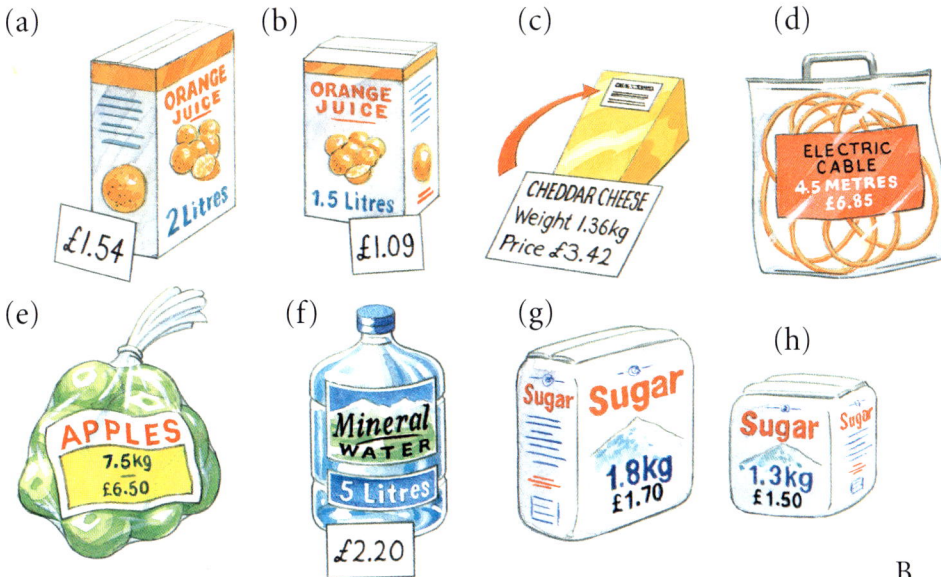

(a) ORANGE JUICE 2 Litres £1.54

(b) ORANGE JUICE 1.5 Litres £1.09

(c) CHEDDAR CHEESE Weight 1.36kg Price £3.42

(d) ELECTRIC CABLE 4.5 METRES £6.85

(e) APPLES 7.5kg £6.50

(f) Mineral WATER 5 Litres £2.20

(g) Sugar 1.8kg £1.70

(h) Sugar 1.3kg £1.50

F4 A shop sells two different sizes of rose food.
Pack A – a 1.2 kilogram box for £2.00
Pack B – a 3 kilogram box for £3.99
(a) In which pack is rose food the best value?
(b) How did you decide?

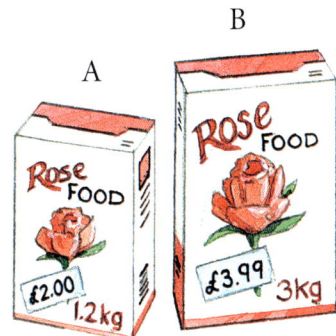

A

Rose FOOD £2.00 1.2 kg

B

Rose FOOD £3.99 3kg

133

F5 Which pack in each pair gives you more for your money?
Explain why in each case.

(a)

(b)

(c)

(d)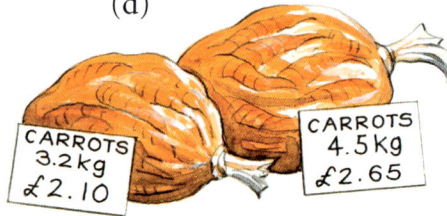

(e)

(f)

G Mixed questions

G1 Creme eggs are sold
in packs of four.

(a) How much would three packets of creme eggs cost?

(b) Jodie buys one packet of creme eggs and pays with a £5 note.
What is her change?

(c) What is the cost of one egg, correct to the nearest penny?

G2 Cable costs £1.15 per metre. Calculate the cost of 4.8 metres.

G3 Saul bought 2.4 kg of parsnips. He paid £2.52.
Calculate the cost of 1 kg of parsnips.

G4 2.6 metres of cloth costs £6.37. Calculate the cost of 1 metre.

G5 Paraffin costs £1.09 per litre. Calculate the cost of 3.4 litres.

G6 June bought some material. It cost £2.65 per metre.
She bought 3.2 metres. How much did she pay?

G7 (a) What is the cost of two Family packs of biscuits?

(b) What is the cost of a Standard pack and a Large pack?

(c) Work out to the nearest penny the cost of a biscuit in each of these.

(i) a Standard pack   (ii) a Large pack   (iii) a Family pack

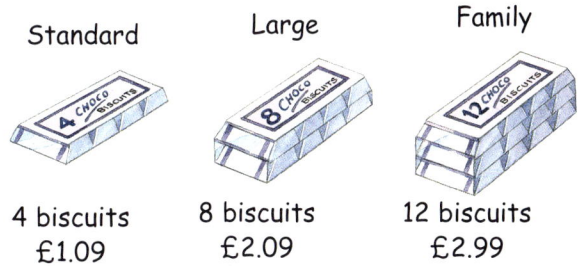

Standard   Large   Family

4 biscuits   8 biscuits   12 biscuits
£1.09   £2.09   £2.99

G8 (a) Work out the cost per litre for each can of paint.

(b) Which can is the best buy?

(c) How much would two 2.5 litre cans cost?

(d) How much do you save by buying a 5 litre can instead of two 2.5 litre cans?

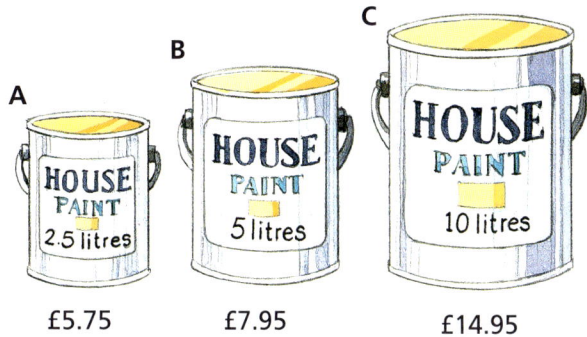

A   B   C

HOUSE PAINT 2.5 litres   HOUSE PAINT 5 litres   HOUSE PAINT 10 litres

£5.75   £7.95   £14.95

(e) How much do you save by buying a 10 litre can instead of two 5 litre cans?

What progress have you made?

Statement

I can calculate with decimals without using a calculator.

Evidence

1 Work these out.

(a) $3.6 + 2.5$ (b) $8 - 2.3$ (c) 2.4×100

(d) $231 \div 100$ (e) 0.5×9 (f) 3.6×5

(g) $12.4 - 6.8$ (h) $5.6 \div 8$ (i) $1.8 \div 4$

2 Work these out.

(a) $25.6 + 9.91$ (b) $16.7 - 5.93$

(c) 3.56×2 (d) 12.65×8

(e) $16.24 \div 4$ (f) $34.7 \div 5$

3 (a) Convert 560 grams to kilograms.

(b) Convert 3.4 m to centimetres.

I can use a calculator to calculate with decimals.

4 Bananas cost £0.97 per kg. Calculate the cost of 2.4 kg correct to the nearest penny.

5 A piece of cheese weighing 3.8 kg costs £8.17. Calculate the cost per kg.

135

⑲ Three dimensions

This work will help you
- ◆ describe, make and draw 3-D objects
- ◆ draw nets and find the surface areas of 3-D objects

A Describing three-dimensional objects

For pupils working in pairs

Each person in the pair has some multilink cubes.

Sit back to back. No looking round!
One of you make an object with the cubes.
Then describe it to your partner.
The partner has to make it from the description.

When the partner has finished, compare your objects.

B Drawing three-dimensional objects

B1 This object is made with four cubes.   Draw it on triangular dotty paper.

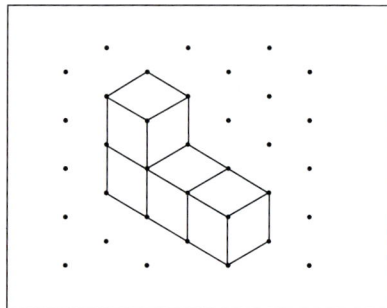

B2 (a) Copy and complete these letters so they are all one cube thick.

(b) Draw a letter F the same way.

(c) Choose a letter of your own to draw the same way.

(d) How many cubes are used for each letter?

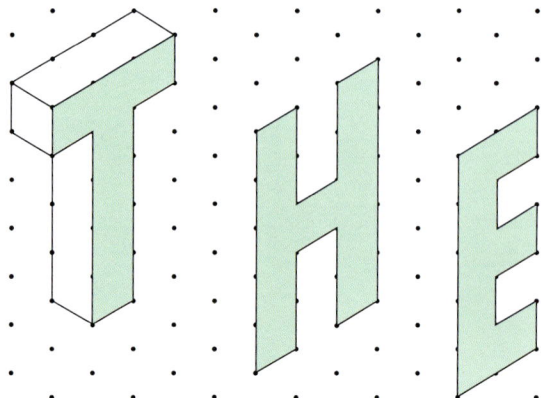

B3 The shape in question B1 was made with four cubes.

What other shapes can be made from four cubes?
Try to make them all and draw them on dotty paper.

B4 Draw these shapes on triangular dotty paper.

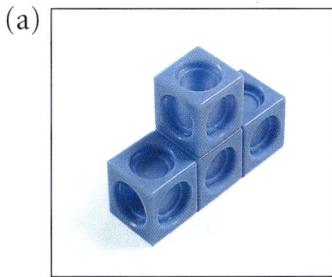

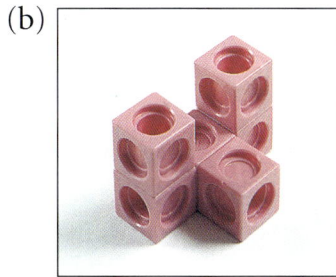

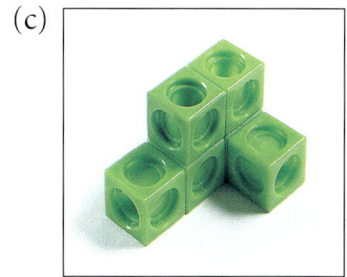

(a)

(b)

(c)

C Views

Three people are looking at a shape.

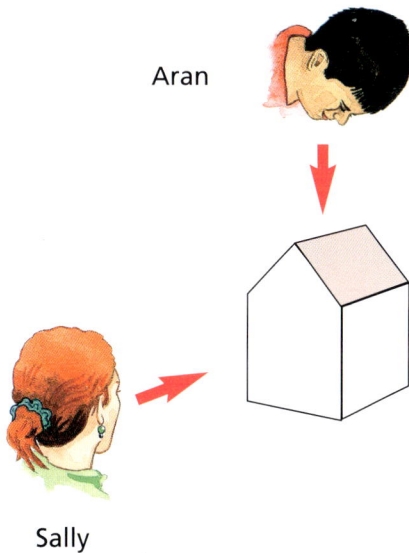

Aran

Sally

Keith

Sally sees this.
It is a **front view**.

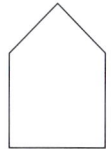

Keith sees this.
It is a **side view**.

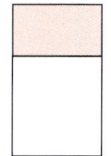

Aran sees this.
It is a **top view**
or **plan view**.

C1 This shape is made with five cubes.
This is the front view of the shape.

(a) Draw the top view.
(b) Draw the side view.

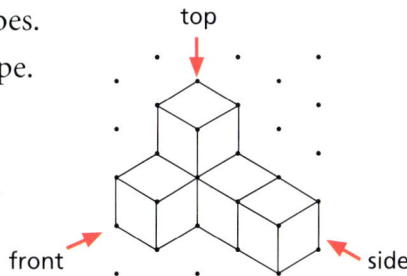

top

front

side

C2 Draw a front, side and top view of each of these shapes.
Make the shape out of multilink first, if it helps.
Label the views clearly.

(a)
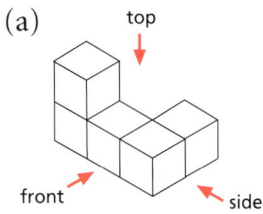

(b)
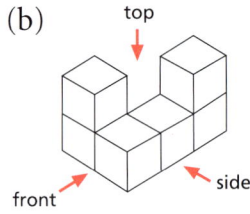

(c)
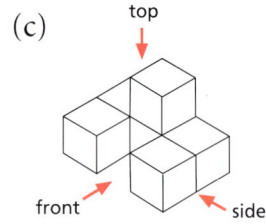

C3 Four views of a model building are drawn below.

(a) Match each view to one of
the directions shown by arrows.

(b) The view from one direction is missing.
Draw this view.

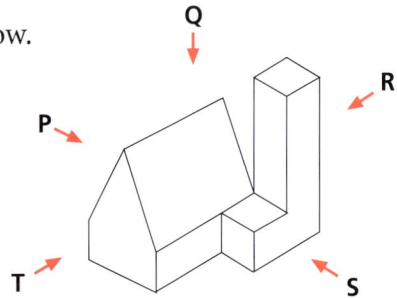

A
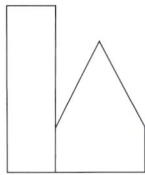

B
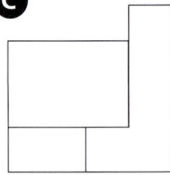

C
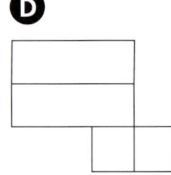

D

C4 These are views of some everyday objects.
For each object there are two views, which may be front, side or top.
Identify the objects and sketch the missing view of each one.

A
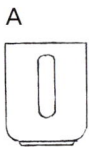

B

C
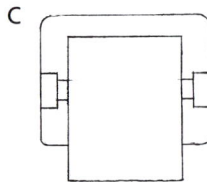

D

E
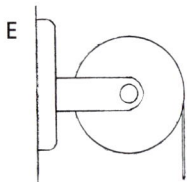

F

G
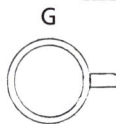

H
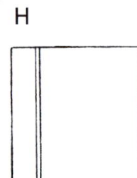

D Nets

A flat shape that can be folded up to make a three-dimensional shape is called a **net** of the three-dimensional shape.

Here are three nets, P, Q and R.

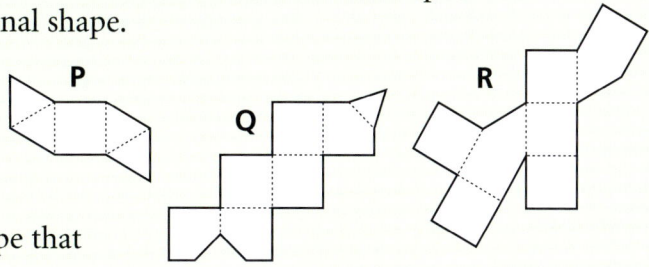

Sketch the three-dimensional shape that you would make with each net.

D1 A cuboid is a shape that has rectangles for all its faces.
Write whether each shape below could be a net of this cuboid.

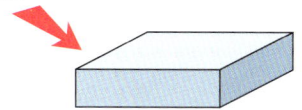

(a)

(b)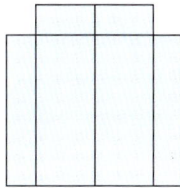

(c)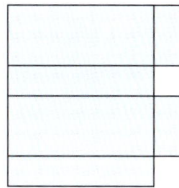

(d)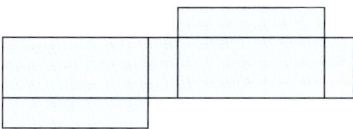

(e)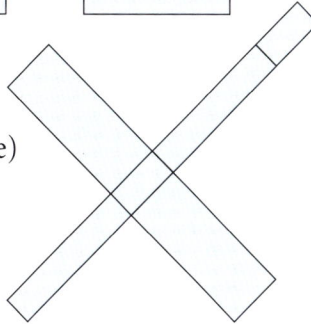

D2 (a) The shaded shape is an incomplete net of a cuboid.
The dotted line shows one possible position for the missing face.
Copy the diagram and show all the other possible positions for the missing face.

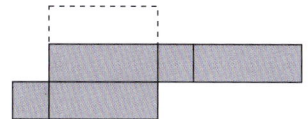

(b) Copy this incomplete net of a cuboid and show all the possible positions for the missing face.

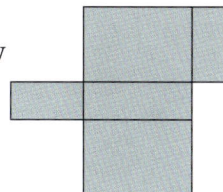

D3 (a) Is each of these a net of a cube?

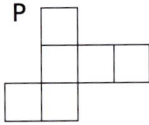

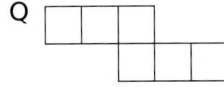

P

Q

R

(b) How many different nets of a cube can you find?

D4 This cube has a cross on the bottom and an arrow
on each of the four vertical faces.
All the arrows point to the left.
Copy and complete these two nets of the cube showing
the cross, and all the arrows pointing the correct way.

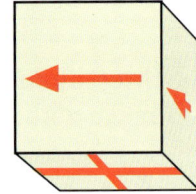

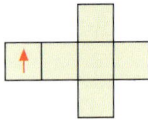

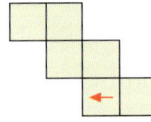

D5 Here are the nets of some three-dimensional shapes.
Sketch each shape and write its name if you know it.

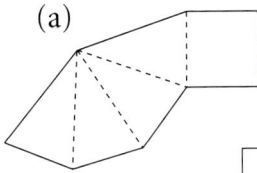

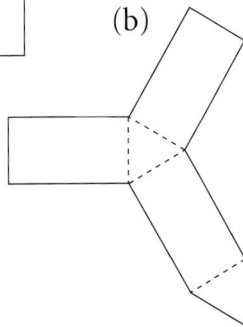

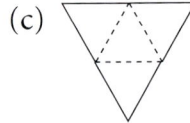

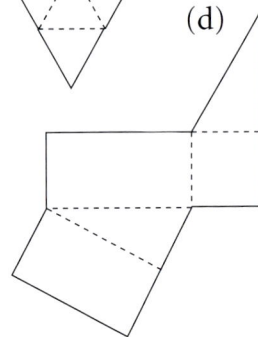

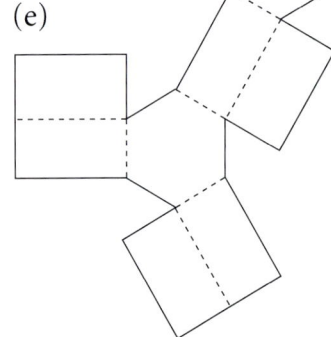

(a)

(b)

(c)

(d)

(e)

D6 The top and bottom of a box are identical quarter-circles.

(a) Copy and complete this sketch of a net that
could be folded up to make the box.

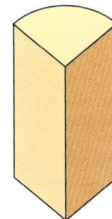

(b) Sketch a different net that could be folded up to make the box.

D7 The ends of this box are right-angled triangles.
Sketch a net of the box.

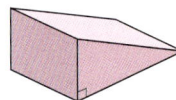

E Surface area

The **surface area** of a solid is the total area of all its surfaces …

… which is the same as the area of its net.

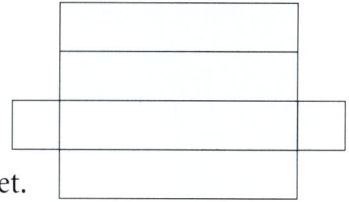

E1 Here is the net of a cuboid.
What is the surface area of the cuboid?

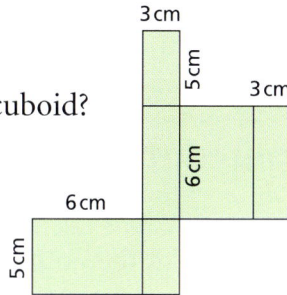

3 cm
5 cm
3 cm
6 cm
6 cm
5 cm

E2 What is the surface area of this cuboid?

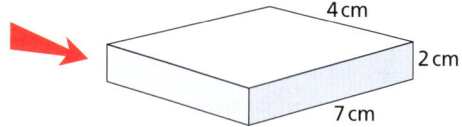

4 cm
2 cm
7 cm

E3 What is the surface area of each of these cuboids?

(a) 2 cm by 3 cm by 4 cm   (b) 4 cm by 3 cm by 7 cm

(b) 9 cm by 4 cm by 5 cm   (d) 3 cm by 5 cm by 8 cm

*E4 The surface area of this cuboid is 332 cm².
What is its height?

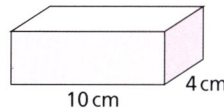

10 cm
4 cm

What progress have you made?

Statement	Evidence
I can draw three-dimensional objects.	1 Make an object with five cubes. (a) Draw it on triangular dotty paper. (b) Draw top, front and side views of it.
I can work with nets of solids.	2 Sketch a net of this shape.
I can find the surface area of a cuboid.	3 Find the surface area of a cuboid 5 cm by 4 cm by 2 cm.

⓴ Percentage

This work will help you

◆ change a percentage to a decimal

◆ calculate a percentage of a quantity

◆ calculate one quantity as a percentage of another

◆ construct pie charts from percentages

A Understanding percentages

Most cheeses contain fat.
Some contain a greater proportion of fat than others.

Danish Blue is 28% fat.

50 g of Blue Stilton contains 18 g of fat.

A 20 g piece of Edam has 5 g of fat in it.

21% of Camembert is fat.

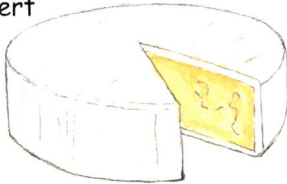

There is 18 g of fat in 40 g of Mascarpone.

Red Leicester is one third fat.

2% of Cottage Cheese is fat.

Cheddar cheese is about 30% (30 per cent) fat.

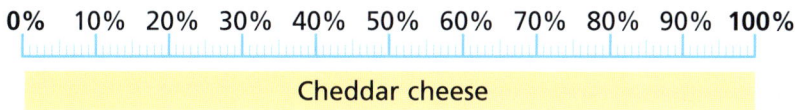

This bar represents a piece of cheese, divided into 100 equal parts. Each part is 1% of the cheese.

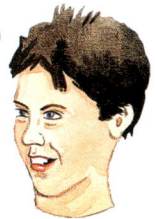

So 1% is the same as $\frac{1}{100}$ ...

0%   10%   20%   30%   40%   50%   60%   70%   80%   90%   **100%**

Cheddar cheese

.... and 30% is the same as $\frac{30}{100}$.

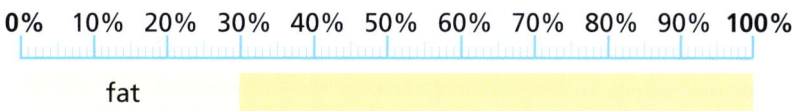

0%   10%   20%   30%   40%   50%   60%   70%   80%   90%   **100%**

fat

A1 This bar shows the nutritional content of processed cheese.

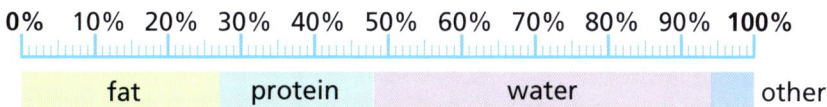

0%   10%   20%   30%   40%   50%   60%   70%   80%   90%   **100%**

fat   protein   water   other

(a) What percentage of processed cheese is fat?

(b) What makes up the greatest part of processed cheese?

(c) What percentage of processed cheese is protein?

A2 (a) Which of these bars are 20% coloured? (There may be more than one.)

(b) Which bars are 40% coloured?

(c) Which bars are 60% coloured?

(d) Which bars are 80% coloured?

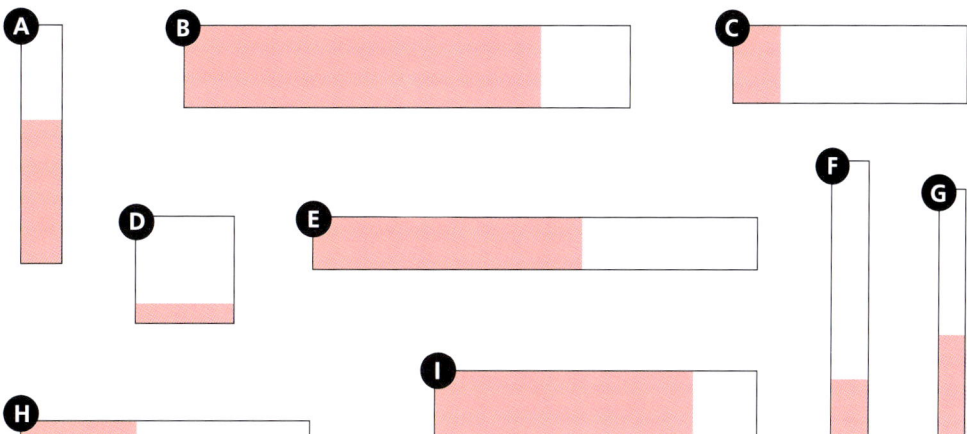

A3 Estimate what percentage each of these bars is coloured.

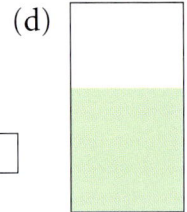

(a)

(b)

(c)   (d)

(e)

(f)

B Percentages in your head

B1 50% of something is the same as $\frac{1}{2}$ of it.

What fraction is the same as

(a) 25%　　　(b) 75%　　　(c) 10%　　　(d) 90%　　　(e) 20%

B2 Write the proportions in these statements as percentages.
(Some of them may have to be approximations.)

(a) About half of cream cheese is fat.

(b) About $\frac{1}{10}$ of a slice of granary bread is protein.

(c) 1 part in 4 of brown toast is water.

(d) Three quarters of custard is water.

(e) Although about one third of Double Gloucester cheese is fat,
a quarter is protein.

B3 63% of pupils in a school have school dinners.
What percentage do not?

B4 28% of the members of a choir are male.
What percentage are female?

B5 Work these out in your head.

(a) 50% of £30　　　　　(b) 50% of £84　　　　　(c) 50% of £35

B6 Work these out in your head.

(a) 25% of £40   (b) 25% of £84   (c) 25% of £70

B7 (a) Explain how you work out 10% of a number in your head.
Use 10% of 60 and 10% of 65 as examples.

(b) How do you work out 5% of a number in your head?
Find out from some other people how they do it.

B8 (a) What is 1% of £1?

(b) So what is 3% of £1?

(c) What is 37% of £1?

B9 (a) What is 7% of £1?

(b) So what is 7% of £3?

C Percentages and decimals

This diagram shows a bar representing 1 unit.
It is divided up to show fractions, decimals and percentages.

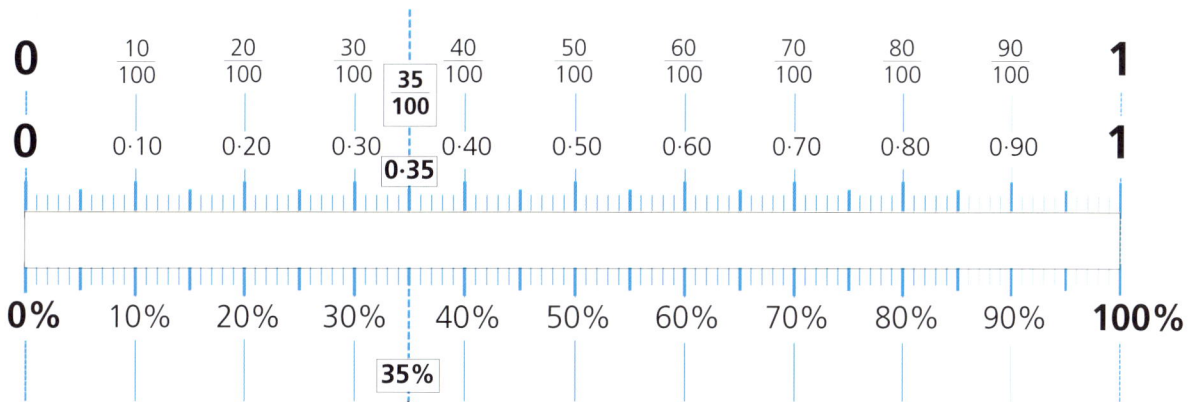

35% of something means the same as $\frac{35}{100}$ of it.
But $\frac{35}{100}$ as a decimal is 0.35, so **35% is equal to 0.35**.

C1 What decimal is equal to

(a) 50%   (b) 25%   (c) 65%   (d) 78%

(e) 10%   (f) 1%   (g) 4%   (h) 40%

C2 What percentage is equal to

(a) 0.3   (b) 0.8   (c) 0.83   (d) 0.03

Do the following questions without looking at
the diagram on the previous page.

C3 Copy and complete this table.

Fraction		Decimal		Percentage
$\frac{70}{100}$	=		=	
$\frac{45}{100}$	=		=	
	=	0.57	=	
	=	0.85	=	
$\frac{5}{100}$	=		=	
	=		=	63%
	=	0.07	=	

C4 Write each of these percentages as a decimal.

(a) 44%   (b) 26%   (c) 90%   (d) 84%

(e) 55%   (f) 5%   (g) 11%   (h) 1%

(i) 73%   (j) 20%   (k) 6%   (l) 19%

C5 Write these decimals as percentages.

(a) 0.72   (b) 0.31   (c) 0.5   (d) 0.01

(e) 0.13   (f) 0.4   (g) 0.02   (h) 0.92

(i) 0.04   (j) 0.85   (k) 0.14   (l) 0.56

C6 Put these in order, starting with the smallest.

0.1   15%   0.25 $\frac{12}{100}$ 1% $\frac{45}{100}$ 0.3

C7 Put these in order, starting with the **largest**.

0.51   65%   0.4 $\frac{78}{100}$ 5%   0.75   0.08

C8 Change each of these fractions (i) to hundredths and (ii) to a percentage.

(a) $\frac{3}{10}$ (b) $\frac{2}{5}$ (c) $\frac{7}{10}$ (d) $\frac{1}{5}$

(e) $\frac{3}{5}$ (f) $\frac{3}{20}$ (g) $\frac{13}{20}$ (h) $\frac{7}{20}$

C9 Put these in order, starting with the smallest.

$\frac{3}{4}$ $\frac{1}{10}$ 0.08   74%   0.2   0.56   15%

D Calculating a percentage of a quantity

There are different types of fat, but for a balanced diet it helps to know how much fat we are eating.

This Stilton cheese is 35% fat.
I wonder how much fat there is in a 40 g piece?

Joe works out 35% of 40 g like this:

35% of 40 g

$= \frac{35}{100} \times 40\,g$ ← You can leave out this step.

$= 0.35 \times 40\,g$

$= 14\,g$ ← Use a calculator for this step.

D1 Calculate these.

(a) 45% of 360 g   (b) 61% of 420 g   (c) 29% of 230 g   (d) 70% of 134 g

(e) 14% of 190 g   (f) 22% of 160 g   (g) 96% of 210 g   (h) 11% of 480 g

D2 Calculate these.

(a) 3% of 75 g   (b) 7% of 96 g   (c) 8% of 45 g   (d) 6% of 28 g

D3 Butter is 82% fat. How much fat is there in a 500 g tub?

D4 White bread is 2% fat. How much fat is there in a 30 g slice?

D5 Fred said: 'Percentages? Easy! To find 10%, just divide by 10. For 5%, just divide by 5, and so on.'

Quickly convince Fred that he is wrong.

D6 This **pie chart** shows the nutritional content of milk chocolate.

Calculate the amounts of sugar, fat and protein in

(a) a 35 g bar

(b) a 150 g bar

(c) a 500 g bar

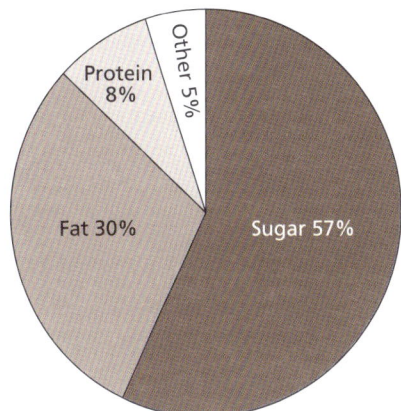

E Changing fractions to decimals

The fraction $\frac{1}{5}$ means 1 unit divided by 5.

Doing $1 \div 5$ on a calculator gives 0.2, which is the **decimal equivalent** of $\frac{1}{5}$.

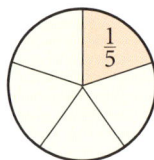

The fraction $\frac{2}{5}$ can be thought of as 2 times $\frac{1}{5}$.

It can also be thought of as **2 units divided by 5**. You can look at it this way.

2 pizzas are to be shared equally between 5 people. Each pizza is cut into fifths.

Each person gets $\frac{1}{5}$ of the first pizza and $\frac{1}{5}$ of the second.

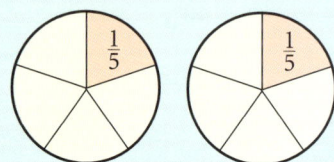

That's $\frac{2}{5}$ altogether for each person.

So $2 \div 5 = \frac{2}{5}$

So to change $\frac{2}{5}$ to a decimal, **divide 2 by 5**: $\frac{2}{5} = 2 \div 5 = \mathbf{0.4}$

E1 Change each of these fractions to decimals.

(a) $\frac{1}{4}$ (b) $\frac{1}{8}$ (c) $\frac{1}{20}$ (d) $\frac{4}{5}$ (e) $\frac{3}{8}$

(f) $\frac{7}{8}$ (g) $\frac{7}{25}$ (h) $\frac{3}{20}$ (i) $\frac{11}{50}$ (j) $\frac{15}{16}$

E2 Put these fractions in order of size, smallest first.

$\frac{5}{8}$ $\frac{3}{5}$ $\frac{13}{20}$ $\frac{29}{50}$

E3 Put these in order of size, largest first.

$\frac{17}{20}$ $\frac{3}{4}$ $\frac{19}{25}$ $\frac{39}{50}$

E4 Change each of these fractions to a decimal.
Round them to two decimal places.

(a) $\frac{1}{7}$ (b) $\frac{4}{7}$ (c) $\frac{1}{9}$ (d) $\frac{5}{9}$ (e) $\frac{7}{11}$

(f) $\frac{4}{15}$ (g) $\frac{1}{13}$ (h) $\frac{5}{13}$ (i) $\frac{7}{17}$ (j) $\frac{20}{23}$

F One number as a percentage of another

.**Problem**   3 out of 7 jelly babies are red.
           What percentage of the jelly babies are red?

Solution $\frac{3}{7}$ of the jelly babies are red.

(Change the fraction to a decimal ...)   (...and the decimal to a percentage.)

$\frac{3}{7} = 3 \div 7 \;=\;$ | 0.4285714 | $= 42.85714...\% = \mathbf{43\%}$

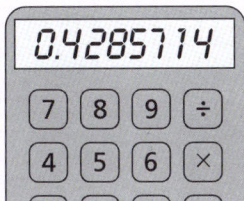

                                        to the nearest 1%

This diagram shows that the answer is right.

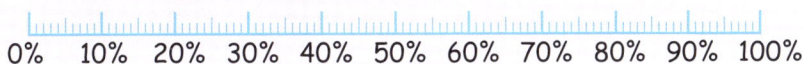

0%   10%   20%   30%   40%   50%   60%   70%   80%   90%   100%

F1   Five out of seven jelly babies are red.

    (a)   What fraction of the jelly babies are red?

    (b)   What percentage of the jelly babies are red?
        Check your answer using the diagram above.

F2   Match these fractions and percentages. Some percentages will be left over!

    (a) $\frac{3}{5}$ (b) $\frac{7}{20}$ (c) $\frac{7}{8}$ (d) $\frac{1}{3}$ (e) $\frac{2}{3}$

         3%   3.5%   6%   35%

      about 33%   about 67%   87.5%   60%

F3   Change these fractions into percentages, to the nearest 1%.

    (a) $\frac{2}{7}$ (b) $\frac{7}{9}$ (c) $\frac{3}{13}$ (d) $\frac{7}{17}$ (e) $\frac{1}{19}$

In questions F4 to F10, round percentages to the nearest 1%.

F4 In a survey, Kim asked her friends what their favourite vegetable was.
She asked a total of 32 people.
8 said potatoes and 6 said carrots.

(a) What fraction of Kim's friends said potatoes?

(b) What percentage said potatoes?

(c) What percentage said carrots?

F5 Frank bought 23 tomatoes, of which 7 were bad.

(a) What percentage of his tomatoes were bad?

(b) What percentage were edible?

F6 In a class of 29 pupils, 25 can swim.

(a) What percentage of the class can swim?

(b) What percentage cannot swim?

F7 Dina has done 8 miles out of a 27-mile sponsored walk.
What percentage of the walk has she done?

F8 This season, Peter attended 19 out of 23 practice sessions
for the school football team.
Carol attended 21 out of 27 practice sessions for the netball team.

Use percentages to show who has the better attendance record.

F9 This information about washing machines was
recorded by an electrical dealer.

	Model A	Model B	Model C	Model D
Number of machines sold	78	230	85	42
Number reported faulty within one year	2	9	7	6

Use percentages to show

(a) which model of washing machine seems most reliable

(b) which model seems least reliable

*F10 The world's population is about 6000 million.
It is reckoned that 950 million people are hungry all the time.

(a) What percentage of the world are hungry all the time?

(b) Imagine that the people in your class represent all the people in the world.
How many of them would be hungry all the time?

G Drawing pie charts

You need a pie chart scale.

Pie charts are often a good way of displaying percentage information.
They are very useful when making comparisons.
For example, these pie charts show the nutritional content of cheese slices
and cheese spread.

**Nutritional content
of cheese slices**

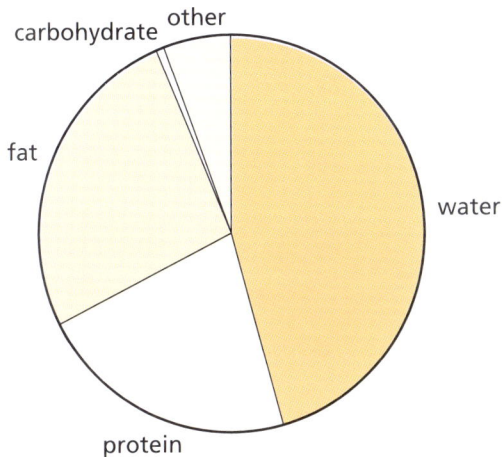

**Nutritional content
of cheese spread**

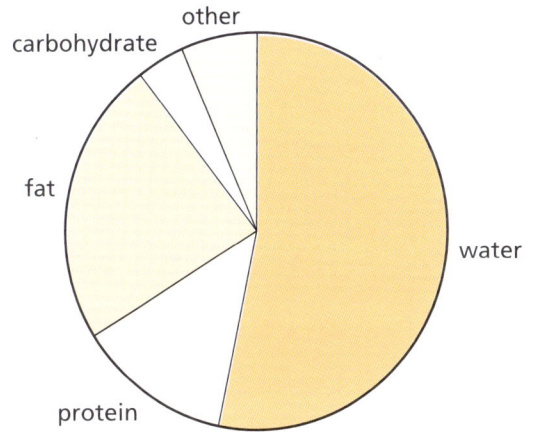

G1 Write in a couple of sentences what you can see from the pie charts.

G2 The actual percentages may be read off
from a pie chart using a pie chart scale.

Use a pie chart scale to find
these percentages from the
two pie charts above.

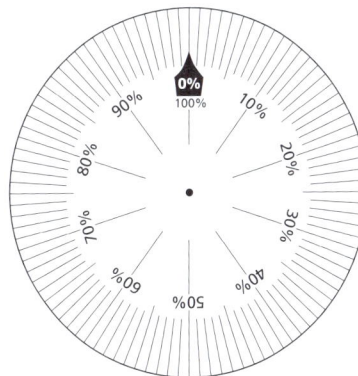

(a) Fat in cheese slices

(b) Fat in cheese spread

(c) Water in cheese slices

(d) Water in cheese spread

G3 Use a pie chart scale to draw a pie chart to illustrate this data.

Nutritional content of cheese and tomato pizza				
Water	Protein	Fat	Carbohydrate	Other
52%	9%	12%	25%	2%

G4 This pie chart shows how the average household in England in 1995 spent money on types of food.

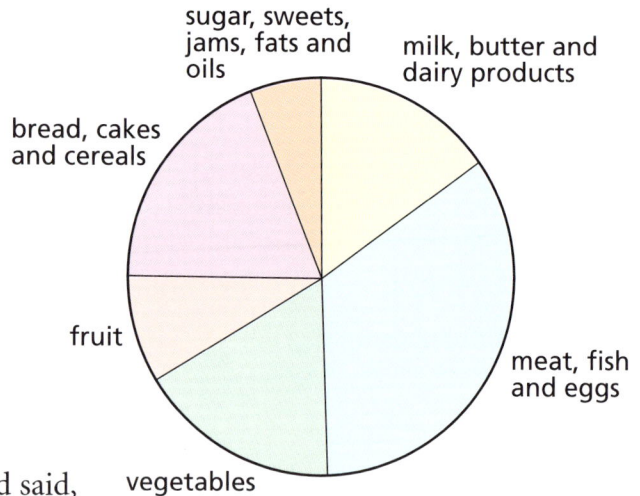

(a) Which type of food was most money spent on?

(b) What percentage was spent on fruit?

(c) Clio looked at the pie chart and said, 'People ate about twice as much meat, fish and eggs as they did vegetables.' Is this a reasonable conclusion?

G5 Here is how the Siddiqi family spent money on food in one week.

Calculate the percentage of the total food bill that is spent on each type of food.

Draw a pie chart to illustrate the data.

Milk, butter, dairy products	£ 8
Meat, fish, eggs	£28
Vegetables	£12
Fruit	£ 8
Bread, cakes, cereals	£20
Sugar, sweets, jams, fats, oils	£ 4
Total	**£80**

G6 This table shows how the pages of a newspaper were allocated.

	Home news	Foreign news	Sport	Entertainment	Finance
Number of pages	11	7	5	3	6

(a) What was the total number of pages?

(b) What percentage of the total number of pages were devoted to home news? Give your answer to the nearest 1%.

(c) Calculate the percentage for each of the other headings and draw a pie chart.

G7 This table gives information about Parinda's CD collection.

	Pop	Hard rock	Jazz	Easy listening	Classical
Number of CDs	13	4	8	3	9

Draw a pie chart to show this information.
Label each slice with its percentage.

What progress have you made?

I understand what percentage means.

1 Which of these bars is

    (a) about 40% green

    (b) about 20% green

    (c) about 60% green

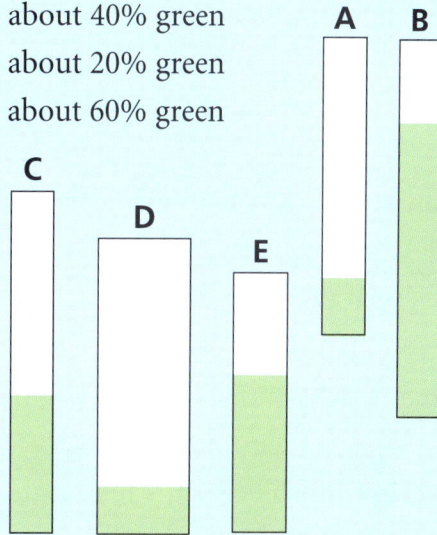

I can change percentages into decimals.

2 Change these percentages into decimals.

    (a) 50%   (b) 45%   (c) 4%   (d) 7%

I can calculate percentages of quantities, both in my head and using a calculator.

3 Calculate these in your head.

    (a) 50% of £10   (b) 25% of 8 kg

    (c) 75% of 12 kg   (d) 10% of £20

4 Use a calculator to find these.

    (a) 38% of 180 g   (b) 4% of 325 g

I can calculate one quantity as a percentage of another.

5 Ann has 44 apple trees.
32 of them are affected by a disease.
What percentage of the trees are affected, to the nearest 1%?

6 Which is the better record,
21 successes out of 25 tries, or 30 out of 37?
Explain why.

I can draw a pie chart.

7 Draw a percentage pie chart to show this information about a football team.

    Wins: 24   Losses: 6   Draws: 10

Review 3

Do not use a calculator for questions 1 to 20.

1 This object is made with five cubes.
Draw it on triangular dotty paper.

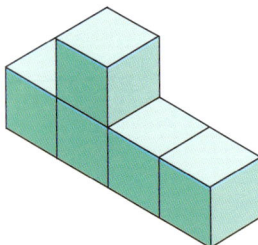

2 Melvyn ate $\frac{3}{4}$ of a bar of chocolate.

   (a) What percentage of the chocolate bar did he eat?

   (b) What percentage is left?

3 Ruthie gives birth to twins.
James weighs 2.8 kg and Julie weighs 3.25 kg.

   (a) What is their total birthweight?

   (b) How much heavier is Julie than James?

4 A hamburger weighing 2500 kg was made in the USA in 1989.

   (a) How heavy was the hamburger in grams?

   (b) Joe makes jumbo sized hamburgers that weigh 250 grams each.
       How many of Joe's hamburgers would weigh the same as the giant one?

5 A piece of cheese that weighs 2.4 kg is cut into eight equal pieces.
How heavy is each piece in kilograms?

6 The smallest recorded marine fish is the dwarf goby at 8.6 mm long.

   How long would be a line of a hundred dwarf goby fish, placed end to end?
   Give your answer in centimetres.

7 (a) Sue sends 42 Christmas cards altogether.
       She puts a 27p stamp on each one.

       How much does she spend on stamps altogether?

   (b) Liam buys a pack of six cards for £2.52.
       How much does each card cost?

8 If this net was folded to make
a cube, what would be on the
face opposite the triangle?

9

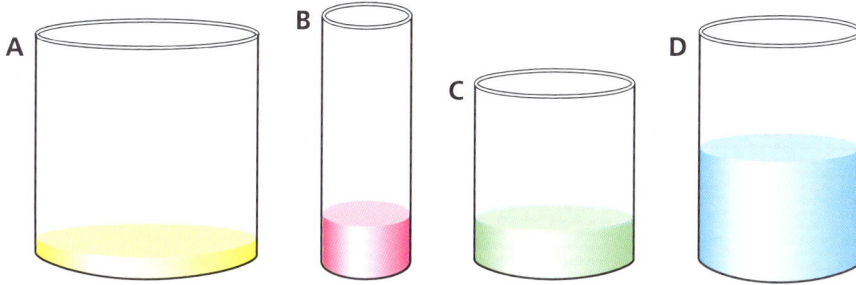

Which cylinder is

(a) 50% full   (b) 25% full   (c) 10% full   (d) 20% full

10 This table shows the weights of some new born baby girls.

A new born baby is expected to double its weight in about 6 months.

How much would you expect each baby to weigh in about 6 months?

Name	Weight (kg)
Phoebe	3.37
Hayley	3.5
Jennifer	3.52
Kate	4.05

11 Dave has a bottle that holds 0.3 litres of medicine.
He takes 15 ml of medicine every day.

How long will this bottle of medicine last him?

12 Match up each fraction with a percentage.

$\frac{1}{2}$ $\frac{1}{4}$ $\frac{1}{5}$ $\frac{3}{5}$ $\frac{3}{10}$ 25%   20%   50%   30%   60%

13 Hamish weighs 3.4 kg at birth.
A baby is expected to lose 10% of its birthweight in the first few days of life.

(a) How much weight will Hamish lose in the first few days of his life?

(b) How heavy will he be after his weight loss?

14 Kazuo's bamboo plant grows 72 cm each day.
At this rate, how long does it take to grow 16.56 metres?

15 Geena gets £60 for her birthday.
She spend 40% of her money on clothes.

How much money does she spend on clothes?

16 A specimen of *Dioon edule*, a Mexican evergreen shrub,
was found to be growing only 0.76 mm in a year.

At this rate, how many centimetres would it grow in 100 years?

17 An object is made with six cubes. The diagrams on the right show the top, front and side views.

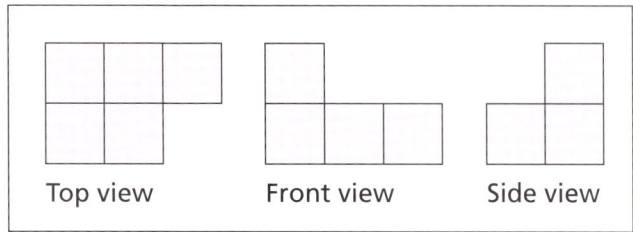

Top view   Front view   Side view

Which of these is the object described above?

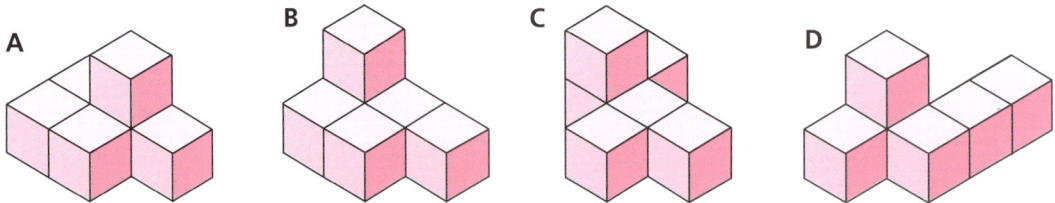

A   B   C   D

18 Put these in order, starting with the smallest.

30% $\frac{4}{5}$ $\frac{1}{4}$ 90%   0.42   0.03

19 In the year 2000, the average British male smoker smoked 114 cigarettes each week.

(a) How many cigarettes will the average male smoker smoke in one year? (There are 52 weeks in one year.)

(b) How many cigarettes is this to the nearest thousand?

20 Put the following volumes in order, smallest first.

225 ml   0.175 litres   0.2 litres   150 ml   0.30 litres

21 (a) Sketch a net for this cuboid. Show the dimensions on your sketch.

(b) Use a calculator to work out the surface area of this cuboid, correct to one decimal place.

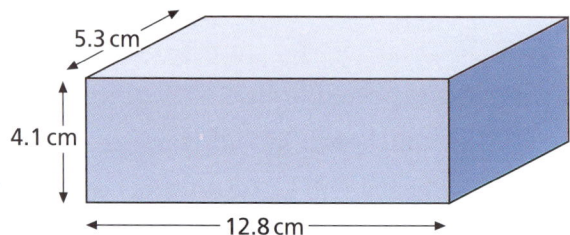

5.3 cm
4.1 cm
12.8 cm

22 A seal needs about 6% of its body weight in food each day. How much food does a seal that weighs 245 kg need each day?

23 On 25 December 1997, a 2300 kg Christmas log was made and eaten in Thailand.

(a) It contained 300 kg of sugar. What percentage of the log was sugar (to the nearest 1%)?

(b) The log was cut into 19 212 equal portions.

(i) How heavy was each portion in kilograms, correct to three decimal places?

(ii) What was the weight of each portion in grams?

21 Fair to all?

This work will help you

◆ calculate the mean of a list of numbers
◆ calculate the mean from a frequency table
◆ Calculate the mean, median and mode and decide which value is the most representative average

A How to be fair

Which group do you think did better?

Ann's group

Name	Number of 1 kg bundles collected
Ann	3
Carren	6
Diana	3
Ian	8

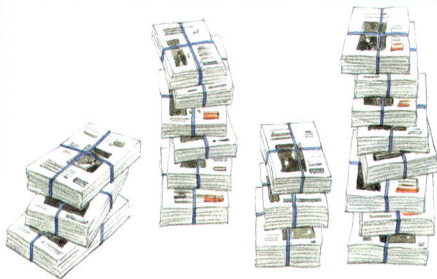

Ben's group

Name	Number of 1 kg bundles collected
Ben	8
David	3
Debbie	7

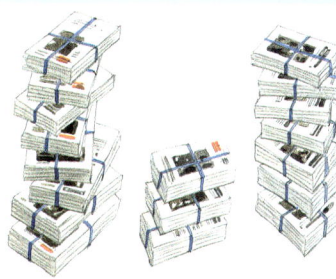

A1 Some pupils in Year 9 held a similar paper collection competition.

Sharon 10 kg
Amy 3 kg
Rajit 6 kg
Mark 5 kg

Jason 9 kg
Isha 3 kg
Purva 10 kg
Krush 6 kg
Rik 8 kg
Nina 6 kg

(a) What was the mean amount collected by Sharon's group?

(b) What was the mean amount collected by Jason's group?

(c) Whose group did better?

A2 Here are the results of rolling a dice.

What is the mean result?

A3 Julie did a survey of how many goldfish
some of her friends had.
Here are her results:

15, 10, 9, 12, 12, 8, 20, 14, 9, 11

What is the mean number of goldfish?

A4 Lewis recorded the number of pupils using the school minibus.
Here are his results for one week:

Weekdays
Number of pupils each journey   10, 7, 4, 9, 10

Weekend
Number of pupils each journey   11, 8, 11, 6

(a) What was the mean number of passengers on weekdays?

(b) What was the mean number of passengers at the weekend?

A5 Ruth grows peppers in a growing bag.
She has 5 plants.
She picked a total of 35 peppers.

What was the mean number of peppers per plant?

A6 Holly planted four pepper plants. She says:

> The mean number of peppers
> on my plants is twenty-four
> divided by three.
>
> This gives a mean of eight
> peppers per plant.

11   0   6   7

But Ruth says the mean is only six peppers.
Who is right and why?

A7 Here are the points scored by three people playing a computer game.

Use these figures to help you decide who you think is the best points scorer. Give a reason for your choice.

Pat Mitchele	10	7	7	8		
Jon Simpson	11	0	15	8	5	
Wayne Beeza	20	5	10	8	4	4

A8 Forms 8L and 8N collected bottles and cans for recycling.
Here are the record sheets for each form.
They show the number of cans and bottles collected by each person.

8L
Cans   2 3 2 5 0 1 2 5 2 0 0 4 3 1 1 2 0 0 6 1
Bottles   1 0 1 3 4 3 3 4 4 2 1 5 4 2 4 1 1 0 4 3

8N
Cans   1 1 2 1 4 1 1 2 0 3 1 0 4 5 6 1 0 2 3 1 1 3 2 2 8
Bottles 3 1 1 4 2 0 1 6 0 5 6 1 5 0 2 0 0 0 4 1 4 0 2 2 10

> This shows someone who collected 3 cans and 0 bottles.

(a) Which form deserves the prize for collecting cans?

(b) Which form deserves the prize for bottle collecting?
Explain your decision.

(c) Which form did better overall?
How did you decide?

A9 (a) Which team is working hardest?

(b) Which team has the easiest job?
Give reasons for your answers.

Mean tricks

A game for 2, 3, 4 or 5

You need a pack of playing cards without Jacks, Queens or Kings.
Aces count as 1.

The object of the game is to use as many cards as you can to get a target mean.

- Decide how many rounds you will play
  Deal 7 cards each.

  Turn over the top card from the ones that are left.
  This is the target mean.

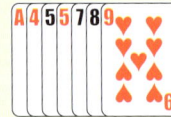

Sue's cards

- Each player then puts down cards whose mean is
  the same as the target mean.

  The number of cards you put down is your score.
  (So the more the better!)

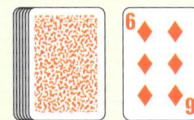

The target mean is 6

- Keep a record of the scores.

  The player with the highest total score wins.

Sue plays ...

She scores 5

B Means from frequencies

Here are the players in a football team.

70 kg 70 kg 70 kg 71 kg 71 kg 72 kg 72 kg 72 kg 72 kg 73 kg 73 kg

Here is a frequency table for the weights.

> Use the numbers in this table to answer the questions.

Weight in kg	Frequency
70	3
71	2
72	4
73	2

> This is the number of players.

- How many players are there in the team?
- There are three players who each weigh 70 kg.
  What is the total weight of these players?
- What is the total weight of those players who weigh 72 kg each?
- What is the total weight of all players in the team?
- What is the mean weight of the players in the team?

B1 This table gives information about a rugby team.

(a) How many players are there altogether in the team?

(b) How many players weigh 78 kg?

(c) Calculate the total weight of all the players. Show how you found your answer.

(d) Calculate the mean weight of the players.

Weight in kg	Frequency
75	1
76	4
77	3
78	5
79	2

B2 This data comes from a survey of birds' nests.

(a) How many nests were surveyed?

(b) Find the total number of eggs in all the nests

(c) What is the mean number of eggs per nest?

This is the number of nests.

Number of eggs in nest	Frequency
3	17
4	15
5	3

B3 Jackie wants to find the mean number of goals scored by her favourite ice hockey team last season.

This is a frequency table of the goals scored.

(a) How many games did they play last season?

(b) In how many games did they score more than one goal?

(c) How many goals did they score altogether?

(d) What was the mean number of goals scored by her team?

Number of goals	Tally	Frequency
0	卌	5
1	卌 卌 //	12
2	卌 卌 ///	13
3	卌 ///	8
4	//	2

B4 This tally table gives information about Rashid's tomato plants.

(a) How many tomato plants does Rashid have altogether?

(b) How many tomatoes are on Rashid's plants altogether?

(c) Calculate the mean number of tomatoes on a plant, correct to 1 d.p.

Number of tomatoes	Tally	Frequency
4	卌 //	7
5	卌 ////	9
6	卌 卌 /	11
7	卌 卌	10
8	///	3

B5 Leroy counted the number of Smarties in some tubes. Here are his results.

Number of Smarties in tube	26	28	29	30
Frequency	2	22	13	13

What was the mean number of Smarties in a tube?

B6 Every time Marie went to the market, she kept a record of the price she paid for a cabbage.

The prices were

57p, 60p, 58p, 59p, 59p, 61p, 59p, 57p, 58p, 60p,
61p, 59p, 58p, 61p, 57p, 61p, 58p, 60p, 58p, 59p

(a) Make a frequency table for Marie's information.

(b) Calculate the mean price she paid for a cabbage.

B7 Calculate the mean of this list of numbers, correct to 2 d.p. Describe the method you used.

3 3 3 3 4 4 4 4 4 4 4 4

5 5 5 5 5 6 6 6 6 7 7 7

8 8 8 8 8 8 8 9 9 9 9 9

B8 Jon has fifteen tomato plants.
Two of them have 8 tomatoes each, three have 7 tomatoes, nine have 6 tomatoes and one has 5 tomatoes.

Calculate the mean number of tomatoes on a plant.

B9 This frequency bar chart gives information about the numbers of people in cars passing a traffic census point.

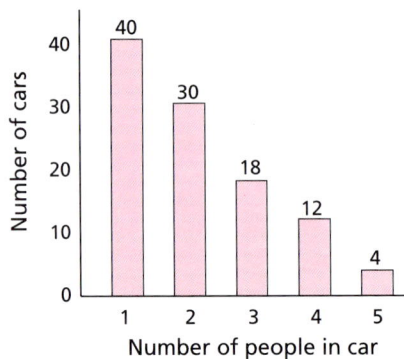

Calculate the mean number of people in a car, correct to 1 d.p.

B10 A firm that makes matches received a complaint that the statement 'Average contents 50 matches' on a box of matches was misleading.

They counted the matches in many boxes.
Here are their results.

Number of matches in box	48	49	50	51	52
Number of boxes	10	27	39	67	34

(a) Find the mean number of matches per box, correct to 1 d.p.

(b) Do you think the statement is misleading?

B11 Write down a list of five numbers less than 10.

    (a) Find the mean of your set of numbers.

    (b) What happens to the mean if you add 2 to each of the numbers in your list?

    (c) Experiment with some other sets of numbers.
       What can you find out?

    (d) Without using a calculator find the mean of
       9761,   9763,   9760,   9762,   9764.

B12 Ms Rees's choir has fifty members.

Age in years	11	12	13	14	15	16
Number of boys	3	4	4	5	2	2
Number of girls	3	5	4	3	7	8

    (a) What is the mean age of the boys?

    (b) What is the mean age of the girls?

    (c) What is the mean age of the choir?

B13 A junior chess team has three members aged 11, four members aged 12, and one aged 13.

    (a) What is the mean age of the team?

    (b) Another person now joins the team.
       The new mean age of the team is 12.

       How old is the new member?

Investigation

Investigate one of these statements:

'The mean sentence length is smaller in The *Mirror* than it is in The *Guardian*.'

'English words are shorter than German words.'

C Averages

What do you think these statements mean?

Mary is of average height.

The average maximum daily temperature in London in January is 7°C.

The average family uses about 400 litres of water a day.

There are three kinds of average we can use: **median mean mode**

This dot plot shows the weekly pocket money of 11 young people.

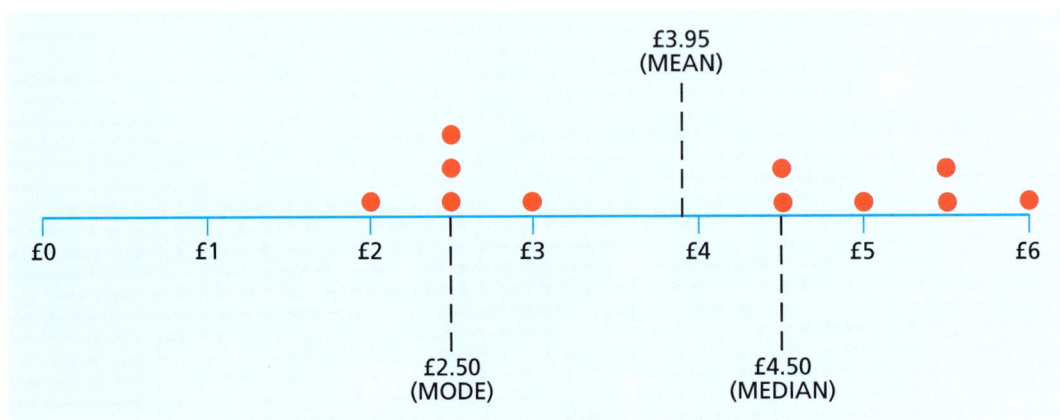

Median The median is the middle value when the amounts are arranged in order of size.

So the median amount of pocket money is **£4.50**.

Mean To find the mean you add up the amounts and divide by how many there are.

So the mean amount of pocket money is £43.50 ÷ 11 = **£3.95** (to the nearest penny).

Mode The mode is the amount which occurs most often.

So the **modal** amount of pocket money is **£2.50**.

C1 Which average would you use if

(a) you had £3 pocket money and thought you should have more

(b) you were a parent of a child with £4.50 pocket money and thought they should have less

C2 These are amounts of weekly pocket money for some young people.

£2.50 £3.00 £3.00 £0.50 £0.50 £3.00 £2.50 £3.50 £2.50 £3.50

£3.50 £0.50 £1.00 £2.50 £3.00 £0.50 £4.50 £2.00 £3.00 £2.00

(a) Find the median amount of pocket money.

(b) Find the mean amount.

(c) Find the modal amount.

(d) Which average would you use if you had £1.50 pocket money and thought you should have more?

C3 These are the ages of the members of a swimming club.

13 17 19 24 15 39 49 34 25 34 18 20 25 16 44

21 37 18 15 13 22 54 18 20 38 26 17 46 24 33

(a) Find
   (i) the median age   (ii) the mean age   (iii) the modal age

(b) Explain why the modal age is not a good representative value for the ages of this group of people.

(c) Group people into ages 10–19, 20–29, etc.

   Find the modal age group.

C4 Averages are often used to compare sets of data.
Here are the hours of sunshine for the days of August in two seaside towns.

Blackmouth								Bournepool							
5	6	8	2	7	5	8	4	3	2	4	5	8	7	1	9
4	1	5	4	8	3	1	9	7	7	9	7	1	4	3	5
3	6	3	4	9	10	5	9	8	6	4	8	6	4	8	8
4	10	5	11	11	9	10		9	1	5	7	8	7	7	

(a) Find the median, mean and modal number of hours of sunshine for each town. Compare the towns using averages.

(b) Write a short advert for each town, showing that it is 'better' than the other one.

Challenge

- Find a set of seven different positive whole numbers whose mean is 8, median 5 and range 20.

- How many different sets can you find?

- Now make up a similar problem and try it on somebody.

What progress have you made?

Statement	Evidence

I can calculate the mean of a set of data.

1 The Ransoms' paper bills for the last seven weeks were

£4.95   £5.35   £5.85   £4.95

£5.35   £4.95   £5.84

Calculate the mean amount spent on papers per week during this period.

I know what is meant by mean, mode and median.

2 Here are the total hours of sunshine recorded during April 1992 in London.

10	2	1	6	8	0	0	9	11	8
10	3	2	0	5	6	0	6	3	8
5	2	5	1	8	1	7	3	7	0

(a) Calculate the mean, mode and median (correct to 1 d.p. where necessary).

(b) Which average do you think best represents the daily hours of sunshine in London for April 1992? Why?

I can calculate the mean from a frequency table.

3 Ms Scott kept a record of the number of calculators that were brought to her lesson.

Here are the results.

Number of calculators	Number of lessons
20	5
21	2
22	6
23	15
24	14
25	8

What is the mean number of calculators brought per lesson?

㉒ Negative numbers

This work will help you
- ◆ compare positive and negative numbers
- ◆ add and subtract negative numbers

A High and deep

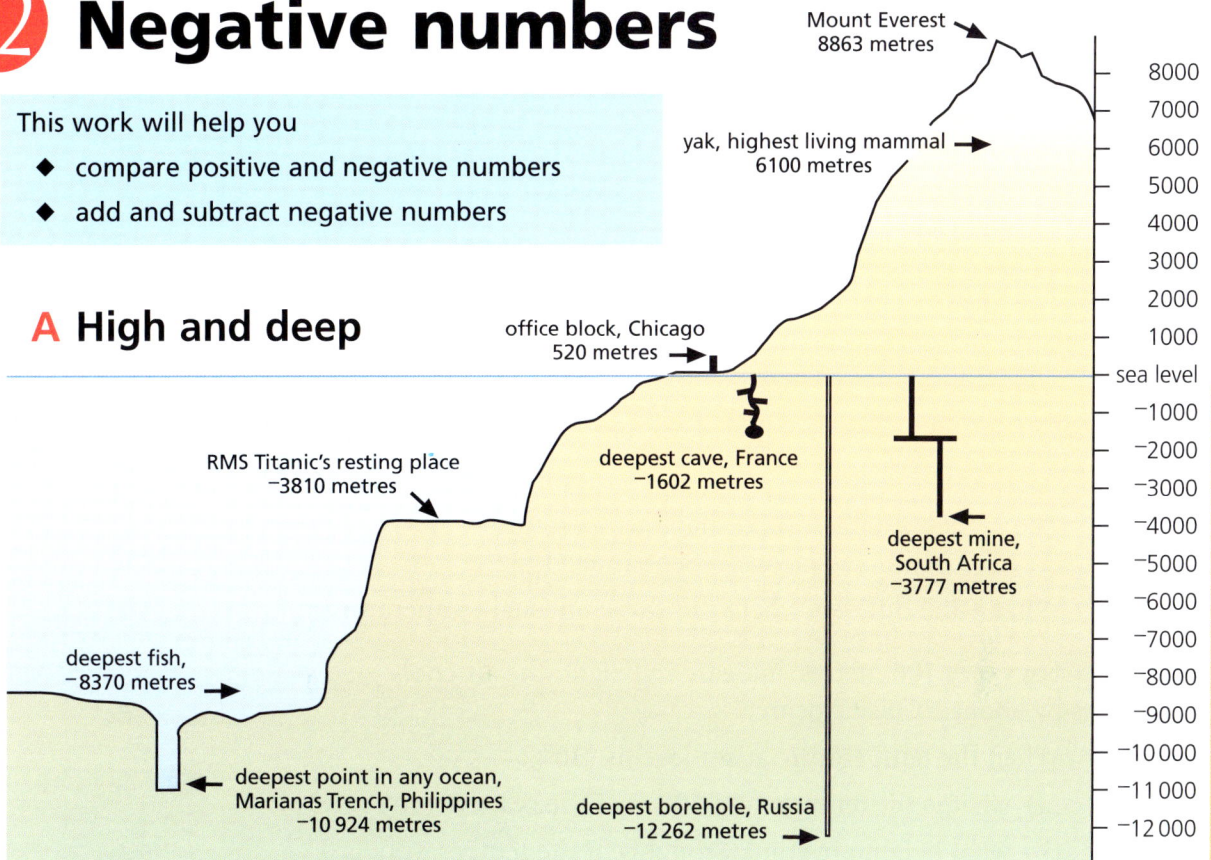

Mount Everest 8863 metres

yak, highest living mammal 6100 metres

office block, Chicago 520 metres

RMS Titanic's resting place −3810 metres

deepest cave, France −1602 metres

deepest mine, South Africa −3777 metres

deepest fish, −8370 metres

deepest point in any ocean, Marianas Trench, Philippines −10 924 metres

deepest borehole, Russia −12 262 metres

8000
7000
6000
5000
4000
3000
2000
1000
sea level
−1000
−2000
−3000
−4000
−5000
−6000
−7000
−8000
−9000
−10 000
−11 000
−12 000

A1 Heights on Earth are usually measured from sea level.
The Snowdon Mountain Railway rises to 1064 metres above sea level.
The rails in the Channel Tunnel go to 127 metres below sea level ($^-$127 metres).
What is the difference between these heights?

A2 This table shows the highest and lowest points in each continent.

Continent	Highest	(metres)	Lowest	(metres)
Europe	Mt Elbrus	5633	Polders	−4
Asia	Mt Everest	8848	Dead Sea	−393
Africa	Mt Kilimanjaro	5889	Qattarta depression	−133
N America	Mt McKinley	6194	Death Valley	−86
S America	Mt Aconcagua	6960	Rio Negro	−30
Australasia	Mt Carstenztoppen	5000	Lake Eyre	−12
Antarctica	Vinson Range	5140	Interior	−2500

(a) In which continent is the lowest point in the world?

(b) What is the difference in metres between the highest and lowest points in Europe?

(c) Make up, and try out on a friend, some questions of your own from the table. Make sure you can answer them yourself.

B Hot and cold

B1 Which of these temperatures is lowest? $^-5°C$, $^-4°C$, $^-10°C$, $0°C$

B2 The temperature outside my house at 6 p.m. was 2°C.
By midnight the temperature had dropped 7 degrees.

What was the temperature at midnight?

B3 The greatest change in temperature in Britain in a single day
happened in Tayside in 1978.
The temperature changed from $^-7°C$ to 22°C.

By how many degrees did the temperature change?

B4 In Omyakon in Siberia the temperature fell to $^-68°C$ in 1933.
The highest ever recorded shade temperature is 58°C
(at Al'Aziziyah, Libya, on 13 September 1922).

What is the difference between these unusual temperatures?

B5 For every 100 metres' increase in height, the air cools
by about 1 Celsius degree.

When the temperature at sea level is $^-10°C$,

(a) what is the temperature 500 m above sea level, roughly?

(b) what height are you at, roughly, if the temperature is 0°C?

(c) what height are you at, if the temperature is 7°C?

(d) what height are you at, if it is $^-3°C$?

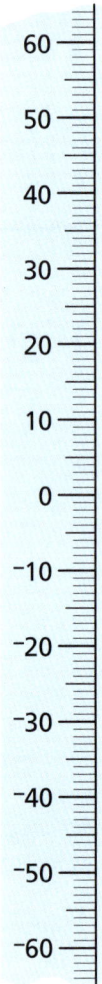

Scientists can measure temperatures very accurately, to decimals of a degree.

B6 What are the temperatures
marked (a), (b) and (c)?

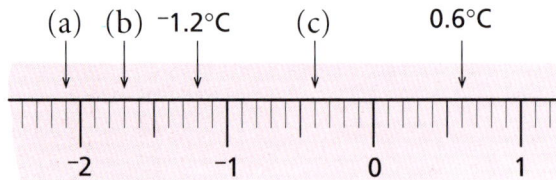

B7 List these temperatures in order, lowest first.

$^-1.3°C$ $0.3°C$ $^-0.7°C$ $^-1.4°C$ $^-2.3°C$

B8 In an experiment, the temperature rises from $^-4.8°C$ to 3.4°C.
By how much has it risen?

B9 In another experiment, the temperature falls from $^-7.8°C$ to $^-13.3°C$.
How far has it fallen?

B10 Which of these temperatures is the lowest?

$^-0.2°C$ $0.01°C$ $^-0.3°C$ $0.001°C$

C Adding negative numbers

Dana's class have a joke contest. The judges give points.

When they think a joke is good
they give scores like 4 or 6.

When they think a joke is awful
they can give negative scores.

The scores are added up.

What is the total score in each of these?

(a) Total

(b) Total

(c) Total

(d) Total

(e) Total

(f) Total

C1 What is the total score in each of these pictures?

(a)

| 5 | ⁻6 | Total |

(b)

| ⁻6 | ⁻5 | Total |

(c)

| 2 | ⁻2 | Total |

(d)

| ⁻3 | 2 | Total |

C2 Do these additions.

(a) ⁻2 + ⁻1 + 6   (b) 2 + ⁻2 + 3 + ⁻1 + ⁻1   (c) ⁻1 + ⁻1 + ⁻2 + 7 + 3

(d) 4 + ⁻2 + ⁻5 + ⁻1   (e) ⁻6 + 9 + 1 + ⁻4 + ⁻3   (f) 5 + ⁻1 + ⁻3 + ⁻4

(g) ⁻3 + ⁻1 + 10   (h) 13 + ⁻2 + 3 + ⁻4 + ⁻1   (i) ⁻10 + ⁻2 + 8 + 7

C3 The temperature at midday in a garden was recorded every day for a week in January.

   5°C   ⁻1°C   5°C   3°C   ⁻2°C   5°C   6°C

What was the mean midday temperature for that week?

C4 The midnight temperatures were also recorded.

   2°C   ⁻5°C   ⁻6°C   1°C   ⁻7°C   1°C   ⁻7°C

What was the mean midnight temperature?

C5 In a magic square each row, each column and each diagonal adds up to the same total (called the 'magic number').

Copy and complete these magic squares.

(a)

4		0
	1	
2	3	

(b)

1		⁻1
	2	
5		3

(c)

⁻2	3	⁻4
⁻3		
		0

C6 Make a magic square with magic number ⁻6.
Use these numbers:

   2   1   0   ⁻1   ⁻2   ⁻3   ⁻4   ⁻5   ⁻6

D Subtracting negative numbers

Here are the points for Jo's joke.

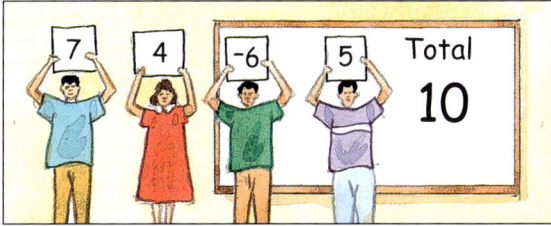

The score of ⁻6 is taken off.

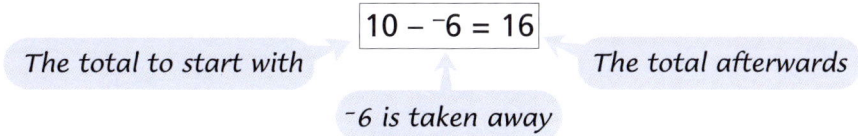

$$10 - {}^-6 = 16$$

The total to start with

⁻6 is taken away

The total afterwards

- What happens when a negative score is taken away from one of your class's joke totals?

- What subtraction can you write?

D1 This is what happens with Elly's joke.

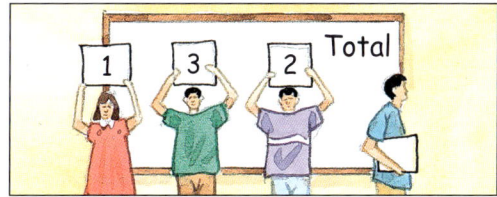

Copy and complete the subtraction.

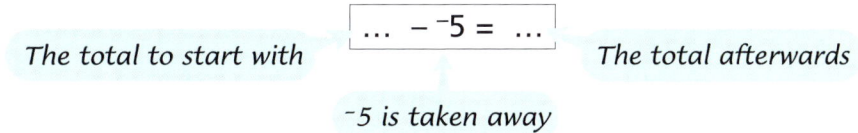

$$... - {}^-5 = ...$$

The total to start with

⁻5 is taken away

The total afterwards

D2 This happens with Dai's joke.

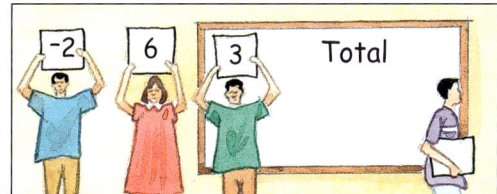

Write the subtraction.

D3 Zak got these scores: 3 ⁻2 1

   (a) What is the total?

   (b) The score of ⁻2 is taken away. What is the new total?

   (c) Write the subtraction.

D4 Pippa got these scores: $^-8$ $^-4$ 3

(a) What is the total?

(b) The score of $^-8$ is taken away. What is the new total?

(c) Write the subtraction.

D5 What is an easy way to subtract a negative number?

D6 Work out (a) $8 - {}^-4$ (b) $14 - {}^-8$ (c) $5 - {}^-27$ (d) $26 - {}^-34$ (e) $21 - {}^-19$

D7 Calculate (a) $^-5 - {}^-11$ (b) $^-11 - {}^-5$ (c) $^-4 - {}^-2$ (d) $^-23 - {}^-48$ (e) $^-53 - {}^-36$

D8 Work these out.

(a) $11 + {}^-3 - {}^-7 + {}^-9$ (b) $^-11 + 6 + {}^-5 - 6$ (c) $26 - {}^-7 + {}^-13$

(d) $223 + {}^-104 - {}^-150$ (e) $47 + {}^-12 - {}^-35$ (f) $437 - {}^-526 + {}^-130$

D9 (a) Subtract $^-43$ from $^-56$. (b) Subtract $^-11$ from the sum of $^-6$ and 15.

(c) Add 34 to $^-17$ then subtract 8. (d) Add $^-61$ to 98 then subtract $^-52$.

D10 Write a subtraction which begins with $^-10$ and has an answer of $^-2$. $^-10$ $= {}^-2$

D11 During the day the temperature on the Moon can reach 110°C, but at night it drops to $^-155$°C.

(a) Which of these calculations gives the difference between these two temperatures?

$^-110 - {}^-155$ $^-155 - {}^-110$ $155 - 110$ $110 - {}^-155$

(b) Use the correct calculation to work out the temperature difference.

What progress have you made?

Statement	Evidence
I can compare positive and negative numbers.	**1** List these numbers in order, lowest first. $^-0.7$ 0.4 $^-1.2$ $^-2.5$ $^-0.9$
I can add negative numbers.	**2** Do these additions. (a) $^-3 + {}^-4 + 7$ (b) $^-11 + {}^-3 + 9 + {}^-6$ (c) $^-15 + 23 + {}^-7$ (d) $^-132 + {}^-97$
I can subtract negative numbers.	**3** Work these out. (a) $12 - {}^-9 + {}^-8 + 7$ (b) $39 + {}^-17 - {}^-49$ **4** (a) Subtract $^-67$ from $^-90$. (b) Add 24 to $^-19$ then subtract $^-13$.

23 Transformations

This is about reflecting, rotating and sliding shapes ('transformations').

The work will help you

- ◆ follow instructions for transformations
- ◆ describe transformations clearly

A Reflection

- Cats A, B, C and D are mirror images of Dinah. Can you work out where the mirror was for each one?

- What are the images of Dinah in mirrors M1 and M2?

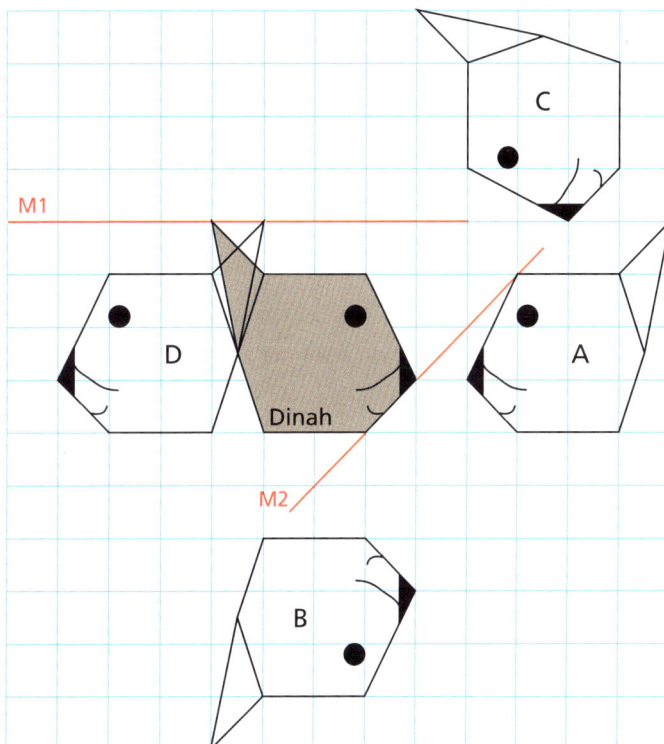

A1 Copy this L-shape and mirror lines on to squared paper.

Draw a mirror image of the L-shape for each of the mirror lines.

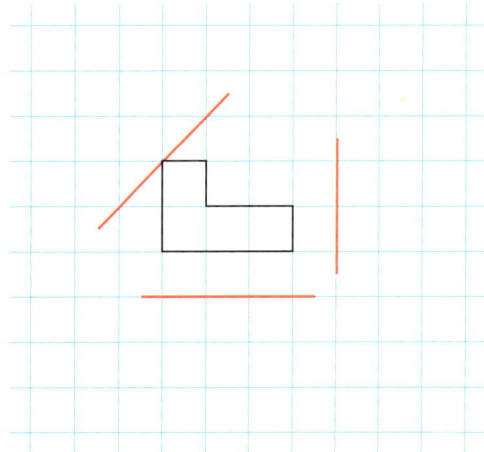

173

A2 Shapes U, V, W and X are all mirror images of shape T.
Which do you get by reflecting shape T

(a) in line M1 (b) in line M2

(c) in line M3 (d) in line M4

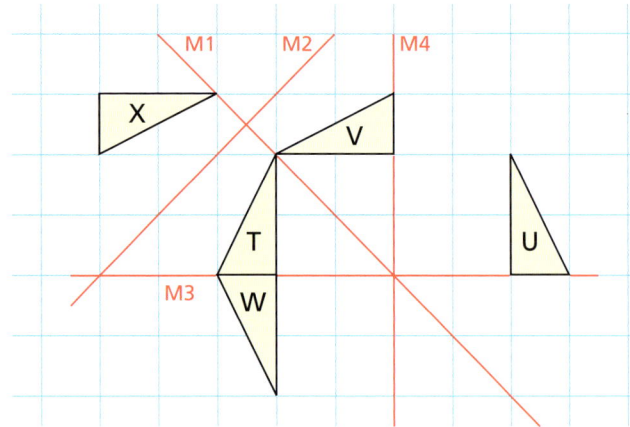

A3 Here, shape H is the mirror image of shape G in the line M3.

Which shape is the mirror image when you reflect

(a) shape D in line M3

(b) shape D in line M5

(c) shape E in line M4

(d) shape I in line M3

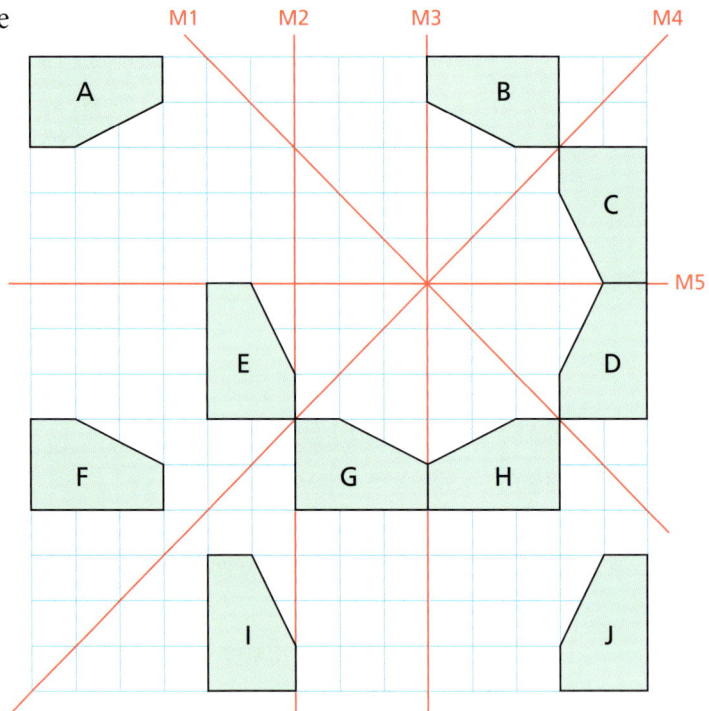

A4 Which mirror line would reflect

(a) shape I on to shape F

(b) shape B on to shape H

(c) shape C on to shape G

(d) shape H on to shape D

A5 Draw and label a grid like this.

(a) Draw a triangle with vertices at the points (5, 1), (7, 3) and (10, 2).

(b) Draw a straight line that goes through (1, 4) and (11, 4).

(c) Draw the image of the triangle when it is reflected in the line.

(d) Write the coordinates of the vertices of the image.

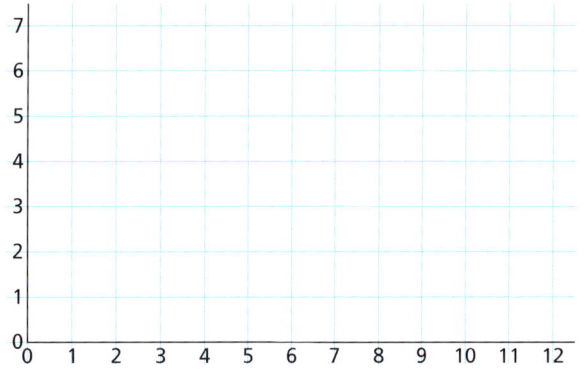

A6 Draw and label a grid like this.

(a) Draw a pentagon with vertices at the points (1, 2), (4, 1), (5, 4), (3, 6) and (1, 5).

(b) Draw the image of the pentagon when it is reflected in the vertical axis.

(c) Write the coordinates of the vertices of the image. How are they related to the coordinates of the original vertices?

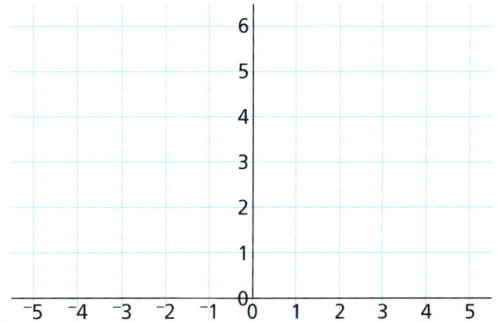

B Rotation

What is the image of this quadrilateral

- after a half turn with point A as the centre of rotation
- after a half turn with point B as the centre of rotation
- after a half turn with point C as the centre of rotation
- after a half turn with point D as the centre of rotation

What about quarter turns?

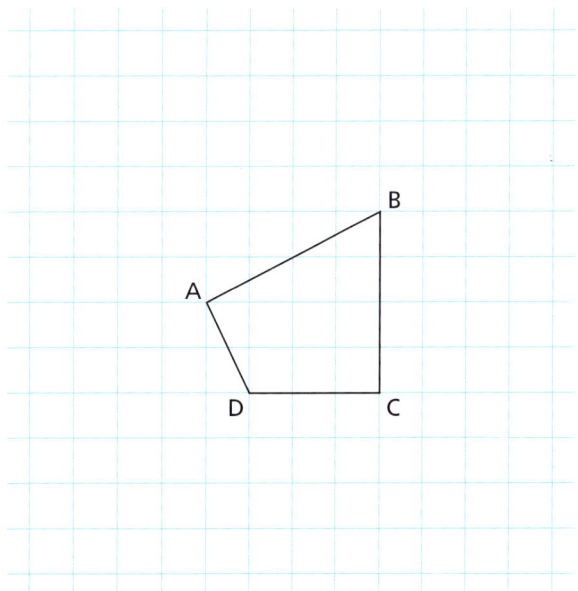

175

B1 Copy this shape on to squared paper leaving some space around it.

Draw the image of the shape

- after a 90° turn clockwise about C
- after a 90° turn anticlockwise about C
- after a 180° turn about D
- after a 90° turn anticlockwise about E

Label each image with the description of the transformation.

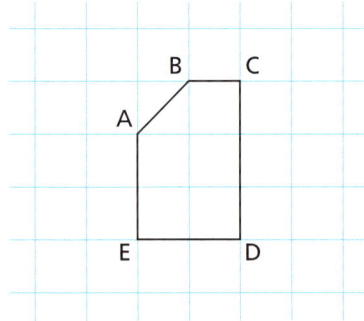

B2 Follow the instructions on sheet 173.

B3 Which image do you get by rotating shape S
  - (a) a quarter turn clockwise about D
  - (b) a half turn about C
  - (c) a quarter turn anticlockwise about C
  - (d) a half turn about E
  - (e) a quarter turn clockwise about E

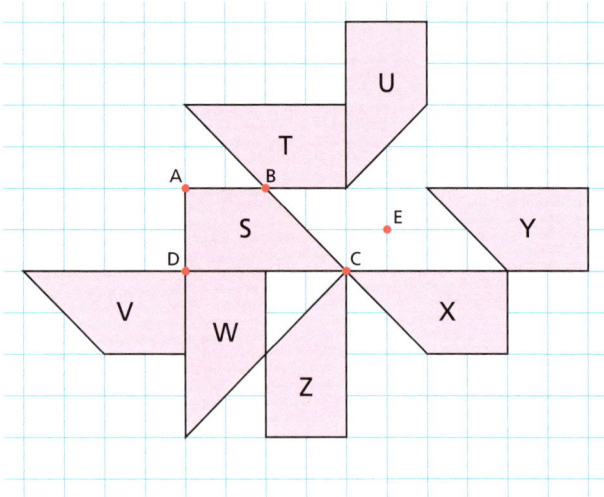

B4 Which centre of rotation and what angle (clockwise or anticlockwise) would you use to rotate
  - (a) shape P to shape R
  - (b) shape Q to shape R
  - (c) shape R to shape S
  - (d) shape T to shape P

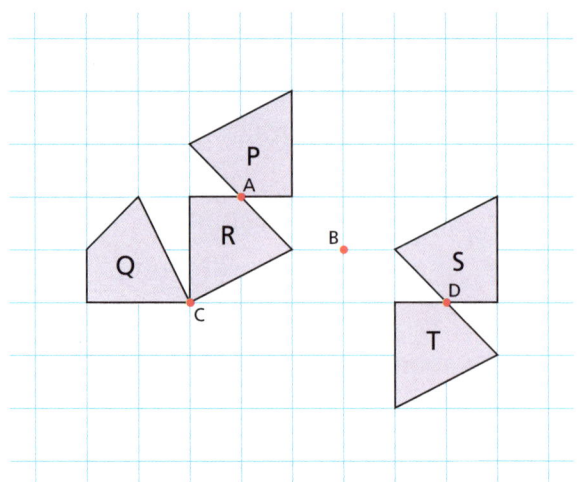

B5 Draw and label a grid like this.

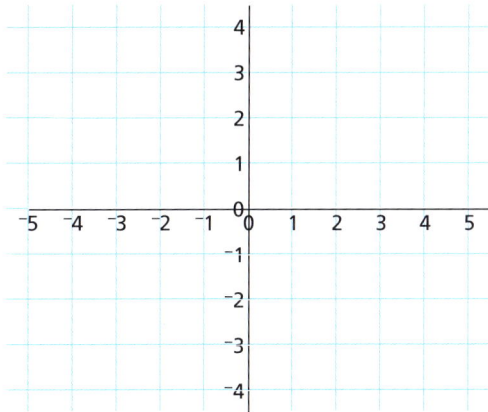

(a) Draw a hexagon with vertices at the points
(1, 1), (1, 3), (2, 4), (4, 4), (5, 2) and (4, 1).

(b) Draw the image of the hexagon when it is rotated through
180° with (0, 0) as the centre of rotation.

(c) Write the coordinates of the vertices of the image.
How are they related to the coordinates of the original vertices?

Transformation code

- Each transformation in the list below takes you
from **where you are** to the next shape.

  What word do the letters of the shapes spell?

  Start at shape S

  Rotate a half turn, centre C

  Rotate a quarter turn anticlockwise, centre C

  Reflect in M2

  Rotate a quarter turn anticlockwise, centre C

- Starting at shape N, what does this spell?

  Reflect in M2

  Rotate a quarter turn anticlockwise, centre C

  Reflect in M4

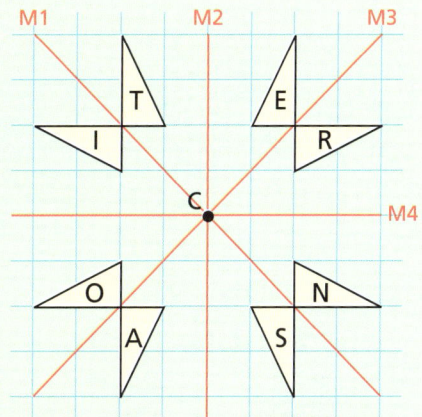

- Starting at shape T, what transformations spell TASTE ?

- Starting at shape R, what transformations spell ROTATE ?

Try using the diagram to write transformation code for some other words.
See if a partner can decode what you have written.

C Translation

Translating a shape means sliding it without rotating it.

The translation that moves shape P to shape Q can be described as

   1 unit left, 2 units up.

Left/right first   *Up/down next*

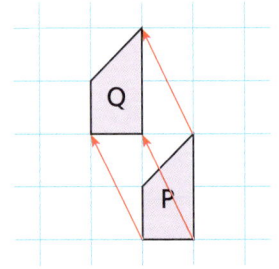

C1 Which shape does A move to with each of these translations?

  (a) 3 units left, 1 unit down

  (b) 2 units left, 1 unit up

  (c) 1 unit right, 2 units up

  (d) 2 units right, 1 unit down

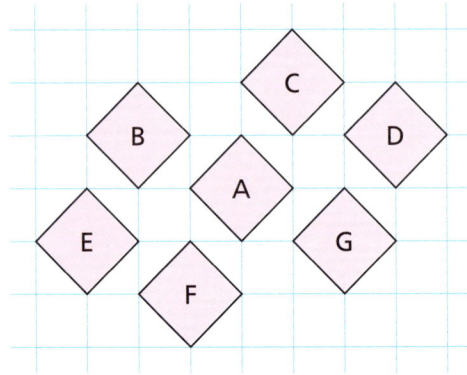

C2 Karl thinks the translation that moves triangle F to triangle G is '3 right, 1 up'. Is he correct? If not, what is it?

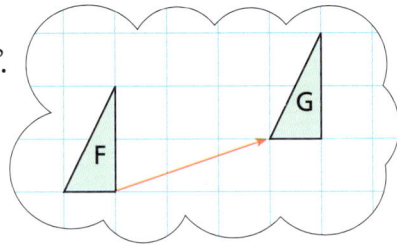

C3 Describe the translation

  (a) that moves P to Q

  (b) that moves P to R

  (c) that moves P to S

  (d) that moves P to T

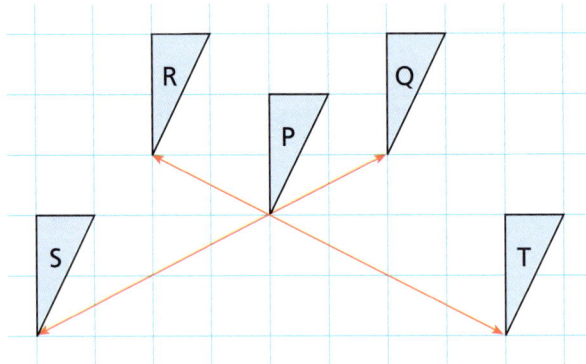

C4 Copy shape A on to squared paper.

  (a) Translate A 3 units right, 1 unit down. Label the new position B.

   Translate A 1 unit left, 2 units up. Label the new position C.

  (b) Describe the translation that moves B to C.

  (c) Describe the translation that moves C to B.

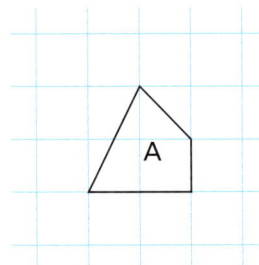

Patterns with transformations

- Copy the design and complete the pattern according to the instructions.

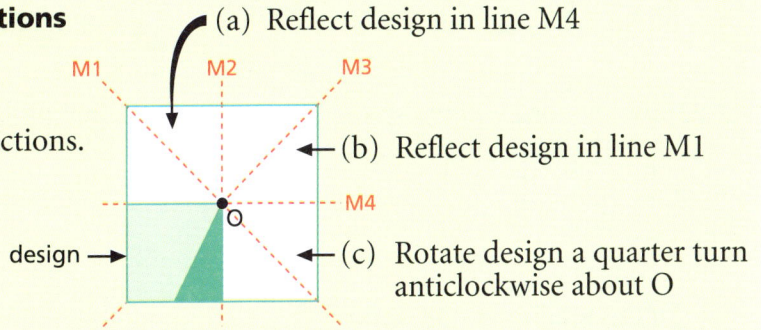

(a) Reflect design in line M4

(b) Reflect design in line M1

(c) Rotate design a quarter turn anticlockwise about O

design →

- For each of these, describe how the design in the bottom left-hand corner has been transformed to make (a), (b) and (c).

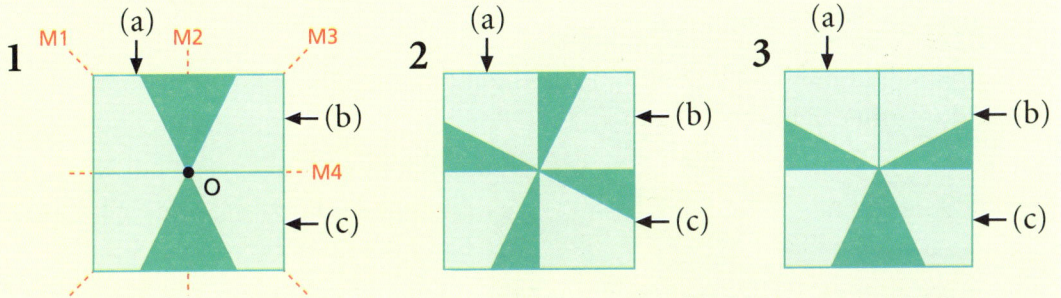

1 M1 (a) M2 M3 ← (b) ← M4 O ← (c)

2 (a) ← (b) ← (c)

3 (a) ← (b) ← (c)

- Use transformations to make some patterns of your own. Describe the transformations you used.

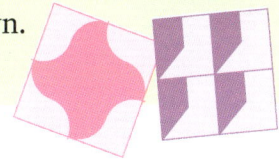

What progress have you made?

Statement

I can reflect, rotate and translate shapes.

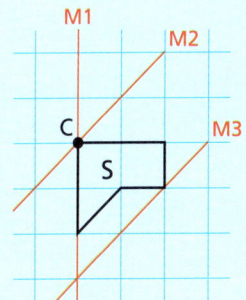

I can describe transformations.

Evidence

1 Copy this diagram.

(a) Reflect shape S in the line M2. Label the image T.

(b) Reflect shape S in the line M3. Label the image U.

(c) Rotate S 90° anticlockwise about C. Label the image V.

2 (a) What type of transformation would take T to U?

(b) Describe fully the transformation that takes V to T.

179

24 Functions and graphs

This work will help you

◆ draw a graph based on a rule

◆ find the equation of a straight-line graph

A From table to graph

Teacher-led discussion

Notice: spacewalks
1 kilogram of gas lasts 2 hours.
You must have 1 hour's worth of gas
left in your tank when you return.

Gas in tank (kg)	Hours away from base
1	1
2	3
3	
4	

A1 (a) The table above shows how many hours you can be away from base.
Complete the table up to 7 kilograms.

(b) Plot the points from your table on graph paper.
The points should all lie on a straight line.
Draw the line through the points.

(c) Suppose you have $4\frac{1}{2}$ kg of gas in your tank.
Use the graph to find how many hours you can be away from base.

(d) You want to be away from base for 10 hours.
How many kilograms of gas should you put in your tank?

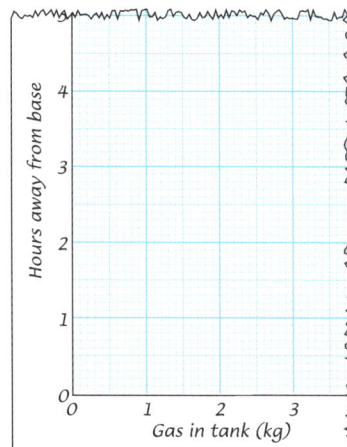

A2 Petra sees a snail crawling up a post.
When she first sees it, it is 20 cm from the ground.

She measures its height from the ground every hour and finds that it climbs 30 cm in each hour.

(a) Copy and complete this table, showing the time that has passed in hours (t) and the height of the snail in cm (h).

t	0	1	2	3	4	5	6
h	20	50					

(b) Draw a graph to show the time that has passed and the snail's height in centimetres.

(c) Use the graph to find how high the snail is when $1\frac{1}{2}$ hours have passed.

(d) How much time has passed when the snail is 35 cm up the pole?

(e) Use the graph to find t when $h = 100$.

(f) What is h when $t = 2.5$?

Height of snail in cm (h) / Time passed in hours (t)

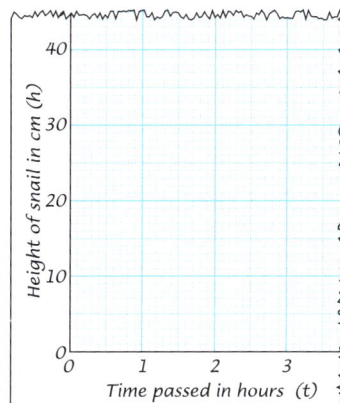

A3 A candle is 28 centimetres long when it is new.
It burns down 2 centimetres every hour.

(a) Copy this table showing the time that has passed in hours (t) and the length of the candle in centimetres (l).

t	0	1	2	3	4	5	6
l							

(b) Draw a graph to show the time that has passed and the candle's length in centimetres.

(c) Use the graph to find how long the candle is when $3\frac{1}{2}$ hours have passed.

(d) How much time has passed when the candle is 17 cm long?

(e) Use the graph to find t when $l = 25$

(f) What is l when $t = 4.5$?

B Using formulas

A taxi firm charges £3 per mile plus a £1 pick-up charge.

We can use the letter d for the distance travelled in miles and show what happens in their way of charging like this.

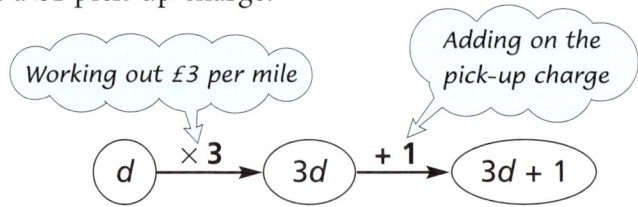

Working out £3 per mile

Adding on the pick-up charge

$$d \xrightarrow{\times 3} 3d \xrightarrow{+1} 3d + 1$$

So if we use the letter c to mean the amount charged in pounds, we can write a **formula**, like this.

$$c = 3d + 1$$

B1 Taxi firms in different places have different ways of charging. Write a formula, using c and d, for each of these ways.

(a) £4 per mile plus a £2 pick-up charge

(b) £3 per mile plus a £3 pick-up charge

(c) £5 per mile but no pick-up charge

B2 A taxi firm uses this formula.

$$c = 4d + 3$$

What is the cost of each of the following journeys?

(a) 2 miles   (b) 5 miles   (c) 12 miles   (d) 17 miles   (e) $2\frac{1}{2}$ miles

B3 A different firm uses this formula.

$$c = 5d + 1$$

(a) Copy and complete this table up to $d = 7$.

d	1	2					
c							

(b) Draw a graph to show the distance travelled and the amount charged. It should be a straight line. Label the line '$c = 5d + 1$'

(c) From your graph, how much would it cost to travel $5\frac{1}{2}$ miles?

(d) If a passenger was charged £18.50, how far had she travelled?

B4 As a special offer, a taxi firm decides to charge £4 per mile less a discount of £2 on each journey.

Their formula is

$$c = 4d - 2$$

(a) Draw a graph with d going up to 6 on the across axis.

(b) How far can you go for

  (i) £18   (ii) £12   (iii) £15

(c) What do you pay if your journey is half a mile?

(d) What if it is a quarter of a mile?

B5 Dina did an experiment with a spring.
She hung different weights on the spring and measured its length each time.

This graph shows her results. ➤

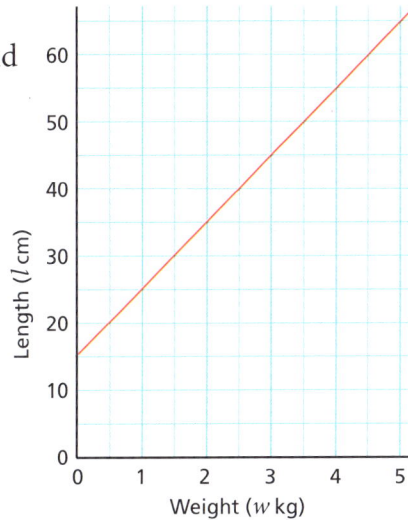

(a) Copy this table and fill in results from the graph.

Weight on spring, w kg	0	1	2	3	4	5
Length of spring, l cm						

(b) Write a formula linking l to w.

$$l = \ldots$$

Bill did an experiment with a stronger spring than Dina's.

This graph shows his results. ➤

(c) Make a table as in part (a) but fill it in with results from Bill's graph.

(d) Write a formula linking l to w.

$$l = \ldots$$

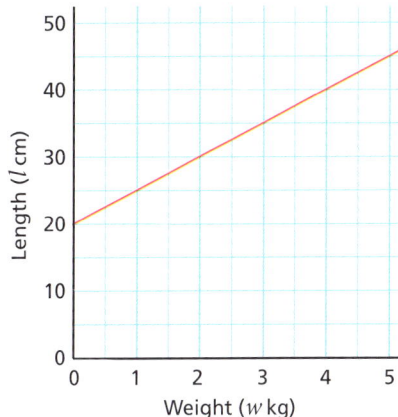

183

C Functions

You can think of the equation $y = 2x + 1$ as a rule, or **function**, linking x and y.

For each value of x, you can find the value of y.

Here is a **table of values** of x and y.

x	0	1	2	3
y	1	3	5	7

When you plot x and y as coordinates, the points lie on a straight line.
This line is the **graph** of $y = 2x + 1$.

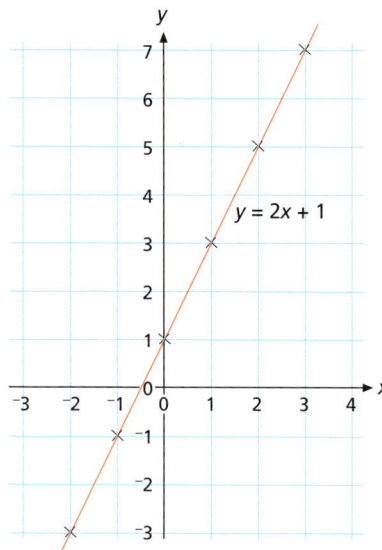

C1 Draw axes with x (across) and y (up) from 0 to 7.

(a) Copy and complete this table of values for the function $y = x + 1$.

x	0	1	2	3	4	5	6
y	1						

Plot points from the table.
Draw and label the graph of $y = x + 1$.

(b) Copy and complete this table of values for the function $y = 2x - 1$.

x	1	2	3	4
y				

Plot points on the axes as your first graph.

Draw and label the graph of $y = 2x - 1$.

(c) Copy and complete this table of values for the function $y = 5 - x$.

x	0	1	2	3	4	5
y	5					

Plot points. Draw and label its graph on the same axes.

C2 Draw axes with x and y from 0 to 5.

On these axes, draw and label the graphs of these functions.

$y = x + 2$ $y = 2x$ $y = 4 - x$

A 'Think of a rule' activity for the whole class is described in the teacher's guide.

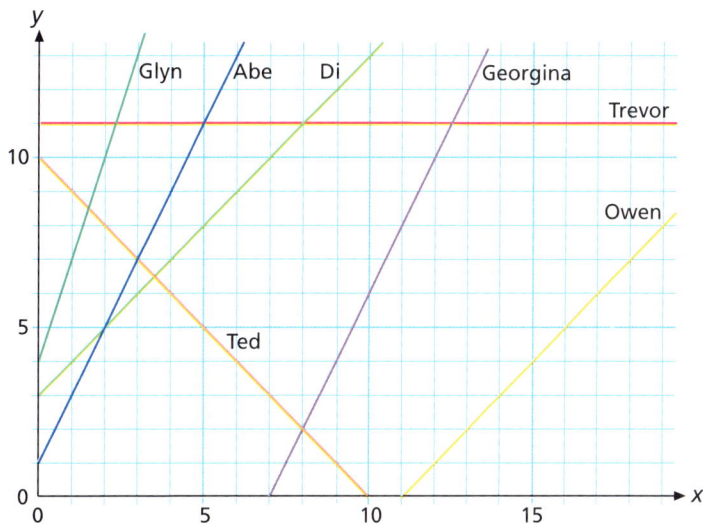

Georgina's rule was $y = 2x - 14$.
Here are some of her points.

x	y
7	0
10	6
13	12

C3 Look at the graph for Glyn's rule.
Copy and complete this table of coordinates for points on the graph.

x	0	1	2	3
y	4	7		

Find the equation of Glyn's graph.

C4 One person's rule was $y = 10 - x$.
Copy and complete this table of coordinates for this rule.

x	0	1	2	3	4
y	10				

Find the line that goes through these points and write whose rule it was.

C5 What rule did Abe use? (It may help to make a table of the coordinates of some of the points on the graph.)

C6 What rule did Di use?

C7 Who used the rule $y = x - 11$?

C8 One person used the rule $y = 11$.
So whatever value of x he was given,
he always said '11' for the value of y.

Who was it?

D Negative numbers on graphs

D1 Peter uses this rule in a game:

$$y = 2x - 7$$

(a) Copy and complete this table for his rule.

x	0	1	2	3	4	5
y	-7					

He works out
$2 \times 0 - 7$.

You need to work out
$2 \times 1 - 7$.

(b) Draw axes like these on squared paper.
Plot points from the table and draw a graph.

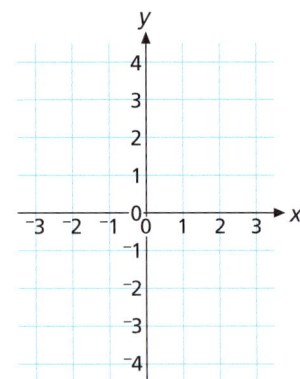

(c) What is y when $x = 4\frac{1}{2}$?

(d) What is x when $y = {}^-2$?

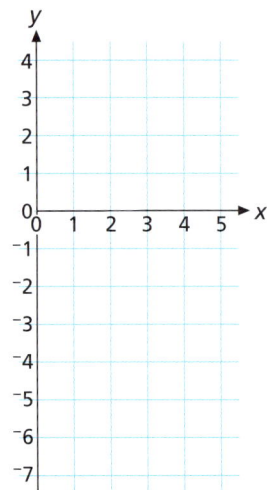

D2 Charlotte uses the rule $y = x - 3$.

(a) Copy and complete this table for her rule.

x	0	1	2	3	4	5
y						

(b) Draw axes like those for question D1.
Plot points from the table and draw a graph.

D3 Carol uses the rule $y = x + 1$.

She wants to see what happens if x is allowed to be negative.

(a) Copy and complete this table for $y = x + 1$.

x	-3	-2	-1	0	1	2	3
y	-2						

She works out
$^-3 + 1$.

You need to work out
$^-2 + 1$.

(b) Draw axes like these on squared paper.
Plot points from the table and draw a graph.

D4 Kevin uses the rule $y = x - 1$.

(a) Copy and complete this table for his rule.

x	-3	-2	-1	0	1	2	3
y							

(b) Draw axes like those for question D3.
Plot points from the table and draw a graph.

What progress have you made?

Statement

For a situation described in words
I can write a table of values
and draw a graph.

Evidence

1 For each job, a plumber charges £10 for a
call-out, plus £15 per hour.

   (a) Copy and complete this table
   to show the time taken in hours (t)
   and the cost in pounds (c).

t	0	1	2	3	4	5
c						

   (b) Draw axes with t going across to 5
   and c going up to 90.
   Draw a graph of the plumber's charges.

I can find information from a graph.

2 From the graph in question 1,
how long was the job if the
plumber charged £62.50?

I can draw the graph of a function
like $y = x + 3$.

3 Draw the graph of the function $y = x + 3$
for values of x from 0 to 4.

I can draw graphs that involve
negative numbers.

4 Draw the graph of the function $y = 2x + 3$,
for values of x from $^-4$ to 4.

I can find the equation of a straight-
line graph.

5 Find the equation of each line below.

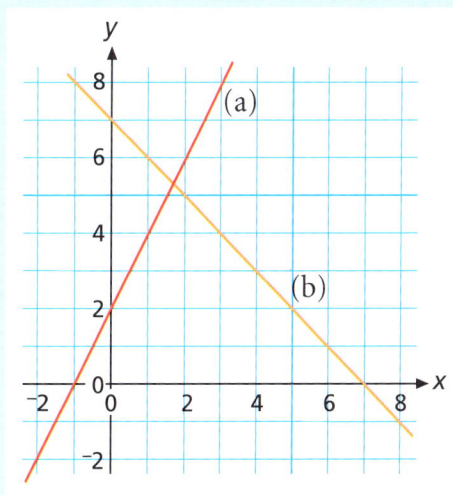

㉕ Multiples and factors

This work will help you

♦ understand multiples and factors, including common multiples and factors

♦ recognise prime numbers

A Multiples

A **multiple** of 3 is a whole number of 3s.

12 is a multiple of 3 (because 12 is 4×3).

You need to know about multiples to play 'Nasty multiples'.

The rules and board are on sheet 174.

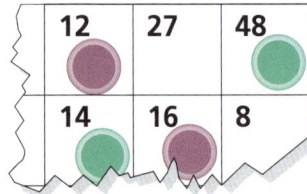

12	27	48
14	16	8

A1 Which numbers in this list are multiples of 3?

3, 5, 9, 10, 12, 14, 16, 30, 31, 33, 35

A2 Which numbers in this list are multiples of 8?

4, 8, 10, 12, 16, 20, 24, 25, 48, 49, 50, 56

A3 (a) Write down five multiples of 10.

(b) Pick out the multiples of 10 from this list.

70, 90, 100, 103, 110, 148, 170, 220, 316

(c) How can you tell by looking at a number that it is a multiple of 10?

A4 Here is a list of numbers.

6, 8, 15, 18, 20, 24, 36, 60

(a) Which numbers are multiples of 2?   (b) Which are multiples of 3?

(c) Which are multiples of 4?   (d) Which are multiples of 5?

A5 Pioneer Buses decide to make all their fares multiples of 5p.

Which of these fares will have to be changed?

15p, 20p, 33p, 45p, 59p, 66p, 75p, 90p

A6 What different ways can you complete these?

(a) 12 is a multiple of …   (b) 15 is a multiple of …

(c) 24 is a multiple of …   (d) 30 is a multiple of …

B Factors

You need the factor chart on sheet 175.

> 8 can be divided exactly by 2.
> We say 2 is a **factor** of 8.
> Other factors of 8 are 1, 4 and 8.

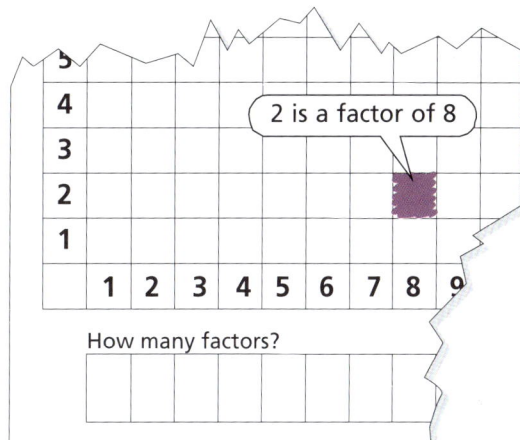

2 is a factor of 8

How many factors?

- Complete the factor chart by shading the factors of each number from 1 to 16.

- Write about what you see in your chart.

> For example ◊ Which numbers have lots of factors?
>
> ◊ Are any numbers special? Why?
>
> ◊ What patterns are there?

> Here are all the factors of 20, in order.
>
> 1   2   4   5   10   20
>
> They are paired off, so that each pair multiplies to make 20.

B1 Draw a diagram, similar to the one above, for the factors of
(a) 12 (b) 18 (c) 24 (d) 30

B2 (a) Draw a diagram for factors of 36. What is special about it?
(b) Does 36 have an odd or even number of factors?
(c) Find three numbers with an odd number of factors.
(d) What is special about these numbers?

B3 Draw a diagram for 7. What is special about this diagram?

B4 A number with only two factors, itself and 1, is called a **prime** number.
(1 is not classed as a prime number; it has only one factor.)

List all the prime numbers between 1 and 16.
(You might find your factor chart useful.)

B5 What are all the prime numbers between 20 and 30?

B6 Find a prime number which, when its digits are reversed, is also prime.

The sieve of Eratosthenes

You need a hundred square (sheet 134).

- Put a ring round 2.
  Then cross out all the other multiples of 2
  (4, 6, 8, …).

- The first number after 2 which isn't crossed out is 3.
  Ring 3. Then cross out all the other multiples of 3.
  (Some will be crossed out already. Why?)

- The first number after 3 which isn't crossed out is 5.
  Ring 5. Then cross out all the other multiples of 5.

- Carry on like this as far as you can.

- What kind of numbers have rings round them?
  Can you explain this?

1	2	3	4	5	6	7	
11	12	13	14	15	16	17	18
21	22	23	24	25	26	27	28
31	32	33	34	35			
41	42	43	44	45			
51	52	53	54	55			
			64	65			

C Multiples and factors

If you sometimes mix up multiple and factor,
this diagram may help.

20 is a multiple of **5** is a factor of **20**

C1 Which word, 'multiple' or 'factor', goes in each of these?

(a) 6 is a … of 2.   (b) 6 is a … of 30.   (c) 10 is a … of 60.

(d) 8 is a … of 32.   (e) 8 is a … of 4.   (f) 36 is a … of 9.

C2 Which numbers in the loop are

(a) factors of 25

(b) multiples of 25

2   5   25   80
1
10   75   50   100   150

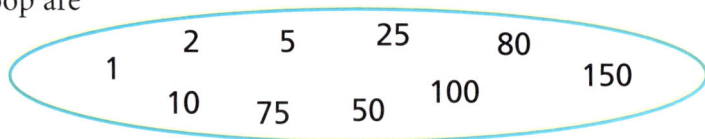

C3 Which of these numbers are multiples of 40?

2, 3, 4, 5, 8, 10, 20, 40, 60, 80, 100, 120

C4 Which of these numbers are factors of 60?

1, 2, 3, 4, 5, 6, 7, 10, 12, 40, 60, 120, 180, 200

C5 (a) List four multiples of 6.

(b) List four factors of 6.

Multiples and factors maze

The rules for the maze are printed on sheet 176.

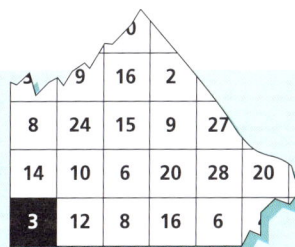

9	16	2	
8	24	15	9	27
14	10	6	20	28	20
3	12	8	16	6

D Divisibility

D1 (a) Without doing any calculation, list the numbers in the list below that are divisible by 2.

562, 3334, 3108, 874, 678, 4893, 400 098, 67 924

(b) How can you tell, without doing any calculation, whether a number is divisible by 2?

(c) Explain how you can tell that 54 729 167 263 533 316 is divisible by 2.

D2 (a) Explain how you can tell whether a number is divisible by 10.

(b) Explain how you can tell whether a number is divisible by 5.

(c) (i) Which numbers in the loop are divisible by 10?

(ii) Which numbers in the loop are divisible by 5?

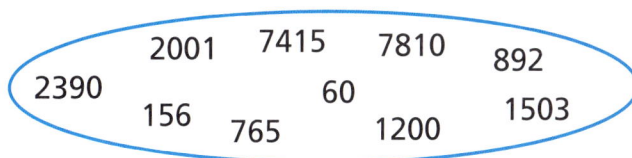

2001 7415 7810 892
2390 156 765 60 1200 1503

D3 (a) Use a calculator to decide if 782 654 is divisible by 3.

(b) (i) Copy and complete this table.

Number	Is the number divisible by 3?	Digit sum	Is the digit sum divisible by 3?
4056	Yes	15	Yes
1101			
692			
9218			

Add up the digits to find the **digit sum**. So the digit sum for 4056 is $4 + 0 + 5 + 6 = 15$

(ii) Continue the table for some of your own numbers.

(c) How can you tell whether a number is divisible by 3?

(d) Decide which of these are divisible by 3.

562, 3334, 3108, 874, 678, 4893, 400 098, 67 924

D4 (a) Write down some numbers that are divisible by 9.
Work out the digit sum for each number.

(b) Write down some numbers that are not divisible by 9.
Work out the digit sum for each number.

(c) How can you tell whether a number is divisible by 9?

(d) Decide which of these are divisible by 9.

69, 402, 504, 21 348, 5631, 39 285, 10 234, 61 236

D5 You need a hundred square (sheet 134).

(a) Underline each number that is divisible by 2.

(b) Circle each number that is divisible by 3.

(c) List all the numbers that are divisible by 6.
What do you notice?

(d) (i) Which numbers in the loop
are divisible by 2?

(ii) Which are divisible by 3?

(iii) Which are divisible by 6?

1	2	3	4	5
11	12	13	14	15
21	22			

138   625   135 912

106   1314   213   5012

*D6 Can you find a way of telling if a number is divisible by   (a) 4   (b) 8

E Common multiples

Common multiples of two numbers are numbers that are multiples of **both** numbers.

For example

- multiples of 6 are   6, 12, 18, **24**, 30, 36, 42, **48**, 54, 60, 66, **72**, …
- multiples of 8 are   8, 16, **24**, 32, 40, **48**, 56, 64, **72**, 80, 88, …

Common multiples appear in **both** lists.
So common multiples of 6 and 8 are 24, 48, 72, …

The smallest number in this list is 24.
So 24 is the **lowest common multiple** of 6 and 8.

E1 Emma is finding common
multiples of 3 and 5.

Multiples of 3	3	6	9	12
Multiples of 5	5	10	15	

(a) Copy and complete the lists to show the first ten multiples of each number.

(b) Find three common multiples of 3 and 5.

(c) What is the lowest common multiple of 3 and 5?

E2 (a) List the first ten multiples of 4.

(b) List the first ten multiples of 6.

(c) What are three common multiples of 4 and 6?

(d) What is the lowest common multiple of 4 and 6?

E3 (a) List four common multiples of 2 and 5.

(b) What is the lowest common multiple of 2 and 5?

E4 What is the lowest common multiple of

(a) 2 and 3   (b) 6 and 9   (c) 3 and 6

E5 What is the lowest common multiple of

(a) 2, 3 and 5   (b) 2, 3 and 4   (c) 2, 3 and 6

F Common factors

Common factors of two numbers are numbers that are factors of **both** numbers.

For example

- the factors of 12 are   **1, 2, 3**, 4, **6**, 12
- the factors of 18 are   **1, 2, 3, 6**, 9, 18

Common factors appear in **both** lists.
So the common factors of 12 and 18 are 1, 2, 3 and 6.

The largest number in this list is 6.
So 6 is the **highest common factor** of 12 and 18.

F1 (a) List the factors of 15.

(b) List the factors of 20.

(c) What are the common factors of 15 and 20.

(d) What is the highest common factor of 15 and 20?

F2 (a) Find the common factors of 12 and 30.

(b) What is the highest common factor of 12 and 30?

F3 What is the highest common factor of 10 and 12?

F4 What is the highest common factor of

(a) 6 and 9   (b) 16 and 40   (c) 8 and 15

F5 What is the highest common factor of 12, 20 and 28?

G Common factors and multiples

G1 (a) Find the lowest common multiple of 4 and 10.

(b) Find the highest common factor of 4 and 10.

G2 (a) Find the lowest common multiple of 3 and 8.

(b) Find the highest common factor of 3 and 8.

G3 Two bell-ringers ring their bells like this:

Peter – every 4 seconds
Imran – every 5 seconds

If they both start at the same time, how long will it be
before both bells ring at the same time?

G4 Harry has 20p. Amit has 36p.
Both boys buy some Fruit Chews. They both spend all their money.

What is the maximum possible cost of a Fruit Chew?

G5 A bag of sweets can be shared between 5 or 6 people with no left-over sweets.
What is the smallest number of sweets that could be in the bag?

G6 Julie wants to tile a small table-top with square tiles.
She doesn't want to cut or break any tiles and wants them all to be the same size.

Her table-top measures 66 cm by 42 cm.
What are the largest tiles she can buy?

G7 In each diagram, the number in each square is found by
multiplying the two numbers in the circles on either side of it.

Copy and complete each diagram.

(a) 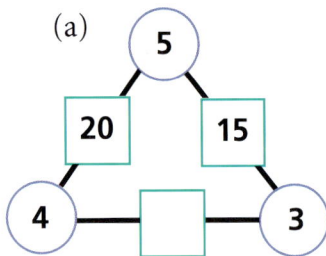 (b) 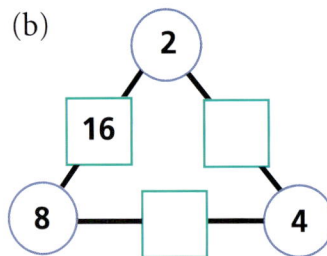 (c)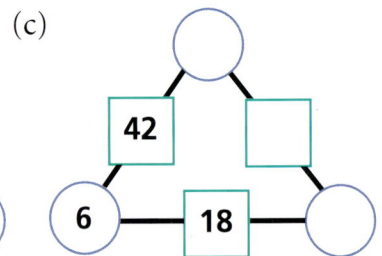

(d) 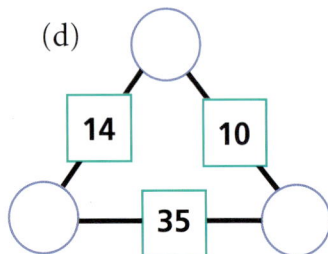 (e) 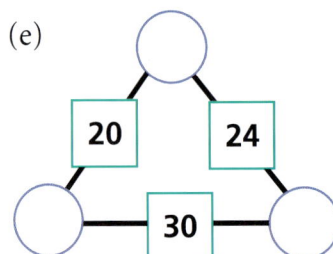 (f)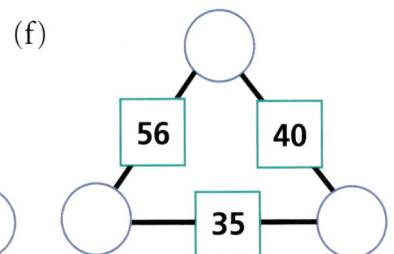

H Polygon wheels

You need polygon tiles (sheet 177).

1 Mark a dot on a square and a pentagon.
  Put the polygons edge to edge with the dots together.

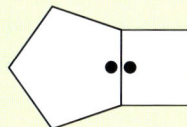

2 Keep the pentagon still. Roll the square around it.

Start rolling   *After 1 turn*   *After 2 turns*   *After 3 turns ...*

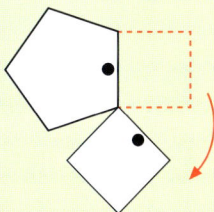 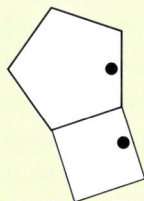 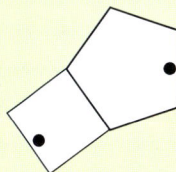 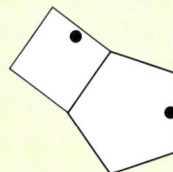

3 How many turns does it take to get the dots together again?
  Will it make any difference if the square is kept still and the pentagon
  is rolled round it?

4 Repeat for other pairs of polygons.
  Can you find any rules for the number of turns?

What progress have you made?

Statement

Evidence

I know what 'multiple' means.

1 Write down three multiples of 5.

I know what 'factor' means.

2 Write down three factors of 24.

I know what a prime number is.

3 Write down all the prime numbers between 1 and 20.

I can use some tests for divisibility.

4 Explain how you can tell that 103 976 is not a prime number.

I know what 'lowest common multiple' means.

5 Find the lowest common multiple of 3 and 7.

I know what 'highest common factor' means.

6 What is the highest common factor of 24 and 36?

195

26 Know your calculator

This work will help you
- use a calculator effectively, including the bracket, square, square root, memory and sign-change keys
- learn rules to find the value of expressions with more than one operation

A In order

A `9` `−` `5` `−` `2`

B `8` `÷` `4` `÷` `2`

C `5` `+` `2` `×` `3`

D `9` `−` `6` `÷` `3`

E `6` `×` `4` `−` `1`

F `6` `÷` `2` `+` `1`

G `5` `−` `3` `+` `2`

H `6` `×` `9` `÷` `3`

I `7` `+` `4` `÷` `2`

J `8` `−` `3` `×` `2`

K `8` `÷` `2` `×` `4`

What result do you think your calculator would give for each set of key presses?

A1 For each set of key presses
- predict the result your calculator will give
- check with your calculator

(a) `3` `+` `4` `−` `2`

(b) `4` `×` `3` `−` `5`

(c) `1` `+` `3` `×` `2`

(d) `4` `+` `6` `÷` `2`

(e) `8` `÷` `4` `−` `2`

(f) `3` `×` `4` `÷` `2`

A2 Which of these sets of key presses will give 12 as the result?

A `6` `+` `2` `×` `3`

B `1` `8` `÷` `3` `×` `2`

C `2` `+` `1` `×` `4`

D `1` `5` `−` `6` `−` `3`

E `2` `0` `−` `4` `×` `2`

F `6` `+` `1` `2` `÷` `2`

Check with your calculator.

A3 Find three different sets of key presses that give 8 as the result.

196

Do not use a calculator for A4 to A7.

A4 Work these out.

(a) $6 + 3 - 5$	(b) $2 \times 5 - 3$	(c) $4 + 3 \times 2$
(d) $10 - 2 \times 4$	(e) $10 - 4 - 2$	(f) $12 \div 3 + 1$
(g) $4 + 8 \div 2$	(h) $2 \times 3 \times 5$	(i) $3 + 5 \times 4$
(j) $14 \div 2 + 5$	(k) $12 - 9 \div 3$	(l) $16 \div 4 \div 2$
(m) $3 \times 8 - 4$	(n) $20 - 3 \times 5$	(o) $10 + 15 \div 5$

A5 Find the missing number in each of these calculations.

(a) $8 + 2 - \blacksquare = 4$	(b) $3 + 2 \times \blacksquare = 15$	(c) $\blacksquare \times 5 - 4 = 6$
(d) $12 \div \blacksquare - 1 = 2$	(e) $6 + \blacksquare \div 3 = 9$	(f) $\blacksquare - 5 - 1 = 2$
(g) $\blacksquare + 3 \times 3 = 21$	(h) $8 + 16 \div \blacksquare = 12$	(i) $20 - \blacksquare \times 2 = 10$

A6 In the expression below, you can replace each diamond with $+$, $-$, $\times$ or $\div$.

$$12 \blacklozenge 6 \blacklozenge 2$$

You must not use brackets or
change the order of the numbers.

*For example, replace the
diamonds with $\div$ and $+$ to make
$12 \div 6 + 2 = 4$*

Replace the diamonds with operations
to make an expression with a value of

(a) 16   (b) 70   (c) 24   (d) 15

A7 Play the game on sheet 179.

B Brackets

Always evaluate expressions in brackets first.

Example $2 \times (3 + 4)$
$= 2 \times 7$
$= 14$

If there are no brackets, then
- *multiply or divide before you add or subtract*
- *otherwise, work from left to right*

Example $3 + 4 \times 2$
$= 3 + 8$
$= 11$

Do not use a calculator for these questions.

B1 Work these out.

    (a) $2 \times (1 + 5)$ (b) $(8 - 2) \div 3$ (c) $10 - (7 + 1)$

    (d) $(7 - 2) \times 3$ (e) $8 \div (1 + 3)$ (f) $(6 + 2) \div 4$

    (g) $7 - (4 - 1)$ (h) $2 \times (11 - 3)$ (i) $15 \div (6 - 1)$

B2 Work these out.

    (a) $3 \times (5 - 1)$ (b) $3 \times 5 - 1$ (c) $(9 + 6) \div 3$

    (d) $9 + 6 \div 3$ (e) $20 \div (5 - 1)$ (f) $20 \div 5 - 1$

    (g) $12 - (6 + 1)$ (h) $12 - 6 + 1$

B3 Find the missing number in each of these calculations.

    (a) $(\blacksquare + 5) \times 2 = 16$ (b) $\blacksquare + 5 \times 2 = 16$

    (c) $16 - \blacksquare \times 2 = 10$ (d) $(16 - \blacksquare) \times 2 = 10$

B4 The expression $8 + (6 \times 2)$ has the same value as $8 + 6 \times 2$
so brackets are not needed.

Which of these expressions do not need brackets?

    A $8 + (6 - 2)$ **B** $(8 + 6) \times 2$ **C** $8 - (6 \div 2)$

        D $(8 - 6) \div 2$ **E** $(8 \times 6) - 2$ **F** $8 - (6 - 2)$

C A thin dividing line

For division, we can use a line like this.

$$6 + 4 \div 2 = 6 + \frac{4}{2} \qquad\qquad 6 \div 4 + 2 = \frac{6}{4} + 2$$

$$(6 + 4) \div 2 = \frac{6 + 4}{2} \qquad\qquad 6 \div (4 + 2) = \frac{6}{4 + 2}$$

C1 Find four matching pairs of expressions.

    A $(20 - 4) \div 2$ **B** $20 - \frac{4}{2}$ **C** $\frac{20 - 4}{2}$ **D** $\frac{20}{4 - 2}$ **E** $\frac{20}{2} - 4$

    F $20 \div (4 - 2)$ **G** $20 - 4 \div 2$ **H** $20 \div 4 - 2$ **I** $\frac{20}{4} - 2$

C2 Write these expressions using a line to show division.

(a) $10 + 6 \div 2$ (b) $(18 - 2) \div 4$ (c) $(8 + 4) \div 3$

(d) $12 - 10 \div 5$ (e) $5 \div (3 - 1)$ (f) $12 \div 4 + 2$

C3 Work these out, without using a calculator.

(a) $\dfrac{6 + 8}{2}$ (b) $12 + \dfrac{8}{4}$ (c) $\dfrac{15}{3} - 1$

(d) $\dfrac{24}{6 + 2}$ (e) $\dfrac{19 - 9}{5}$ (f) $15 - \dfrac{9}{3}$

(g) $\dfrac{30}{5 - 2}$ (h) $\dfrac{20}{2 + 8}$ (i) $20 - \dfrac{10}{2}$

D All keyed up

D1 You can find the value of $(3 + 4) \times 2$ with these key presses.

$$\boxed{(}\ \boxed{3}\ \boxed{+}\ \boxed{4}\ \boxed{)}\ \boxed{\times}\ \boxed{2}$$

For each set of key presses below

• predict the result your calculator will give

• check with your calculator.

(a) $\boxed{1}\ \boxed{0}\ \boxed{-}\ \boxed{(}\ \boxed{5}\ \boxed{+}\ \boxed{3}\ \boxed{)}$

(b) $\boxed{3}\ \boxed{\times}\ \boxed{(}\ \boxed{6}\ \boxed{-}\ \boxed{1}\ \boxed{)}$

(c) $\boxed{(}\ \boxed{6}\ \boxed{+}\ \boxed{4}\ \boxed{)}\ \boxed{\div}\ \boxed{2}$

D2 The value of $\dfrac{9 - 3}{2}$ can be found with these key presses.

$$\boxed{(}\ \boxed{9}\ \boxed{-}\ \boxed{3}\ \boxed{)}\ \boxed{\div}\ \boxed{2}$$

With brackets keys where necessary, use your calculator to find the value of these.

(a) $\dfrac{16 + 24}{8}$ (b) $\dfrac{14}{7} + 3$ (c) $42 - \dfrac{20}{4}$

(d) $\dfrac{13 - 7}{1.5}$ (e) $8 + \dfrac{108}{4}$ (f) $\dfrac{11 + 6}{3.4}$

D3 You can find the value of $\dfrac{9}{4-1}$ with these key presses.

$$\boxed{9}\ \boxed{\div}\ \boxed{(}\ \boxed{4}\ \boxed{-}\ \boxed{1}\ \boxed{)}$$

With brackets keys where necessary, use your calculator to find the value of

(a) $\dfrac{36}{3+1}$ (b) $\dfrac{36}{3}+1$ (c) $\dfrac{72}{12-4}$

(d) $\dfrac{52}{7+6}$ (e) $8+\dfrac{36}{1.8}$ (f) $\dfrac{6-0.4}{3.5}$

D4 (a) Find the result of each set of key presses below.

(i) $\boxed{4}\ \boxed{+}\ \boxed{5}\ \boxed{\times}\ \boxed{3}$ (ii) $\boxed{4}\ \boxed{+}\ \boxed{5}\ \boxed{=}\ \boxed{\times}\ \boxed{3}$

(iii) $\boxed{6}\ \boxed{+}\ \boxed{9}\ \boxed{\div}\ \boxed{3}$ (iv) $\boxed{6}\ \boxed{+}\ \boxed{9}\ \boxed{=}\ \boxed{\div}\ \boxed{3}$

(b) Describe the effect of using the '=' key in the middle of a calculation.

D5 For each set of key presses below
   - predict the result your calculator will give
   - check with your calculator.

(a) $\boxed{4}\ \boxed{-}\ \boxed{1}\ \boxed{=}\ \boxed{\times}\ \boxed{5}$

(b) $\boxed{3}\ \boxed{+}\ \boxed{7}\ \boxed{=}\ \boxed{\div}\ \boxed{2}$

(c) $\boxed{1}\ \boxed{8}\ \boxed{-}\ \boxed{6}\ \boxed{=}\ \boxed{\div}\ \boxed{6}$

D6 Which sets of key presses below could you use to find the value of $\dfrac{9+1}{5}$.

A $\boxed{9}\ \boxed{+}\ \boxed{1}\ \boxed{=}\ \boxed{\div}\ \boxed{5}$ **B** $\boxed{9}\ \boxed{+}\ \boxed{1}\ \boxed{\div}\ \boxed{5}$

C $\boxed{(}\ \boxed{9}\ \boxed{+}\ \boxed{1}\ \boxed{)}\ \boxed{\div}\ \boxed{5}$

Check with your calculator.

D7 Write down a set of key presses you could use to find the value of $\dfrac{9-3}{2}$?

D8 Find the value of these.

(a) $\dfrac{2.8+9.8}{1.4}$ (b) $52.5-\dfrac{23.4}{3.6}$ (c) $\dfrac{9.25}{6.1-2.4}$

(d) $(3.1+5.4)\times 2.6$ (e) $\dfrac{11-1.5}{2.5}$ (f) $\dfrac{3.2}{16\times 0.4}$

(g) $\dfrac{1.3+3.6}{0.7}$ (h) $(9-6.5)\times 1.6$ (i) $\dfrac{50-2}{3.2}$

E Memory

The calculator's **memory** can store numbers to use later.

One key **stores** the number on the calculator in the memory.
It is labelled 'M in' or 'STO' on some calculators.

Another key **recalls** the number stored in the memory.
It is labelled 'MR' or 'RCL' on some calculators.

For example, $\dfrac{630}{5 - 3.74}$ can be done like this.

| 5 | − | 3 | . | 7 | 4 | = | Min | 6 | 3 | 0 | ÷ | MR | = |

Use the memory on your calculator to do this calculation.

E1 Use the memory to work out each of these.

(a) $\dfrac{2242}{57 - 19}$ (b) $\dfrac{534}{74 + 193}$ (c) $\dfrac{36}{0.8 \times 180}$

(d) $\dfrac{75.6}{2.45 + 3.15}$ (e) $\dfrac{249.28}{3.2 \times 9.5}$ (f) $\dfrac{1031}{14 - 3.69}$

E2 Use your calculator to work out these, choosing your own method each time.

(a) $\dfrac{306}{15 \times 17}$ (b) $4.9 \times (2.01 + 3.29)$ (c) $\dfrac{392 - 50.6}{5.69}$

(d) $\dfrac{99.84}{12.1 + 3.26}$ (e) $498 - \dfrac{377}{13}$ (f) $\dfrac{672.84}{25.2 - 9.18}$

E3 One way to change litres to gallons is to divide by 4.546.

Store 4.546 in the memory and use it to convert the
following amounts to gallons, correct to one decimal place.

(a) 7 litres   (b) 24 litres   (c) 12.5 litres   (d) 180 litres

F Squares

Calculators have a special key for working out squares.
It is labelled 'x^2' on some calculators and is called the **square** key.

For example, 29^2 can be done like this: | 2 | 9 | x^2 |

Use your calculator for these questions.

F1 Use the square key on your calculator to find the value of these.

(a) 21^2 (b) 63^2 (c) 108^2 (d) 311^2 (e) 50^2

F2 Find a number that fits each statement.

   (a) $\blacksquare^2 = 361$ (b) $\blacksquare^2 = 784$ (c) $\blacksquare^2 = 90\,000$ (d) $\blacksquare^2 = 4489$

F3 576 is a square number because $24^2 = 576$.
   What is the next square number after 576?

F4 (a) What is the next square number after 2209?

   (b) What is the square number that comes before 2209?

F5 Use a calculator to work out the shaded areas.

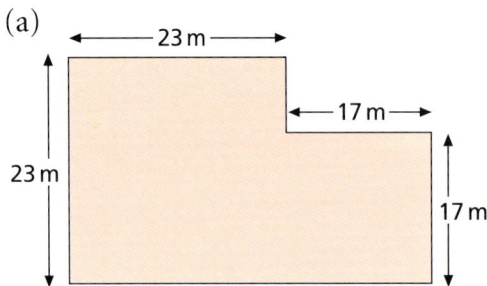

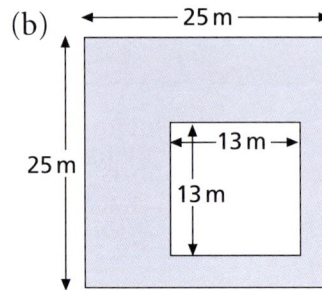

(a)

23 m — 23 m, 17 m — 17 m

(b)

25 m — 25 m, 13 m — 13 m

F6 Can 289 square paving stones be arranged to make a square patio?
   If so, how many stones will be on each side?

F7 Can 200 square paving stones be arranged to make a square patio?
   If so, how many stones will be on each side?

F8 Work these out.

   (a) 3.2^2 (b) 5.7^2 (c) 1.46^2 (d) 0.8^2 (e) 0.12^2

F9 Find a number that fits each statement.

   (a) $\blacksquare^2 = 3.61$ (b) $\blacksquare^2 = 23.04$ (c) $\blacksquare^2 = 0.81$ (d) $\blacksquare^2 = 1.1025$

G Square roots

Finding the **square root** of a number is the opposite of squaring.

For example, the square root of 9 is 3, because $3^2 = 9$.

The symbol for square root is $\sqrt{}$. We write $\sqrt{9} = 3$.

G1 Without using a calculator, write down the square root of

   (a) 25   (b) 4   (c) 49   (d) 100   (e) 1

G2 Without using a calculator, write down the value of

   (a) $\sqrt{16}$ (b) $\sqrt{81}$ (c) $\sqrt{36}$ (d) $\sqrt{64}$ (e) $\sqrt{144}$

G3 Find the square root ($\sqrt{}$) key on your calculator.
On some calculators this key is pressed after the number.

Use your calculator to find these.

(a) $\sqrt{121}$ (b) $\sqrt{225}$ (c) $\sqrt{400}$ (d) $\sqrt{4761}$ (e) $\sqrt{3481}$

G4 Use the $\sqrt{}$ key on your calculator to find these.

(a) $\sqrt{42.25}$ (b) $\sqrt{13.69}$ (c) $\sqrt{1.6384}$ (d) $\sqrt{0.36}$ (e) $\sqrt{0.0016}$

G5 The population of Belgium is about 9 000 000.

(a) Suppose everyone in Belgium stood
on a giant square board.
How many people would be along
one edge of the square?

(b) If each person stands in a square that is
big enough to fit them, estimate how
long each side of the board would be.

Show how you found your answer.

H Negative numbers

The '**sign-change**' key changes a positive number to a negative, and
a negative to a positive.

It is labelled '±' or '(−)' on some calculators.

On some calculators this key is pressed after the number.

H1 (a) Use your calculator to do each of these.

(i) $8 + {}^-3$ (ii) ${}^-5 + 9$ (iii) $2 + {}^-7$ (iv) ${}^-2 + {}^-4$

(b) Check your results by doing each addition without a calculator.

H2 Work these out using your calculator.

(a) ${}^-2 + 3$ (b) ${}^-6 + 1$ (c) ${}^-7 + {}^-1$ (d) ${}^-3 + {}^-9 + 8$

(e) ${}^-5 - 1$ (f) ${}^-3 - 4$ (g) ${}^-2 + 5 - 7$ (h) ${}^-4 + {}^-15 - 1$

H3 Work these out using your calculator.

(a) $7 - {}^-3$ (b) $3 - {}^-5$ (c) ${}^-5 - {}^-2$ (d) ${}^-11 - {}^-12$

(e) ${}^-5.4 - 3.1$ (f) ${}^-3.6 + {}^-4.5$ (g) ${}^-1.3 - {}^-6.2$ (h) ${}^-7.5 - {}^-3.4$

H4 Find the missing number in each calculation.

(a) ${}^-6 + \blacksquare = {}^-4$ (b) $\blacksquare + {}^-8 = {}^-10$ (c) ${}^-7 - \blacksquare = {}^-12$

(d) $3 - \blacksquare = 10$ (e) $\blacksquare - {}^-5 = 0$ (f) ${}^-8 - \blacksquare = {}^-3$

I Complex calculations

I1 Without using a calculator, work these out.

(a) $(2 + 3)^2$ (b) $20 - 4^2$ (c) 2×5^2 (d) $10 + 2 \times \sqrt{36}$

(e) $\sqrt{4^2 - 7}$ (f) $5 \times 3^2 - 20$ (g) $(3 \times 2)^2 + {}^-1$ (h) $(\sqrt{16} - {}^-3) \times 5$

(i) $\dfrac{6^2}{3}$ (j) $\dfrac{32}{4^2} + 9$ (k) $\dfrac{6^2}{12 - 3}$ (l) $\dfrac{12}{\sqrt{49} - 3}$

I2 For each set of key presses below
- predict the result your calculator will give
- check with your calculator.

(a) [2] [×] [3] [x²]   (b) [(] [2] [×] [3] [)] [x²]

(c) [2] [7] [÷] [3] [x²]   (d) [(] [2] [7] [÷] [3] [)] [x²]

I3 Write down a set of key presses you could use to work these out.

(a) 5×7^2 (b) $5 + 7^2$ (c) $\dfrac{100}{5^2}$

I4 Use your calculator to work these out.

(a) $2.4^2 + 6.3$ (b) $(33 - 8)^2$ (c) $62.5 - 1.5^2$

(d) $(62.5 - 1.5)^2$ (e) 8.1×4.6^2 (f) $5.3 \times \sqrt{1.44} + {}^-2.8$

(g) $\sqrt{28.77 + 5.8^2}$ (h) $\dfrac{4.2 + 0.3^2}{2.86}$ (i) $\dfrac{2.4 \times 9^2}{5.4}$

(j) $10 - \dfrac{3.2^2}{4}$ (k) $\dfrac{\sqrt{1521}}{2.4^2 - 4.46}$ (l) $\dfrac{11^2 + {}^-4}{\sqrt{6.76} \times 5}$

I5 Copy and complete the crossnumber puzzle.

Across

1 $\dfrac{26^2 - 76}{6} + 5$

4 $\dfrac{^-40 + 32^2}{3}$

5 $^-8 + 22^2$

7 $\left(\dfrac{126}{9}\right)^2 + 2$

Down

1 $\dfrac{\sqrt{36} \times 8}{\sqrt{16}}$

2 $(77 \times \sqrt{9}\,)^2$

3 $\dfrac{\sqrt{144}}{1.2} - {}^-8$

5 $2 \times 5^2 - 1$

6 $3 + \dfrac{45^2}{27}$

What progress have you made?

Statement

I can work out the value of an expression that involves more than one operation and may include brackets.

Evidence

1 Without using a calculator, work out

(a) $12 + 4 \times 2$ (b) $12 \div 4 - 2$

(c) $12 + 4 \div 2$ (d) $12 \times 4 + 2$

(e) $(12 + 4) \times 2$ (f) $12 - (4 + 2)$

(g) $12 - \dfrac{4}{2}$ (h) $\dfrac{12 + 4}{2}$

(i) $12 - (4 - 2)$ (j) $\dfrac{12}{4 + 2}$

(k) $\dfrac{12 + 4^2}{2}$ (l) $\dfrac{(12 - 4)^2}{2}$

(m) $\sqrt{12 + 4} \times 2$ (n) $(12 + {}^-4) \times 2$

I can use a calculator to find the value of an expression.

2 Use a calculator to find the value of these.

(a) $6 - (1.2 + {}^-0.53)$ (b) $(7.9 - 1.4) \times \sqrt{0.36}$

(c) $\dfrac{(9 - 2.7)^2}{18.9}$ (d) $18^2 + \dfrac{13}{2.6}$

(e) $\dfrac{\sqrt{1296}}{2.5}$ (f) $^-6 + \dfrac{11.34}{1.8^2}$

(g) $\dfrac{6^2 + {}^-4}{0.8}$ (h) $\dfrac{15^2 + 27}{1 - {}^-1.8}$

205

Review 4

Do not use a calculator for questions 1 to 10.

1 Two groups of children raise
  money for a local hospice.

  (a) Calculate the mean amount raised
      by the people in group A.

  (b) Calculate the mean amount raised
      by the people in group B.

  (c) Which group did better? How did you decide?

Group A	
Grace	£5.20
Jim	£4.90
Amit	£6.00
Ken	£3.50
Dean	£4.40

Group B	
Grant	£4.80
Tiffany	£5.90
Phil	£4.90
Kathy	£7.50
Bianca	£2.10
Ricky	£0.90
Carol	£3.30

2 Here are some
  number cards.

  ⁻4   ⁻3   1   5   ⁻2

  (a) List the numbers in order, starting with the smallest.

  (b) From these cards, find a pair of numbers that add to give
      (i) 2   (ii) ⁻6   (iii) ⁻3

3 Four congruent shapes are shown on a coordinate grid.
  Some transformations are given below.

  Rotation of
  90° clockwise
  about (0, 0)

  Translation
  2 units right,
  6 units down

  Translation
  2 units right,
  3 units down

  Reflection in
  the vertical
  axis

  Rotation of
  180° about
  (1, ⁻1)

  Rotation of
  180° about
  (1, ⁻3)

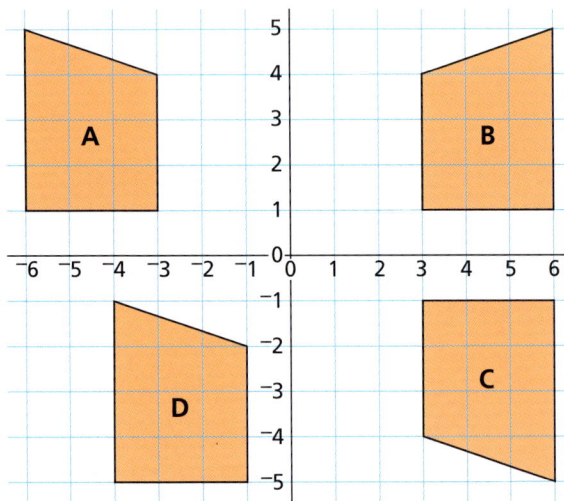

  (a) Which of the transformations above could you use to move each of these?
      (i) Shape A to B   (ii) Shape A to D   (iii) Shape D to C
  (b) Describe the transformation that would move each of these.
      (i) Shape B to C   (ii) Shape A to C   (iii) Shape D to A

4 Which numbers in the loop are

(a) multiples of 3   (b) factors of 12

(c) prime numbers   (d) square numbers

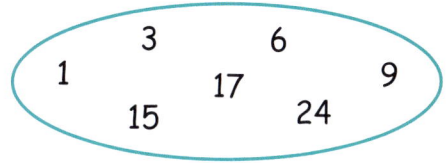

3   6
1   17   9
    15   24

5 For each of these quadrilaterals only three coordinates are given.
Draw a grid going from ⁻6 to 6 in both directions.
Plot the coordinates on the grid and complete each shape.
Write down the coordinates of each fourth point.

(a) Square $(3, {}^-2)$ $(4, {}^-4)$ $(6, {}^-3)$ (b) Rectangle $(0, {}^-2)$ $(2, {}^-2)$ $(2, {}^-5)$

(c) Kite $({}^-1, 4)$ $(1, 3)$ $({}^-1, {}^-1)$ (d) Parallelogram $(0, 1)$ $(3, 1)$ $(4, {}^-1)$

6 Calculate each of these.

(a) $2 - 5$ (b) $2 - {}^-5$ (c) ${}^-2 - {}^-5$

7 Copy shape ABCD on to squared paper
leaving some space around it.

Draw the image of the shape

(a) after reflection in the line BC

(b) after a 90° turn anticlockwise about D

(c) after a translation of
3 units right, 4 units down

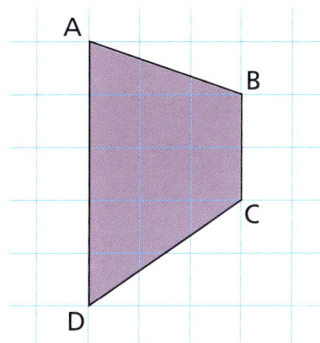

8 Aluna is filling a fish tank.
The tank starts with 5 cm of water in it.
Each minute the hose-pipe adds 2 cm.

(a) Copy and complete
this table.

Time (t min)	0	1	2	3	4	5	6
Depth of water (d cm)	5						

(b) Draw a graph to show the time (t minutes)
and the depth of water (d centimetres).

(c) Use the graph to find the depth of
water in the tank after $3\frac{1}{2}$ minutes.

(d) Use the graph to find t when $d = 8$.

(e) Write a formula linking d to t.

$d = \ldots$

Go up to 18

Go along to 6

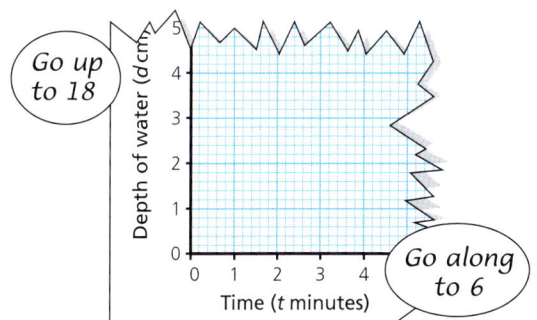

9 (a) What is the lowest common multiple of 4 and 10?

(b) What is the highest common factor of 8 and 36?

10 Draw axes with x and y from 0 to 1

(a) On these axes, draw and label t

$y = x + 3$ $y = 2x$ $y = 8 - x$ $y = 2x + 1$

(b) Which pair of lines are parallel?

11 Work these out.

(a) $1 + 6 \times 3$ (b) $\dfrac{24}{6-2}$ (c) $10 - 3^2$ (d) $(8 + {}^-6) \times 9$

12 Stephen recorded the midnight temperature in his garden for the first week in January. The temperatures were

Day	Mon	Tue	Wed	Thu	Fri	Sat	Sun
Temperature	−3°C	2°C	−7°C	2°C	5°C	−1°C	3°C

(a) Which day had the lowest midnight temperature?

(b) What is the difference between the highest and lowest midnight temperatures?

(c) Find the mean of all the temperatures, correct to one decimal place.

13 Geoff counted the number of paper clips in a sample of boxes. His results are shown in the frequency table.

(a) How many boxes contained exactly 100 paper clips?

(b) How many boxes were in Geoff's sample in total?

(c) How many paper clips did he count altogether?

(d) What was the mean number of paper clips per box in his sample?

Number of paper clips	Frequency
97	3
98	4
99	8
100	5
101	3
102	2

14 Find the value each of these.

(a) $\dfrac{63^2}{31.5} - 20$ (b) $\dfrac{\sqrt{7.29}}{0.9 \times 5}$ (c) $\dfrac{(6.4 + {}^-5.12)^2}{1.2^2 - 0.8}$

15 Some pupils and teachers are members of a school singing group. Their ages in years are

12   15   11   13   11   11   14   12

16   12   12   13   14   32   56   42

(a) Find   (i) the mean age   (ii) the modal age   (iii) the median age

(b) Which average do you think best represents the age of the group? Give reasons for your answer.